DATE			

LET ME TAKE YOU DOWN

LET ME TAKE YOU DOWN

INSIDE THE MIND OF MARK DAVID CHAPMAN, THE MAN WHO KILLED JOHN LENNON

JACK JONES

VILLARD BOOKS

1992

 Published in the United States by Villard Books, a division of Random House, Inc., New York, and simultaneously in Canada by Random House of Canada Limited, Toronto.

Library of Congress Card Catalog Number: 92-53655
ISBN: 679-41144-5

Book Design by Anne Scatto

Manufactured in the United States of America on acid-free paper

9 8 7 6 5 4 3 2

First Edition

IN MEMORY OF HAROLD STEELE

A fool hath no delight in understanding,
But that his heart may discover itself.

—PROVERBS 18:2

The chapters that follow will show readers how a man in the grip of madness and malice was able to plan and carry out an assassination that virtually stopped the world. The work is based on more than two hundred hours of interviews with Mark David Chapman at Attica prison, supported by additional interviews with Chapman's wife and with former friends, therapists, and confidants.

The book re-creates a series of interactions between Chapman and people with whom he spoke before and after the killing of John Lennon. In each case, Chapman's memories of events have been corroborated by previously published material, personal diaries, police records, psychiatric reports, and/or personal interviews with the individuals with whom he conversed.

Chapman's encounters with Lennon fans, police, psychiatrists, and others in Georgia, Hawaii, and New York City are based on the killer's memories and on material obtained under the Freedom of Information (FOI) Law from the New York County District Attorney's Office. Statements made to police investigators by Yoko Ono and other witnesses were likewise obtained from the DA's office under an FOI request. With Chapman's permission, several of his former psychiatrists and psychologists agreed to be interviewed and to provide transcribed material from their case records.

Some of the material on John Lennon was obtained under the FOI from extensive files that the FBI maintained during the rock star's nine years of residence in the U.S.

After a series of meetings at Attica prison, Chapman asked the author to undertake the telling of his story in the hope that it might prevent future tragedy. Neither Chapman nor his family will receive any share of profits, royalties, or other financial or material benefits arising from this book.

ACKNOWLEDGMENTS

For help and advice in the preparation of this book, I wish to thank Jim Kurtz, Kris Bertelsen, Ed Sprigg, Bill Ward, Dr. David Barry, Dr. Duncan Stanton, and Phil Kiefer.

For their trust, love, and inspiration, I am forever indebted to the late Harold Steele, his wife, Dorothy, and Ken Siegel, cofounders of the Cephas-Attica organization.

I also wish to thank Attica superintendent Walter Kelly; deputy superintendent Tim Murray and his secretary, Lisa, for often allowing me into Attica prison on short notice; and the many correction officers who facilitated my visits with Mark David Chapman.

For sharing his collection of Beatles music, I thank Chris Warren. To Kevin Higley, who went out of his way to provide music, books, and other resource materials and to take photographs, I am especially grateful.

For their encouragement over the years, I wish to thank my colleagues and former colleagues in Rochester at *The Democrat and Chronicle.* Especially, I am grateful to the late Rick Tuttle and to Mark Wert, Phil Hand, David Dunkle, Barbara Henry, Claude Werder, Dennis Floss, Carol Ritter, and Lee Krenis More.

I shall be forever grateful to all those named in this book who agreed to be interviewed and to freely share their memories, diaries, medical reports, and legal paperwork.

Special mention is accorded to the librarians and volunteers at Wood

Library in Canandaigua for invaluable research assistance. Thanks to Judy for helping to keep matters organized.

Most of all, for making an idea into a reality, I am indebted to Connie Clausen, my wonderful agent in New York City who agreed to handle a proposal from an unknown writer for a difficult book. In the end, it was Diane Reverand, my editor and publisher at Villard, whose patience, knowledge, and expertise made it all come together.

CONTENTS

PROLOGUE

The death of a man who sang and played guitar
overshadows the news from Poland, Iran,
and Washington tonight.

—WALTER CRONKITE, CBS EVENING NEWS,
DECEMBER 9, 1980

The world will not let go of the memories or music of John Lennon. More than a decade after a death as spectacular as his life, the artist who turned rock 'n' roll into a worldwide crusade for peace and justice continues to be rediscovered, celebrated, and mourned by new generations of fans. Because of the historic dimensions of Lennon's fame, one of his fans decided that he had to die.

Like John Lennon, Mark David Chapman was a child of his times who sought himself in drugs, music, art, poetry, religion, and literature. He, like Lennon, married an Asian woman about five years older than himself. He learned to play guitar, the instrument with which Lennon defined himself and captured the attention of the world. After all other instruments eluded his grasp, Chapman defined himself and got the world's attention with a gun.

Chapman, like Lennon, was a troubled, self-absorbed, and emotionally unfulfilled child. Each came separately of age—Lennon in the rubble of post–World War II England, Chapman in the midst of America's divisive decade-long war in Vietnam—in a confused and hypocritical world. Overcoming abandonment and rejection by both his parents, Lennon etched his image in poetry and music upon the consciousness of an era. Desperate for recognition, Chapman finally smeared his name in Lennon's blood upon the soul of the troubled times.

The killer said, "It almost seems like something that had to happen."

Lennon, as well, seemed to foretell his violent death as something that "had to happen." In radio and magazine interviews he talked repeatedly of the assassinations of public figures who, like he, had spoken out against the evils of war, racial bigotry, sexual discrimination, and other forms of social injustice. He talked in numerous interviews of the steps he believed he had taken to avoid a similar destiny: "So I refuse to lead," he told a reporter, "and I'll always show my genitals or something which prevents me from being Martin Luther King or Gandhi and getting killed."

Lennon urged his fans and followers to look within themselves for the answers to such tragedies: "The struggle is in the mind," he said. "We must bury our own monsters and stop condemning people. We are all Christ and we are all Hitler."

In prison, Chapman has received thousands of letters from John Lennon fans all over the world. Many confide to the killer that they've been unable to "bury their own monsters" and come to grips with the violent death of a man whose music and poetry caused them to imagine a warring world at peace.

Both Lennon and his assassin have shaken and forever altered twentieth-century history. The assassination was an abrupt coda to an age still in search of itself. When he shot John Lennon, Chapman robbed us all of an opportunity to better understand ourselves.

This is the story of how Mark David Chapman, unable to find meaning or hope in his own life, conceived and carried out the assassination of a musician who embodied a universal search for truth. The story is dedicated to Harold Steele, who founded the Cephas-Attica prisoner rehabilitation program after forty-three men died in the bloodiest prison uprising in American history in September 1971. Steele died suddenly of a heart attack on November 30, 1989, at the age of forty-six.

I think John Lennon would have liked Harold Steele. He worked to build the kind of world that Lennon helped us to imagine.

Jack Jones
June 22, 1992

PART I

THE CATCHER GONE AWRY

CHAPTER ONE

I HEARD SHOTS

INVESTIGATION: HOMICIDE OF JOHN LENNON (12/8/80)
SUBJECT: INTERVIEW OF JACK HENDERSON (WITNESS)

. . . I was out for the evening and returned at approximately 10:45 (2245). I heard the shots—don't remember how many. I ran down the stairs and found Joseph (Hastings) and Yoko. Hastings had Lennon in the back office. Yoko said "Please, someone get a doctor." I called our office and told the person there to get an ambulance here as quickly as possible. I never saw the person that shot him. After shots, maybe 15 to 20 seconds and I was at the office. . . .

—*Detective R. Hoffman*

INVESTIGATION: HOMICIDE OF JOHN LENNON M/W/40
SUBJECT: INTERVIEW OF MAURY SOLOMON (WITNESS)

On 12/8/80, while at the scene of occurrence, I interviewed one Maury Solomon. . . . Mr. Solomon was about to go to bed when he heard five shots being fired in rapid succession. He brought it to the attention of his mother and informed her he was going downstairs to investigate. After running down the stairs he entered the front office and as he entered he heard Jose the doorman shout something. . . . Then he exited the office and as he was coming out he noticed for the first time that there were holes in the glass on the door. He began to go out to the street and as he did he observed a male white on the west side of the enclosed entrance. The man appeared to have a smile on his face and was just turning around. . . .

—Detective William Lundon

INVESTIGATION: HOMICIDE OF JOHN LENNON
SUBJECT: INTERVIEW OF FRANKLYN WELSH (WITNESS)

1. On 12/8/80 at about 2330 hours I interviewed the above named subject at the Dakota, One West 72nd St. Statement as follows:

I pulled up in a taxicab to visit my friend in the Dakota at about 11 P.M. I saw a gray limo double parked in front. I recognized John Lennon and Yoko getting out of the limo (I've seen them several times before during other visits) and went into the building. I was paying the cab fare when I heard four gunshots coming from the courtyard. I ran to the gate and saw Jose, the doorman, and another man inside. I also saw a gun on the ground which Jose kicked to the rear of the courtyard. I then ran across the street to the Majestic to have someone call the police. When I returned the police had arrived and had the suspect in custody.

—Detective E. Regan

INVESTIGATION: HOMICIDE (GUN) JOHN LENNON
SUBJECT: INTERVIEW OF RICHARD PETERSON (CAB DRIVER)

On 12/9/80 at about 0020 hours I interviewed at the 20th Police Detective Unit office one Richard Peterson . . . employed as a taxi driver for Valeria Cab Corp. He stated that on the day of the occurrence he had picked up two passengers in Soho and that they were going to the Dakota. As he reached 72nd Street and Central Park West he was behind John Lennon's limo. As the limo stopped in front of the Dakota he pulled up behind it. At this time the passengers in his taxi stated, "There is John Lennon and Yoko." Yoko was in front and John Lennon behind her. The doorman and perpetrator were standing at the entrance to the Dakota. The perpetrator was wearing a black, three-quarter-length coat and a black fur hat. At this time he pointed the gun at Lennon. The perpetrator stood in a three-point stance and fired the gun three or four times. He then threw the gun to the ground and walked around. He takes off his coat and hat and puts a red book in his hand.

—Detective Allen Militz

HOMICIDE: JOHN LENNON

SUBJECT: INTERVIEW OF JOSEPH MANY (ELEVATOR OPERATOR)

I saw the perpetrator hanging out in front of the building for the past two or three days. When I arrived at work at 3:30 P.M., I saw him standing in front of the building talking to a female named Jerri (F/W/22, 4′8″, 160 lbs., blond hair, lives in Brooklyn). At 9:30 P.M. to 10 P.M., I saw him still outside the building. I said, "Why are you still hanging around here, you already got his autograph?" I went downstairs and stayed there until I relieved the clerk in the office, so he could use the men's room. This was about 10:45 P.M. He came back about five minutes later and I went downstairs again. I was downstairs approximately 5 to 10 minutes when I heard three shots. I got my coat and went upstairs with Victor Cruz and Joe Grezik, who are employees. I saw Jose who was motioning toward the gun and saying "Get this out of here." I picked up the gun and brought it downstairs. I hid the gun in the bottom draw of an armoire, which was in the storage closet. Approximately five minutes later I took the police officers down to the storage room and opened the draw where I put the gun. I lifted up a few pictures I put on top of the gun and Officer Blake removed it.

—Officer R. Clark

INVESTIGATION: HOMICIDE OF JOHN LENNON M/W/40 YRS

CONTENTS: INTERVIEW OF MRS. LENNON

[At 5:45 P.M. on December 18, ten days after Mark David Chapman murdered John Lennon, New York City Police investigators interviewed Yoko Ono. The following account of the interview is reprinted verbatim from the handwritten notes of police:]

"We had a radio program which had to do it was about 4:30 to 5 P.M. We went by limousine to Record Plant—asked for ride by people who had limo. John was signing autographs. He got in. Went to Record Plant. Stayed until about 10:30. We wanted to go to restaurant but did not. We came back. We normally go into the gate but did not. Got out walked past gate. John was walking past the door, he was walking faster. I heard shots. I heard shots. He walked to door upstairs. Said "I'm shot." I followed him. He was standing but staggering. I told him to lay down. Sometimes he was ahead sometimes I was. I saw a male by the watchman's box. It was dark and night. He nodded at me—dark grayish clothing. Male/White. He was not small. . . ."

—Detective Peter Mangicavallo

CHAPTER TWO

PORTRAIT OF A CRAZY MAN

"There were gargoyles," the killer remembers. "I leaned against a black rail between them. It's like I was a real gargoyle that had come to life."

Mark David Chapman also remembers pacing in silence among the steel faces studding a black rail that protectively surrounds the Dakota building at the edge of Central Park. It was the first weekend of December 1980, and the festive spirit of Christmas was beginning to settle upon the city of New York.

For the second time in less than two months, Chapman had left his home in Honolulu to come to New York. He had arrived outside the Dakota after taking a taxi from La Guardia Airport earlier in the day. Late on the morning of Saturday, December 6, he had checked into a $16.50-a-night room at the West Side YMCA. His room, a ten-minute walk from the Dakota, was on West 63rd Street near the boulevard of Central Park West.

The cell-like room was furnished only with a sagging bed and a small, battered television set. Upon entering the room, Chapman became quickly depressed. Shoving his suitcase under the bed, he left the crowded hostel and walked nine blocks along a low stone fence bordering Central Park. He arrived at the Dakota, on the corner of West 72nd Street, shortly before noon. Although eager to take up a vigil at the entrance to the building, he paused before crossing the street to study the Dakota's distinctive architecture. He sat down on a bench that was canted in the direction of the Dakota from a confluence of sidewalks leading in and out of Central Park.

The Dakota, a forbidding, Gothic-style building overlooking the park, is the New York City residence of some of the world's wealthiest and most famous celebrities. As Chapman's eyes swept the ornate building floor by floor, he began to imagine what it would look like on the inside. He had studied photographs of the elegant suite where John Lennon lived with Yoko Ono on the top floor. He had etched the images of Lennon's apartment into his brain for nearly two months after borrowing a book from the Honolulu Public Library. The book, by Anthony Fawcett, a former employee of Lennon and Ono, was titled *John Lennon: One Day at a Time.*

Chapman believed he had found the real John Lennon when he found that book. In another book, *The Catcher in the Rye,* the J. D. Salinger novel, he believed that he had found himself. For the past several months, Chapman had etched the pages of *The Catcher in the Rye* into his brain alongside the black-and-white photographs of *John Lennon: One Day at a Time.* That's why he had come to New York. He believed he was destined to enter the pages of *The Catcher in the Rye.* He believed that he would become Holden Caulfield, the hero of Salinger's novel, as soon as he got what he needed from Lennon.

As he lingered on the corner across the street from the Dakota building, Chapman unconsciously began humming a familiar Beatles song he had sung in childhood. Although he knew the song well, he found himself momentarily unable to recall the words or the title. He didn't know why the tune had sprung suddenly into his mind.

Seeing no signs of life behind any of the curtained windows looking from the gabled, fortresslike building, Chapman stood and walked from the park bench. Standing directly across the street in front of the Dakota on West 72nd Street, he turned his attention to a small group of people who loitered near the entrance. A woman with a small child stood talking with two younger women. A doorman in a gilt-edged uniform stood nearby, motionless and staring skyward toward the tops of trees in Central Park. Behind the doorman, a brass sentry booth gleamed like an upended coffin on a stone pedestal at the edge of the driveway. The driveway led from the Dakota entrance into the broad, multilaned thoroughfare of West 72nd Street. Beyond the Dakota drive, ornately sculpted gates of black wrought iron were swung open into a courtyard.

Chapman studied the scene for several minutes. It reminded him of an impressionist painting of a nineteenth-century Parisian neighborhood, like those he had seen in art books he had borrowed from the Honolulu library during the past year. As he continued to study the peaceful scene of urban street life, he experienced a sense of déjà vu.

As Chapman pondered the sense of having been there before, the woman and child got into a Mercedes-Benz station wagon and drove away. The other two women continued to linger at the building entrance. He observed that they were about his age. The women were a good sign. He was smiling when he crossed the street.

Chapman was dressed warmly and neatly in long underwear, a V-necked sweater, wool pants, and a navy-blue London Fog trench coat. His thick black hair was combed straight back and covered with a Russian-style brimless hat of synthetic black fur. An expensive silk scarf was draped around his neck. Overdressed and overweight, he found that he was beginning to sweat as he stepped onto the curb in front of the Dakota. Stuffing his hands into the pockets of the snugly buttoned trench coat, he flashed his most sincere smile as he walked toward the two women. They gazed back at him with no sign of emotion.

"Hi," he said, touching his right hand to the corner of his hat in an absentminded salute. "You gals are waiting for somebody, I'll bet."

He stepped closer and gazed benignly into the eyes of one of the women. She was stout, with blond hair that fell straight to her shoulders.

"As a matter of fact we were waiting for you," she replied.

Startled, he slid his right hand slowly back into the pocket of his coat.

"It wasn't worth it," the woman added, turning abruptly away.

Unsure how to respond to the insult, Chapman smiled abashedly as the two women exploded into a paroxysm of girlish giggles before him. He dropped his head and stared silently away.

"I was only teasing," the woman said a moment later. She held out her hand in a gesture of friendship.

"I'm sorry," she said. "I didn't mean to make you feel bad. We were only teasing. Let's start over. I'm Jude. Jude Stein. This is my friend Jery. Jeryl Moll."

He smiled back and briefly took the woman's outstretched hand.

"Hey, Jude," he said, "don't make it bad. I'll bet nobody ever said that to you before."

The women groaned and Chapman guffawed loudly at his own obvious pun. Sensing he could gain the women's confidence, he asked again if they were waiting for anybody in particular.

"I heard John Lennon lives here," he said. "I was hoping to get his autograph. I was wondering whether he might be in town."

"You can be sure of one thing," Jude answered. "John Lennon is somewhere in New York City."

Chapman explained that he was a visitor from Hawaii. He told the women he had been a Beatles fan since childhood, adding that he had grown up realizing John Lennon was the genius behind the most famous rock band in history. He said he was sure the Beatles would get back together someday.

Still wary because he was a stranger and because this was New York City, the women found themselves nevertheless warming to the awkward, bespectacled fan who said he had come from Hawaii to get an autograph from their idol. Moon-faced and about fifty pounds overweight, Chapman wasn't especially good-looking. He was tall and very personable, though, and the women found him not altogether unattractive.

"You mean you came all the way here from Hawaii," Jery asked, "just to see John?"

"Well, I came here to see John, yes," he answered. "But there's more to it than that. I imagine I'll be doing more while I'm here in New York than just seeing John Lennon."

The conversation slowly trailed off and the three stood silently for several minutes, Jery and Jude talking quietly between themselves. Chapman moved close to the women.

"I can't believe I'm really standing in front of the building where John Lennon lives," he said. "I mean, wow! You know? I'm standing here on the very sidewalk where John Lennon has walked."

The women smiled.

"Jude and I are considered family to the Lennons," Jery boasted.

In the ensuing conversation, the women told Chapman that Lennon and Ono knew them by name. They told him that the celebrity couple would often stop and talk with them on their way across the street to Central Park where Lennon liked to stroll at times in the late afternoon.

Judith Stein and Jeryl Moll had become close friends after they had met, about four years earlier, outside the Dakota. Finding themselves among the most dedicated of Lennon's fans, they made the building where the ex-Beatle lived their shrine. Whenever they planned to see a movie, have lunch, or go shopping together in the city, the two women met at the Dakota in hopes of getting a nod of recognition or a word of greeting from John Lennon or Yoko Ono. The doormen and many Dakota residents, including the Lennons, had come to consider Jery and Jude semipermanent Dakota fixtures. The loyal fans had stood through sun, rain, and snow outside the building on many days during the past four years. On occasion, they were asked to run errands for the building's celebrity occupants.

Chapman watched as the women greeted people coming and going from the building. Each time Jery or Jude tried to strike up a conversation with the doorman or with stylishly dressed men and women who looked as though they might live inside the building, he would move close, looking for an opportunity to include himself. When someone new arrived at the Dakota, he asked if they knew Lennon. He repeated his story of coming from Hawaii in hopes of meeting the musician and getting an autograph.

He told Jery that he was an avid reader and said he wished he'd brought one of Lennon's books so the star could sign it. She suggested that he find a record store and pick up a copy of *Double Fantasy,* the new hit album Lennon had just released.

"Even if you don't get it signed, it's a great album," she said. "The best. John's really proud of it."

"That's a great idea," Chapman said. "Yeah, maybe I'll do that. Back in Hawaii they would never believe I could get John Lennon's autograph on one of his albums."

Tiring of the small talk, the two fans excused themselves and crossed West 72nd Street to have lunch at the Dakota Grill. Chapman declined an invitation to join them. He said he would wait until they returned.

"I'll be here at least until midnight," he promised.

Jery and Jude returned after lunch and found Chapman smiling. With a theatrical flourish, he lifted aside the lapel of his trench coat and surprised the women by withdrawing a fresh, cellophane-sealed copy of *Double Fantasy.* He said he had found the album just around the corner in a Columbus Avenue record store.

At Chapman's urging the trio continued their Lennon watch together. To while the time away, they studied the album he had bought. They played a game, trying to figure out where the ex-Beatle was standing in the picture on the back of the album.

As the afternoon wore on, Jery and Jude excused themselves again to see a matinée at a downtown movie theater. They said they would return before 5:30 P.M. Chapman assured them he would be there and promised to buy them dinner at a Japanese restaurant when they came back.

When Jude and Jery returned to the Dakota at 5:15 P.M., they were surprised and somewhat disappointed to find that the gregarious Beatles fan from Hawaii had abandoned the vigil. They decided to wait another fifteen minutes in case he returned. At 5:30 P.M., weary of the encroaching cold and darkness, the women decided to give up their Lennon watch for the day.

As Jery and Jude turned away and prepared to leave the building, a taxi stopped at the curb before the stone archway above the drive leading into the courtyard. A slender and familiar figure wearing a tan jacket and a slouch hat opened the back door of the taxi and stepped onto the curb. John Lennon exhaled a plume of smoke from an omnipresent cigarette and smiled from behind the thick, circular lenses that had become his trademark. He greeted Jery and Jude by name. To the women's delight, the superstar lingered to chat amiably with them for several minutes. They talked about the sudden popular and critical success of *Double Fantasy.* The new album was Lennon's first musical undertaking in more than five years. Already, less than a month after its release, it had become the talk of the music industry. Lennon said he believed it to be his best work since the Beatles era, more than a decade before.

Echoing the earlier critical and popular successes he had enjoyed after creating the Beatles, Lennon was back on top of the pop music charts with an album of intensely personal ballads about his wife and their five-year-old son, Sean. Fans and critics alike were finding the simple, direct lyrics and straightforward, driving rock 'n' roll melodies of John Lennon a refreshing alternative to the repetitive, counterfeit, and puerile tunes that had flooded the airwaves and passed for rock during much of the 1970s. Lennon was telling friends, fans, and interviewers that he felt truly alive for the first time in twenty years, since the early struggling days when he had first found an identity as a Beatle.

On the evening of December 6, 1980, John Lennon "was in such a good mood," Jery Moll later recalled.

When the rock legend disappeared beneath the archway, up the low stone steps, and into the building, Jery and her friend said goodnight. Jery headed home to Brooklyn. As she left the building, she wondered what had happened to the man who had come from Honolulu to get Lennon's autograph. She had hoped he would show up before she left. She had hoped he would ask her to dinner.

"He was dressed nicely, he looked clean, well mannered, and polite. I would have gone out with him. He was more normal than most of the people we meet there.

"He was so nice. I just couldn't believe he was the one. . . ."

Chapman had intended to wait for the two women to return. After maintaining his watch alone for about two hours, he found himself drowsing on his feet, leaning alternately against parked cars and the gargoyle-studded railings that reach around the Dakota. When Jude and Jery didn't return by 5 P.M., he crossed West 72nd Street and headed reluctantly back toward his cramped and dingy room at the YMCA. Just thinking about the room, he began to feel depressed.

Chapman's depression had turned to anger by the time he shuffled into the cheap cubicle and switched on the television set. The TV was broken, but he left it on anyway after banging it sharply with the side of his hand. Ghostlike figures swam and hissed across the screen as he sat down uneasily on the edge of the bed and took off his ripple-soled shoes. He had bought the orthopedic shoes especially for a mission he knew would require him to spend long hours on his feet.

Chapman lay back on the thin, lumpy mattress against the head of the squeaking, narrow bed. He wanted to rest for a while before going back onto the streets to find a restaurant and have dinner. He couldn't remember the last time he had eaten. His usually voracious appetite seemed to have disappeared. Worrying that the loss of appetite was a sign of illness, he became concerned about his health. He closed his eyes and fell asleep.

Mark Chapman awoke sometime after midnight to the sound of men's voices. The voices were coming from a room directly across the hall. It was the sound of several men talking together softly and laughing out loud. He got up and stepped across the room to switch off the still-flickering television screen. Stepping carefully back across the bare floor in darkness, he pressed his ear against the door and listened closely to the voices from across the hall.

A wave of scarlet rage began to pulsate before his eyes as he stood in the blackness of the unlighted room. He suddenly began to feel dirty under his skin as he understood what the men were talking about—having sex with other men.

After several minutes, Chapman stepped slowly to the side of the bed and reached into the pocket of his coat. He felt bold and powerful with the Charter Arms .38 caliber pistol in his hand. As fury built within him, he struggled against a compulsion to wrench open the door and leap across the hallway. He envisioned a brief scene of fear and panic as he stood above a group of naked men with the gun roaring and blazing in his hand.

With a great effort of self-restraint, he slid his sweating hand from the doorknob and released his grip on the pistol.

"It's not worth it," he whispered angrily to himself. "This is not what we're here for, old buddy. Don't do it. Just don't do it. Not now."

Switching on the room light, Chapman gathered up his coat and hat and took his suitcase from beneath the bed.

The anonymous men in the room across the hall continued to talk and laugh as he slammed the door behind him. He walked from the YMCA building into the night. The men would never know how close their carefree conversation had brought them to death during the early morning hours of Sunday, December 7.

Chapman walked a short distance from the YMCA building beneath a hazy glow of street lamps on deserted city sidewalks along Central Park West. As he continued in the direction of the ever-blazing lights of midtown Manhattan, his suitcase began to grow heavy in his left hand. He began to fear that a robber would leap at him from darkened shadows across the stone fence that separated the street and sidewalk from Central Park. Recalling that he had more than $2,000 cash in his wallet, he waved down a passing taxi.

He told the driver to take him to the Sheraton Centre, a hotel at Seventh Avenue and 52nd Street.

Chapman knew the Sheraton would be expensive. He had spent several nights there during his first trip to New York, the month before. He decided that he could afford to spend the extra money for a clean, quiet room. He knew that John Lennon was in town. He sensed that he wouldn't have to spend much more money on hotels.

During the early morning hours, Chapman checked into room 2730 at the Sheraton. Still fully dressed and wearing his hat, he turned on the television in the quiet, spacious room and drifted back to sleep.

Shortly after 9 o'clock on Sunday morning, Chapman found himself staring from the back window of a taxi stopped for a traffic light beside a newsstand. He saw a headline about Pearl Harbor Day. He thought briefly of his wife and mother back in Honolulu. He recalled the time that he and his mom had toured the Pearl Harbor Memorial and remembered something that had embarrassed her. As he had watched other visitors weep and drop flowers onto the watery World War II gravesite, Chapman had been overcome with emotion. He still didn't know why he had laughed out loud.

"Totally inappropriate emotional response," he thought to himself, recalling the incident. "What's wrong with me?"

Pondering the recollection, his mind took him back through fifteen years, to a childhood memory of his father, David Chapman. He had never been able to understand why his father had called him to the window on the day that a neighbor had committed suicide.

He remembered looking out the window and seeing the dead man's distraught wife. The woman had stood as though frozen onto the concrete driveway outside her home. She made helpless, random motions with her hands, unable to articulate the horror of finding her husband's headless body curled around a shotgun in their bed. She had looked to Chapman like a wounded bird that had fallen suddenly from the sky.

"Totally inappropriate emotional response," he said again to himself as the taxi pulled to a stop in front of the now-familiar Dakota building. "The world just doesn't make any sense."

Steve Hargett, the doorman on sentry duty at the Dakota on Sunday morning, recalled that Chapman was smiling broadly when he got out of a taxi in front of the building shortly after 9:30 A.M. Hargett thought the large man in the navy-blue raincoat looked familiar. It took him a few moments to remember that Chapman had been there before.

"Hey, Buddy," said Chapman. "Steve, right? How you doin'? Remember me?"

As Chapman continued to talk, Hargett recognized him as the friendly but persistent fan from Hawaii who had appeared outside the building several weeks earlier. Chapman was asking the same question he'd asked then.

"Is John Lennon in town?"

Hargett gave Chapman the routine answer that Dakota doormen had been instructed to give the endless parade of fans and star-struck gawkers who stopped at the building day and night to inquire about Lennon or the Dakota's other celebrity residents. Sometimes they asked about Rex Reed, Leonard Bernstein, Gilda Radner, or Lauren Bacall, who also lived in the building. Mostly, they asked about John Lennon.

"Don't really know," Hargett said. "I think he may be out of town."

Chapman gave the doorman a knowing wink. "Do you mind if I wait and see?"

"It's a public sidewalk," Hargett said. "As long as you don't block the driveway you can stand anywhere you want."

Chapman moved obligingly to curbside. He stood silently beside a parked car for nearly three hours, holding Lennon's new album in his left hand. He kept his right hand in the pocket of his coat. When Hargett returned from lunch at 12:30 P.M., Chapman was gone.

It was shortly after noon on Sunday when Chapman suddenly began to feel the hollow pangs of hunger. For the first time in two days he wanted to eat. On foot, he began winding his way back through the city toward the Sheraton, passing several restaurants along the way. He stopped from time to time to look into the windows of the trendy, specialty bistros. With a sense of envy and loneliness that made him think of Holden Caulfield, he studied the trim and well-dressed people, mostly couples, who sat close together at small tables behind the restaurant windows. He decided they all looked like actors in a Woody Allen movie.

Although he was hungry, Chapman was alone and he knew that he would be out of place among the handsome, modishly attired crowds that filled the elegant cafés of the Upper West Side. He would wait until he got back to the Sheraton and have dinner there. He had always thought there was something refined about eating in the restaurant of a good hotel like the Waldorf or the Sheraton in New York City and the Moana in Honolulu. Often, even when he didn't really have the money, he would use a credit card to check into the most expensive hotels in Honolulu and order from room service. When he could afford to eat an expensive meal and stay in a good hotel it made him feel important. It was a good feeling, but it never lasted.

As he ambled among the restaurants, Mark David Chapman wondered how John Lennon was spending the Sunday afternoon. As he thought again of Lennon, his hunger seemed to disappear. Chapman was suddenly seized with an urge to buy a copy of one of the two books that had brought him to New York. He regretted that he had thrown his last copy of *The Catcher in the Rye* down the trash chute in his apartment a month ago, shortly after he had returned from his first trip to New York. He stepped to the curb and waved for a taxi.

Chapman told the driver he was staying at the Sheraton, but that he wanted to find a bookshop. The driver said he could take him to one near the hotel.

Inside the bookstore, Chapman happened unexpectedly upon two items that made him forget about *The Catcher in the Rye.* He saw a poster from his favorite movie, *The Wizard of Oz.* The poster pictured Dorothy tenderly wiping tears from the snout of the Cowardly Lion. As he walked past the magazine rack toward a row of bookshelves marked "Fiction," his eyes fell upon a scene that caused his heart to race. He stared incredulously at a large poster. John Lennon's familiar, chiseled face peered hauntingly back at him from an advertising rack above a stack of *Playboy* magazines. The poster announced that the magazine contained an exclusive interview with Lennon and Ono, the first in-depth interview the couple had given in more than five years.

Late Sunday afternoon Chapman finally returned to the Sheraton and sought out the hotel's restaurant. He was carrying the new January 1981 issue of *Playboy* and a small photograph of Dorothy and the lion from *The Wizard of Oz.* He was surprised to observe that the restaurant seemed empty as he seated himself. It was nearly an hour later when he looked up from the *Playboy* interview. He called to a uniformed man wearing a Sheraton name tag and demanded to know why no one had bothered to take his order. Pointing to a sign displayed prominently on a polished metal stand, the maître d' curtly advised Chapman that he had been sitting in a part of the restaurant that had been closed for some time.

Apologizing for his outburst, Chapman moved to another table and ordered a bottle of Heineken beer. He also ordered a diet plate of ground beef and cottage cheese. Still absorbed in the Lennon interview after the meal, he ordered another bottle of Heineken and a dish of chocolate mousse. He nearly always drank Heineken and ate chocolate mousse when he dined at the restaurants of good hotels.

When he finished reading the Lennon *Playboy* interview, he flipped to the centerfold of the magazine. He studied the glossy, naked skin of the Playmate of the Month while savoring the final sips of his beer. Looking at the Playmate's glowing, pink flesh, he thought again about *The Catcher in the Rye.* He thought about the curious experience that Holden Caulfield, his fictional alter ego, had undergone in a New York City hotel room with a prostitute in a green dress. Suddenly, Chapman was seized with the desire to be alone with a woman.

Returning in haste to his hotel room, he began flipping through the Manhattan Yellow Pages. He looked under *E* and found the listing for "Escort Services," dialing the number of one with a name that he liked. He asked if any foreign women worked for the agency, saying he would prefer someone exotic—a woman from another country—to visit his hotel room for the evening.

"We have a foreign woman and she is very beautiful," the man assured him. "And she works for tips—if you know what I mean."

"That's good," Chapman said. "Yes, I would like a woman who works for tips. But there's only one thing that's important: She's got to be quiet. I don't want someone who will talk. If she doesn't talk, I will tip her very well."

About an hour later, Chapman opened the door to his hotel room. A shapely woman with golden hair and a European accent stepped inside. He noted at once that she was wearing a green dress.

"Thank you for coming," he said, gesturing with his open palm for her to step into the room.

The woman appeared nervous. Chapman told her she could relax.

"I'm not kinky. I'm clean. I'm not weird," he assured her. "I'm not even all that interested in having sex. I just wanted to be in the company of a woman tonight. I'm expecting that tomorrow will be a very difficult day for me."

He offered to order a round of drinks from room service. The woman said she didn't drink.

Chapman told the prostitute he didn't intend to use her for his own sexual gratification.

"This is your night off," he said. "We'll do whatever you want to do."

He offered to give the woman a massage. He asked her to take off her dress and get onto the bed with him. The woman obeyed, but asked if he would turn on the radio. She said she was afraid another hotel guest had seen her come into his room. She said she was afraid of going to jail.

Chapman worked his fingers gently against the woman's smooth flesh for more than a half hour before he felt her tensed muscles begin to relax beneath his touch.

"A real man doesn't have to use a woman," he whispered to the prostitute. "A real man doesn't have to take from a woman. He can give."

Chapman believed himself to be possessed of normal and healthy heterosexual drives, although he had never especially enjoyed the act of intercourse. He enjoyed touching women and he enjoyed being touched by them in turn. There was something about the wet, warm feeling of entering a woman's body, however, that had always frightened him. It made him feel that he was being swallowed up, disappearing into something he didn't understand.

He had been twenty years old when he had had sex the first time. He had been engaged at the time to another woman, one of his childhood friends who was "a strong Christian." The infidelity had caused him to feel shameful and afraid. It was nearly two years after he lost his virginity before he had slept with another woman, a drunken prostitute who had accosted him on a street in Bangkok, Thailand. He could count the number of times in his twenty-five years of life that he had engaged in the act of coitus, even with his wife.

As the prostitute finally moaned and shivered in pleasure beneath his hand, Chapman switched out the light. He guided her hand to himself and lay back in the darkness to try to shut out images of broken objects that flickered and swirled in his brain.

It was nearly 3 o'clock in the morning on Monday, December 8, when the prostitute stood from the bed and wriggled her smooth, naked body back into the snugly fitting dress. Chapman noted again with satisfaction the dress that was the same color as the one Holden's prostitute had worn.

"Synchronicity," he said to himself.

Counting out $190 in large bills from his wallet, he pressed the money into the woman's eager hand, kissed her on the cheek, and walked her to the door.

Moments after the prostitute had left the room, he picked up a telephone handset from the nightstand beside the bed. He wanted to talk to his wife. It was the first time he had called home since saying good-bye to her at the Honolulu airport, nearly three days ago. He called collect.

Gloria Chapman remembered that it was about 10 P.M., Hawaiian time, when the phone rang. She had just finished reading the copy of *The Catcher in the Rye* that her husband had given her several weeks before. He had told her that she would understand him better if she read the book. He had signed the book for her: "Holden Caulfield."

Gloria had been thinking about the similarities between Mark Chapman and Holden Caulfield when the phone rang. Later, she wrote down her memory of the long-distance conversation.

> Late Sunday, Dec. 7, around 10 P.M., Mark called. He said he knew he had said he wasn't going to call but he's always changing his plans. He said he felt lonely. He said I sounded like I was doing okay, and I told him I was. I didn't cry or plead with him to come home, like I did when he first went to New York.
>
> He asked me how this party I went to Saturday was and said he was sorry he did not wish me a happy party when he left, but he wasn't thinking about stuff like that. He asked me how his mom was. I asked him if he had seen any plays and he said no, not yet. He said the weather was real nice

this time, not cold or rainy. He repeated something that he told me the night before he left when I was half asleep in bed.

He said that he loved me very much, more than anyone else and there is no one else, and even though sometimes he may do things which don't make it seem like he does, he always loves me.

He also told me to call up his mom some time and tell her that he loves her and that he was glad to hear that she was feeling better. He said he hoped he didn't wake me, he knew it was late. It was also very late there but he couldn't get to sleep. I told him that I had just gone to bed and was reading my Bible. I told him that he should try and work on his problems one by one and that perhaps the first one he should work on was getting back with Christ again. After that, he only need ask for His help with the other problems. He seemed to agree and said his little Bible was on his nightstand. He apologized for calling collect, said after he had started the call he remembered that he could have put the call on his hotel bill. We finished our conversation by saying "I love you and I miss you."

After hanging up the phone, Chapman took his Bible from his suitcase and opened it to the New Testament Book of John. He picked up a ballpoint pen and wrote the name *Lennon* after the words *The Gospel According to John.*

"They're coming together," he said to himself. "History and time."

Reverently closing the Bible, Chapman set the alarm clock on his nightstand for 9 A.M. and switched off the light.

CHAPTER THREE

THE CATCHER GONE AWRY

Who wants flowers when you're dead? Nobody.

—HOLDEN CAULFIELD

His mind racing too fast for sleep, Mark David Chapman rose early on the morning of December 8 to make final preparations for the event he had planned to stage in New York City. He had already been gone from the Sheraton for nearly an hour when the alarm clock on the nightstand began chiming at 9 A.M. in the empty room.

Before leaving the hotel, Chapman had neatly arranged and left behind a curious assortment of personal items on top of the hotel dresser. In an orderly semicircle, he had laid out his passport, an eight-track tape of the music of Todd Rundgren, and his little Bible, open to the The Gospel According to John (Lennon). He also left a letter from a former YMCA supervisor at Fort Chaffee, Arkansas, where, five years earlier, he had worked with refugees from the Vietnam War. Beside the letter were two photographs of himself surrounded by laughing Vietnamese children. At the center of the arrangement of personal effects, he had placed the small *Wizard of Oz* poster of Dorothy and the Cowardly Lion.

After laying out the mementos, he had walked in and out of the room several times, returning to the dresser and refining the arrangement each time he stepped back through the door. He wanted to be sure it would be the first sight to meet the eyes of the people who, he was sure, would be visiting his hotel room before the day was over. It would let them know that he had, at one time in his life, been more than the failure he was now—more than the creature he sensed he was about to become.

"I woke up knowing, somehow, that when I left that room, that was the last time I would see the room again," Chapman recalled. "I truly felt it in my bones. I don't know how. I had never seen John Lennon up to that point. I only knew that he was in the Dakota. But I somehow knew that this was it, this was the day. So I laid out on the dresser at the hotel room . . . just a tableau of everything that was important in my life. So it would say, 'Look, this is me. Probably, this is the real me. This is my past and I'm going, gone to another place.'

"I practiced what it was going to look like when police officers came into the room. It was like I was going through a door and I knew I was going to go through a door, the poet's door, William Blake's door, Jim Morrison's door. It was like I was going through a giant door. And I was. I was leaving my past. I was leaving what I was, going into a future of uncertainty. There were tremendous feelings of Holden Caulfield and *The Catcher in the Rye.* The paragraphs and sentences of that book were flowing through my brain and entering my blood, influencing my thoughts and my actions. My very soul was breathing between the pages of *The Catcher in the Rye.*"

Satisfied at last with the arrangement on the dresser, Chapman put on his trench coat and hat and draped his silk scarf around his neck. Before leaving the room, he stood before a full-length mirror and studied the outline of the gun in his coat pocket. After tearing, fitting, and discarding several thick pieces of cardboard to try to conceal the telltale image of the deadly chunk of steel, he finally fashioned one that he was satisfied would do the job.

During the previous two days, he had found his hand getting sweaty and uncomfortable when he had to keep it in the coat pocket concealing the pistol for long periods of time. Sliding the cardboard into the coat, he smiled when he saw that it made the weapon seem to disappear. He was pleased with his impromptu craftsmanship.

Spinning like a model before the mirror, Chapman observed that the cardboard remained in place, masking the deadly silhouette even when he moved. Snapping his hand quickly into the pocket, he found that the mask slipped obligingly aside as his fingers closed around the butt of the gun. In the manner that he had been taught as a security guard, Chapman suddenly twisted, crouched, and aimed the pistol at his image in the hotel-room mirror. Gripping the unloaded gun combat style, in both hands, the hammer clicked five times as quickly as he could flex and unflex his finger.

Still watching himself in the mirror, he reached into the pocket of his trousers and withdrew five stubby bullets. Feeling their weight in the palm of his hand, he visually inspected each one. They were hollow-point slugs, dimpled at their leaden tips to ensure that they would shatter on impact. Chapman had flown all the way from New York City to Georgia, during his first trip to the city a month before, to get the special bullets from a friend.

He knew that hollow points vastly increased the destructive power of bullets when they struck any soft target—especially something as soft as a human body.

He inserted the cartridges into the five empty slots in the cylinder of the gun. Still watching himself in the mirror, Chapman held the loaded pistol aloft in his right hand and snapped the chamber shut with a flick of his wrist.

"The Catcher in the Rye of my generation," he announced to his looking glass image. "Chapter Twenty-seven."

He picked up the copy of the new John Lennon album he had purchased on Saturday and slid it snugly under his left arm. Before leaving the hotel room, he turned around for a final look at the items on the dresser. Should he find himself unable ever to speak again, he hoped the assemblage would tell the story of his life. He hoped the story would be told in a way that the world would understand. He wondered whether he should go back and write something, a statement of intent. Remembering that he still had to find and purchase a copy of *The Catcher in the Rye* somewhere in New York City, he decided that he would leave behind no other clues. The book would be his final statement and gift to the world.

As he closed the door behind him and walked down the hall to the elevator on the twenty-seventh floor of the hotel, he reflected to himself: "It's almost like something a person who was going to commit suicide would do. Before they kill themselves, people lay out the things that mean the most to them."

Chapman stepped off the elevator into the lobby of the Sheraton and walked past the checkout desk. Even though he didn't plan on returning to the hotel, he wanted to preserve the room in which his carefully constructed memento collection was enshrined. He believed that everything was in place as he stepped from the hotel and walked along the crowded, Monday-morning sidewalks in search of *The Catcher in the Rye.* It was still early and he walked for several blocks before he found a small stationery store and bookshop that was open.

To his relief, soon after entering the shop he spotted the familiar red jacket of the paperback. The golden letters blazed before him from the bookshelf like a warm and comforting fire:

THE CATCHER IN THE RYE

J. D. SALINGER

It was the only copy on the shelf. Chapman took it reverently into his hands and moved into line behind a woman at a cash register. As he leafed through the first few pages of the book, he realized that he had left his pen back at the hotel and he picked up a new one from the store counter, a black plastic Bic.

Outside the bookstore he eagerly took the book and pen from a paper bag.

Putting his foot against the rim of a webbed, yellow trash basket near the curb, he placed the book and the *Double Fantasy* album on his knee. He held the pen reflectively for a moment in his hand before pressing the tip against the inside cover page of the book.

"This is my statement," he wrote. He paused for a moment and underlined the word *This.* He signed the statement: "Holden Caulfield" and paused again. After several moments, he added "The Catcher in the Rye."

As he wrote in the book, Chapman recalled a letter he had sent several months earlier to James Lundquist, a University of Minnesota literature professor. Chapman had read a critical, unauthorized biography by Lundquist of J. D. Salinger, the enigmatic author who had gone into seclusion shortly after making Holden Caulfield come alive on the pages of the book in which Chapman now sought to live. In his letter, Chapman had thanked Lundquist for writing about Salinger. He said he had gained great insight by reading about the man who wrote *The Catcher in the Rye.* He signed the letter "The twenty-five-year-old Catcher." He wondered if the literature professor had ever gotten the letter. He wondered if he had bothered to read it, or even thought about answering. It didn't matter anymore.

Chapman stood on the sidewalk reading at random from the book the passages that he almost could recite by heart. Near the end of the novel, on page 187, he found the dialogue he was looking for:

> "This fall I think you're riding for—it's a special kind of fall, a horrible kind. The man falling isn't permitted to feel or hear himself hit bottom. He just keeps falling and falling. The whole arrangement's designed for men who, at some time or other in their lives, were looking for something their own environment couldn't supply them with. Or they thought their own environment couldn't supply them with. So they gave up looking."

He felt a chill of meaning as he continued to leaf through the book. On page 197 he read: "It was Monday and all, and pretty near Christmas, and all the stores were open."

"Amazing," he murmured aloud to himself. "The coincidence is just amazing. A Monday. Pretty near Christmas.

"History and time. Synchronicity."

As he slipped the stiff, new paperback into the left pocket of the trench coat, Chapman felt the inky words of J. D. Salinger begin to mingle with his own blood.

He saw his purpose with crystal clarity. Sliding his left hand into the trench coat, caressing the book with the tips of his fingers, he began walking north, toward Central Park and the Dakota.

"I remember actually feeling, thinking perhaps I would become Holden

Caulfield. Not that I would become crazy. That I would actually *become* Holden Caulfield.

"The book is very poignant, very strong. Almost spiritual, it's so strong. Like Holden, I wasn't going to say anything to anyone else.

"I remember feeling like I was going to go into a fetal position, a coma—just kind of vegetate—and it was such a vivid image I had of a man who wouldn't have to have anything to do with the world anymore. A man who just wants it to bc black all around him.

"Something was awry and I was caught up in it."

CHAPTER FOUR

DID YOU SEE HIM?

It was like I lost myself. Not that I purposely set out to be a hypocrite or a phony.

—JOHN LENNON, DECEMBER 8, 1980

During the course of his two trips from Honolulu to New York City, Mark Chapman believed he had become familiar with all of the doormen who maintained the casual, twenty-four-hour guard at the entrance to the Dakota building. As he stepped onto the curb at West 72nd Street some time after 9:30 on the morning of December 8, he was surprised to confront a man he didn't recognize wearing the building's distinctive dark green, gold-trimmed uniform. The doorman he had expected to see, Steve Hargett, who usually worked the morning shift at the building, had called in sick. Dakota maintenance man Patrick O'Loughlin had been pressed into service in Hargett's place.

O'Loughlin had worked at the Dakota sentry booth before. He recognized most of the die-hard John and Yoko zealots who routinely congregated, sometimes day and night, outside the building. He didn't recognize Chapman.

Displaying John Lennon's *Double Fantasy* album prominently in his left hand, Chapman put on his most ingenuous smile as he approached O'Loughlin in much the same manner he had approached the two fans whom he had befriended outside the Dakota two days earlier. Wary of the new doorman, he kept his right hand in his coat pocket, close to his revolver. He had no reason to suspect that his ruse had been discovered, but he didn't want to take any chances. He had seen a lot of movies and read a lot of books and he knew that it wasn't unusual for police investigators to masquerade in the uniforms of doormen and security guards. He also was aware that armed, off-duty policemen sometimes moonlighted as security officers and sentries at hotels and apartment buildings.

For all that Mark David Chapman knew, John Lennon and Yoko Ono employed their own secret security force to work from time to time as Dakota doormen. As a doorman, a security agent would be able to gather a great deal of information about the peculiar assortment of fans that lurked outside the couple's dwelling. On his first trip to New York, Chapman had observed several disheveled and apparently deranged Lennon fanatics who had stood for long hours outside the building, sometimes begging coins from passersby. He had made it a point to dress and to behave with restraint, to avoid suspicion and to distinguish himself from the unbathed and unkempt celebrity worshipers who would be likely to attract a guard's notice. Chapman himself had worked until recently as a guard at an exclusive high-rise apartment building in Honolulu. Years before that, he had worked on security details for rock concerts back home in Atlanta, Georgia. He knew something about the kind of dress and behavior that would arouse concerns. Chapman realized that he was being paranoid. He also knew that he was being cautious.

After pacing back and forth for several minutes in front of the building, observing the unfamiliar doorman from the corner of his eye, he relaxed his guard. He knew he would have little trouble gaining the new man's confidence.

"Mornin'," he said, stressing his Southern accent for the desired effect. "You wouldn't happen to know whether John Lennon might be planning to come out today, would you? I've got this album here. I'm hoping to get it autographed while I'm here in New York."

O'Loughlin explained that he wasn't the regular doorman and said he didn't know much about Lennon. He said he thought the rock star had left the building earlier, before he had come on duty around 8 A.M. In response to Chapman's questions, O'Loughlin said he had no idea where Lennon might have gone or when or whether the musician would be coming back.

"Where you from?" O'Loughlin asked, curious about the pronounced accent that Chapman had affected.

"Believe it or not, I'm from Honolulu," Chapman replied. "Honolulu, Hawaii."

Surprised for some reason that the doorman would ask him a question, Chapman fell into an apprehensive silence. Keeping both hands in his pockets and the album clasped under his arm, he moved from the sentry's view, back against the gargoyle-studded rail of the building where he became lost in an unexpected web of paranoid musings. He stood for what seemed to him a long time and he began to feel confused by thoughts and fears that threatened to derail him from his purpose.

Growing fidgety, Chapman ambled slowly away from the building. He crossed the street to sit on one of the green park benches at the shrub-lined border of a concrete path leading into Central Park. Gazing back at the Dakota, he intently studied the classically bowed windows, oblique towers, soaring flag-tipped pinnacles, and convoluted details of the building's unique architecture. Methodically, he surveyed each of the sixth-floor windows. He imagined that he might catch a glimpse of the rock star who had unwittingly lured him six thousand miles from the sunshine and rainbows of the Hawaiian islands to linger in the chill and urban congestion of New York City in December.

Maybe John Lennon would step onto one of the building's rooftop balconies, Chapman fantasized. He recalled a picture he had seen in a Beatles book or on an album cover. The picture was of the historic musical group's last concert. The Beatles had performed the impromptu concert on the roof of the building that had housed their recording studio, Apple Records, in London. Bickering among themselves, beset by problems caused by their money and fame, the most popular musical group in history had broken up soon after the rooftop jam session. Chapman had inferred from the Anthony Fawcett book about Lennon that it was there, at the Apple building, that the Beatles had stopped being musicians and started becoming a multimillion-dollar business enterprise. John, Paul, George, and Ringo had gone their separate ways to begin merchandising the images of their collective success.

They had parlayed their innocent songs of love and peace, Chapman believed, into a corrupt and vast enterprise of personal wealth and power. In the eyes of the self-made Holden Caulfield, Lennon had come to symbolize the hypocrisy that was the source of the world's problems. Most acutely, he believed it to be the source of his own pain.

Chapman had known since childhood that the Beatles would never have existed without the genius of John Lennon. After studying the Fawcett book, he had begun to believe that the Beatles Generation had all been a sham, orchestrated from the beginning by Lennon, a cunning businessman posing as a rock star. As he gazed at the Dakota, he saw the ostentatious building as a symbol of all the hypocritical things that the "phony adult" had come to symbolize in his newfound Holden Caulfield consciousness. Closing his eyes, he leafed again in his mind through the pages of *John Lennon: One Day at a Time.* He envisioned the rich and powerful man taunting him from the Dakota rooftop.

Chapman abruptly stood and walked away from the bench, seized by the fear that John Lennon would leave the building and that he would be unable to get back across the street in time to meet him. He waited anxiously at the crosswalk for the traffic light to change. Studying a group of commuters that had just exited subway stairs at the corner of the Dakota, he smiled at a pretty Asian girl. The girl reminded him of his wife.

In a moment of anguish, Chapman recalled his wife's tears and confusion upon his return from his last trip to New York, less than a month earlier. Swallowing hard, he struggled against a familiar anchor of sadness and remorse that still threatened to hold him back from the thing he knew he had to do.

"Give me the strength," he prayed silently, searching out the familiar dark spot in his mind, barely moving his lips. He choked back tears that had begun to sting the corners of his eyes. "Please give me the strength to do it. It has to be done. Please give me the strength. The phonies have to know.

"It's pure, it's holy, it's real. I can no longer stand this pain."

Returning to the stone archway of the Dakota, Chapman observed how the building had become blackened and made somehow more elegantly sinister by decades of exhaust fumes and city soot. He remembered reading somewhere that the Dakota had been the backdrop that Hollywood director Roman Polanski had used when filming *Rosemary's Baby.* Chapman had seen the movie years ago. He began to ponder the horrifying tale of a young housewife, played by Mia Farrow, who had unknowingly been seduced by the devil and given birth to the son of Satan. He seemed to recall a scene from the movie in which someone was falling or being pushed from the top of the Dakota to the sidewalk below, where he was standing.

Chapman thought it ironic that Polanski's wife, a beautiful and talented young actress named Sharon Tate, had been murdered not long after he had made the macabre *Rosemary's Baby.* Along with a group of Polanski's friends, she had been stabbed to death by killers who had laughed at her pleas to spare the unborn infant that she was due to deliver in a few weeks. In a further ironic twist, the killers said they had been driven to murder by a drug-hazed message that they had received from John Lennon and the Beatles.

The infamous Tate-LaBianca killings were part of a gory plan that Charles Manson had code-named *Helter Skelter,* after the song of the same name that Lennon had written for the Beatles' untitled "white album." The lyrics to "Helter Skelter," "Piggies," "Blackbird," and other Beatles tunes had been interpreted by Manson as a command from the Beatles to begin slaughtering members of the wealthy and famous Hollywood social elite. The killers had scrawled "Helter Skelter" in their victims' blood on the walls of the expensive homes in which the bodies were found.

Chapman had found the Beatles-Manson-Dakota connection fraught with significance. As he pondered yet another irony in the events that had brought him to New York, he blinked in astonishment at a petite, vaguely familiar woman with soft, large eyes who smiled as she walked in front of him with a group of children. The woman and the children crossed the street in front of the Dakota and disappeared into Central Park. Caught up in his own angry reveries, he didn't trust his eyes until he heard a passerby give voice to his recognition: "Hey, that was that actress. You know. What's her name—Mia Farrow."

Chapman smiled with satisfaction. It was yet another synchronicity, another sign, he thought. Rosemary herself had walked past him in front of the Dakota. To Chapman, it was a confirmation.

"It has to be right," he said to himself. "This has to be the day. I couldn't possibly be imagining all these things."

Chapman snapped to attention when a trim, well-dressed woman with a mane of straight, black hair got out of a taxi and went into the Dakota. Satisfied that he wasn't looking at Yoko Ono, he relaxed and leaned back against the black rail. He looked at his watch and was astonished to discover that it was only 10:30 A.M. He withdrew *The Catcher in the Rye* from his pocket and soon found himself lost in the book.

Moments later, Chapman was almost in tears as he read about an emotionally exhausted Holden Caulfield talking in confusion to Allie, his dead brother, while wandering alone and frightened on the streets of New York: "I'd say to him, 'Allie, don't let me disappear.' "

Several pages later, he found himself chuckling out loud as he read again about Holden's reaction to graffiti scrawled by vandals at his little sister's school and on a mummy exhibit at the museum: "I think, even, if I die, and they stick me in a cemetery and I have a tombstone and all, it'll say 'Holden Caulfield' on it, and then what year I was born and what year I died, and then right under that it'll say 'Fuck You.' "

His mind riveted between the covers of the book, Chapman was only vaguely aware that a taxi had stopped at the curb in front of him. He paid no attention to the slender man in a slouch hat and tan jacket who stepped from the back of the cab. The man nodded and smiled through thick, circular lenses at the Dakota doorman before bounding beneath the stone archway and up low steps leading through shiny glass and brass doors into the sanctuary of the building.

"Did you see him?"

Chapman pulled his eyes reluctantly from the book, like a man awakening from a deep sleep. The doorman asked a second time, "Did you see him?"

"What? See what?"

"Mr. Lennon," the doorman said. "John Lennon. That was him. He just got out of that cab and went inside the building. Just now."

Stunned, Chapman slid the red paperback into his pocket and regained his composure.

"Guess I missed my chance," he said, holding up the Lennon album. "Guess I'll just have to keep waiting."

Chapman was disappointed, but he sensed that his opportunity had not been lost.

"This wasn't the right time anyway," he consoled himself. "When the time is right, it will happen. He'll be back. It won't be long now. I got a feeling."

Jude Stein was surprised to see Chapman standing again in front of the Dakota when she arrived Monday morning shortly after 11:00 A.M. Chapman waved at her and began talking excitedly as she approached. Jude smiled at Chapman and said hello to Pat, the doorman.

"You just missed him," Chapman said. "I missed him too. I was standing here reading. I had my head down, like a dummy. He pulled right up and got out of a cab and walked right by me and I didn't even see him, except out of the corner of my eye. I noticed somebody in a tan jacket, though."

The doorman smiled at Jude and confirmed that Lennon had indeed walked past just moments before her arrival. Jude told Chapman and O'Loughlin that she and Jery had seen John on Saturday. With feigned nonchalance, she added that Lennon had stopped for an amiable chat with her and her friend.

"You weren't here," she said to Chapman, accusingly.

He didn't respond.

A small flurry of activity had erupted outside the Dakota entrance. It was shortly before noon when Jude noticed that another Lennon fan, free-lance photographer Paul Goresh, had arrived. About the same time, she saw Frederic Seaman, Lennon's personal secretary, go into the building. She pointed out Seaman to Chapman. He had moved close to her and was trying to interject himself into a conversation she had struck up with the photographer. Seaman disappeared into the building as Chapman started to approach him with the *Double Fantasy* album.

As he had told everyone he'd met outside the building for the past three days, Chapman apprised Goresh that he was from Hawaii and that he wanted to get John Lennon's autograph.

Goresh, detecting that Chapman spoke with an accent, said he didn't realize people from Honolulu had a Southern drawl.

"Where you staying in New York?" Goresh added.

Chapman was unable to understand the sudden hostility that the photographer's question evoked. "Careful," he told himself, clutching the Lennon album protectively to his chest. "Inappropriate response. Totally inappropriate response," he reminded himself. Unable to conceal the hostility and paranoia that had been triggered by Goresh's question, he stepped close to the photographer's face.

"Why the hell did you ask me that question?" Chapman demanded. "What do you want to know that for?"

His right hand was in the pocket of his trench coat. The knuckles of his left hand were white from the grip he had on the album.

Goresh was taken aback by the sudden mood change that had descended upon Chapman for no apparent reason. As the photographer backed away, the man from Honolulu continued to demand to know why he had asked where he was staying in New York.

"Easy, man," Goresh said at last. "Take it easy. I was only making conversation, you know? I mean, you're the one who started the conversation in the first place."

His camera dangling around his neck, Goresh turned away from Chapman to walk to the other side of the Dakota archway. "Forget it," he said as he walked away. "Just forget it."

Under his breath Goresh muttered quietly to himself, "Big dope. Big damn dope."

After Goresh walked away, Chapman's hostility seemed to burn itself out as suddenly and inexplicably as it had flared. While the photographer puzzled silently over the brief and hostile incident, Chapman followed Jude across the street to the Dakota Grill.

"My treat," Chapman said, as he stepped off the curb behind Jude and walked quickly to her side.

Inside the restaurant, Chapman searched out a table near the window. He wanted to maintain a view of the Dakota entrance. When he sat down, he took off his coat and hat, keeping the coat folded across his lap. He kept the album in front of him on the table.

"Order anything you like," he said, handing Jude a copy of the menu. "I'm buying."

Jude ordered an omelette and coffee. Chapman ordered a hamburger and two bottles of beer.

As Jude sat in the restaurant across from Chapman, she felt awkward at times, unable to reply to the nearly constant stream of questions, advice, and conversation that he seemed compelled to maintain. He talked mostly about Hawaii, about what "a great place" it was and how he also thought that New York was "nice too." He told her that he had traveled around the world. He described the long plane ride and told her of his visit to Tokyo after Jude said she had always wanted to visit Japan.

Jude said she also had dreamed of visiting Hawaii, but that she would probably never be able to afford a vacation there.

"You can if you set your mind to it," Chapman admonished her. "You can do anything if you set your mind to it. The human mind is an incredible thing. Once it's made up, nothing can stop it from doing what it wants to do."

Before they left the restaurant, Jude gave Chapman her address and phone number. She also wrote down her friend Jery's address, along with the names and phone numbers of other Beatles fans in New York City. She wrote the information on a paper napkin that she folded neatly and gave to him. Absentmindedly, Chapman wadded the napkin in his hand and stuffed it into his pocket.

After leaving the restaurant, Chapman and the girl returned to the Dakota where they stood silently for more than an hour. Jude turned and burst suddenly into a smile as an older woman stepped around the ornate gate from the Dakota courtyard and stood beneath the archway. The woman was holding the hand of a doll-like child with large, almond eyes, porcelain skin, and straight black hair. When Jude began talking to the woman, Chapman moved in close behind her.

As Chapman stood smiling forlornly at the child, Jude introduced him to the boy's nanny, Helen Seaman, the aunt of Lennon's personal secretary Frederic Seaman. Jude explained that Chapman was a Beatles fan from Hawaii who hoped to get Lennon's autograph. As he was introduced to John Lennon's son, Chapman stepped forward and uncurled the sweaty fingers of his right hand from around the chunk of steel. Sliding his hand carefully from the deep pocket of his coat, he knelt on one knee before Sean Lennon. He wrapped his fingers around the child's tiny hand.

"I came all the way across the ocean from Hawaii and I'm honored to meet you," he said. The child stared at him blankly and sneezed.

Chapman smiled.

"You'd better take care of that runny nose," he said. "You wouldn't want to get sick and miss Christmas."

Chapman stood near the curb and waved good-bye as Sean and the nanny got into a Mercedes-Benz station wagon and drove away.

"Isn't he the cutest?" Jude asked Chapman.

"Yeah," Chapman said. "John and Yoko must be really proud to have such a beautiful child."

"Oh well," Jude said. "It's been nice meeting you. I hope you get your album signed."

"You're not leaving now, are you?" Chapman asked. "You haven't seen John yet. He's bound to come out today. I got a feeling about it."

"I don't think so," Jude said. "It's getting late and I don't think so. I've got to go."

"No!" Chapman exclaimed. "I mean, wait. We just got to know each other. How about waiting a while longer and then we can go have dinner and see a movie or a play or something. My treat."

He wondered if the woman could hear the desperation he heard in his own voice.

"Thanks, but I've got to be going," Jude said.

"Just a little longer," he pleaded.

"I have to be going," she said with finality. "Good luck getting the autograph."

CHAPTER FIVE

IS THAT ALL YOU WANT?

God, I wish you could've been there.

—HOLDEN CAULFIELD

Jude Stein had no way of knowing what Mark David Chapman had been struggling to tell her.

When he pleaded with her to linger with him through the evening hours of December 8, there was nothing to indicate what he was really trying to say: that it might be her last chance to see John Lennon alive. Until she read the news on the morning of December 9, Jude had no idea that she had struck up a friendship with the self-appointed "Catcher in the Rye" of his generation.

As he watched Jude bounce up the street and disappear into rush-hour crowds, Chapman felt a faint beam of hope go dark inside his mind. Before he could become ensnared again in the maze of his thoughts and beset by the self-doubt that seemed to threaten his carefully plotted purpose, he turned again to Paul Goresh. The large man had continued to loiter outside the Dakota throughout the afternoon with his hands in his pockets and his camera around his neck, consciously ignoring Chapman. It was almost 5:00 P.M. and the dim incandescent lamps had been turned on beneath the shadowy Dakota archway.

Putting on an ingratiating smile, Chapman ambled across the sidewalk and stood penitently before the photographer. Goresh regarded him warily, still angry that the "big dope" had insulted him earlier in the day.

"Well," Chapman said. "Looks like it's down to us die-hard Beatleholics now."

Goresh pretended not to hear the comment. He stared blankly into the darkening sky above Central Park.

"Look," Chapman said. "I'm sorry if I came on a little strong earlier in the day. I've been standing out here for the better part of three days now. I guess I'm just getting a little testy."

The photographer continued to look silently away. As Chapman turned to walk back across the sidewalk, Goresh finally replied.

"What the hell? You start up a conversation with a guy like he's your long-lost cousin, then you get hostile all of a sudden?"

"I'm bored and I'm far away from home, so I try to talk to people for a little companionship," Chapman struggled to explain. "I'm tired, so I guess that's why I flew off the handle. I'm sorry. Okay?"

He laughed in mock self-consciousness. "I guess it does seem pretty weird," he said, shaking his head. "Like I said, I'm sorry. I guess it's because of all those stories I've heard about the people in New York City. You know, you can't be too careful in the city. You never know who you're talking to."

Goresh noticed that Chapman continued to hug the *Double Fantasy* album close to his large body.

"Relax," he told him. "Nobody's going to steal your album around here."

Reaching a truce of sorts, the two men were engaged in small talk when a new doorman relieved O'Loughlin at the Dakota sentry booth. Chapman at once recognized the short, smiling doorman who took O'Loughlin's place. He had met Jose Perdomo several weeks earlier during the first trip to New York.

"Hey!" he said, waving the album in the air. "Jose. How you doin' man? It's me, Mark. Mark Chapman. I'm back."

Chapman reminded Perdomo that he was the Beatles fan from Hawaii.

Perdomo spoke little English. He just smiled back at the big, pale man with the record album in his hand. He saw Chapman as an eccentric, but harmless, buffoon. Although Chapman was more outgoing and talkative than most of the celebrity worshipers who sometimes stalked the Dakota day and night for weeks at a time, Perdomo had dismissed him as just another obsessed John Lennon fan.

When he had first introduced himself to Perdomo outside the Dakota a month before, Chapman had stood talking for long hours with the doorman. He had learned that Perdomo was a refugee from Castro's Cuba. Perdomo had told Chapman that he was lucky to be a citizen of such a great country as the United States and to live in a beautiful place like Hawaii.

Chapman liked Perdomo. The Hawaiian tourist and the doorman soon had struck up a confidence, talking about Fidel Castro, the Cuban missile crisis, and the assassination of former president John Fitzgerald Kennedy. They mused upon the enormities that drive despots like Castro and impel assassins such as Lee Harvey Oswald. They agreed, Chapman recalls, that Castro had probably been involved in the plot to kill Kennedy.

At Chapman's urging, the conversation also had turned frequently to the topic of John Lennon. Chapman said he wanted to find out everything he could about Lennon.

"The Beatles were creative geniuses," Chapman had explained to the politely nodding doorman. "Their music was truly original, truly inspired." He had boasted to Perdomo that he had spared no expense to travel all the way from his home in Hawaii to see Lennon in person.

"It must be incredible seeing a great star like John Lennon all the time," Chapman had said. "John Lennon is probably the most popular person in the world right now. He's like a god or something. I sure wish I had your job."

Chapman recalls that the doorman told him he had met many stars at the Dakota, and that he knew Leonard Bernstein personally. He said Bernstein had given him autographed albums of several of his popular and classical albums, including the Bernstein signature sound track from *West Side Story.* If Chapman wanted autographs, Perdomo assured him, he could get autographs.

Impressed by the doorman's familiarity with Leonard Bernstein, Chapman informed him that Bernstein had been one of the first established and respected musical experts to appreciate Beatles music. While many critics and much of the public had dismissed the British rock group as another of many passing musical fads, Bernstein had predicted that the songs of Lennon and Paul McCartney would endure.

"And Bernstein is right," Chapman had told Perdomo. "The music of the Beatles will someday be known as classics. They'll be ranked alongside the great musical geniuses like Beethoven, Bach, and Mozart. Mark my word."

On the evening of December 8, Chapman showed Perdomo the Lennon album he'd bought on Saturday. He reminded the doorman of the conversations they'd had outside the Dakota the month before. Abruptly, Chapman turned away from Perdomo. A small group of laughing men and women had come out of the Dakota. Some of them were carrying tape recorders. Others held cassette tapes loosely in their hands as they walked to the curb.

Before Chapman had a chance to approach the group, to ask if they knew John Lennon, a limousine pulled to the curb and Perdomo stepped forward to open the door. A man with a British accent thanked Perdomo. Chapman noted that the man slipped several dollar bills discreetly into the doorman's hand before getting into the limo. As he watched other members of the group getting into the limousine, Chapman heard a voice behind him that sounded strangely familiar. The clear, strong voice was tinged with a British accent. Chills began to move along the back of Chapman's thick neck, up and down his spine.

He turned around to see John Lennon and Yoko Ono stepping from the stone stairway onto the pavement outside the Dakota entrance. In an instant, the very odor and color of the air around Mark David Chapman seemed somehow to change as he found himself gazing at last into the eyes of one of the most recognizable and familiar faces in the world. It was the face he had spent months burning into his brain. As Chapman stared in disbelief, Lennon and Ono were quickly enveloped by an entourage that continued to emerge from the building behind them. With wooden feet, the man from Honolulu stepped stiffly aside. His heart thumped rapidly, arrhythmically, in his chest as Lennon strolled in front of him to the edge of the curb and looked in anticipation up and down West 72nd Street.

The doorman explained apologetically to Mr. Lennon that his limousine had not yet arrived. Lennon told Perdomo not to worry about the limousine. He asked the doorman to hail a taxi instead.

Unable to speak, Chapman stood clutching the *Double Fantasy* album in his hand, his mind a virtual blank. He was aware of the flash of a strobe light as Goresh moved around Lennon and Ono, snapping pictures on the darkening sidewalk. The photographer nudged him awake.

"Hey," he said. "I thought you wanted to get your album autographed. What the heck are you waiting for? There he is."

Chapman shuffled obsequiously from the edge of the circle that had formed around Lennon as the photographer prompted him forward. Lennon and Ono had already accepted a ride with the group that had preceded them from the building and entered the limousine. Yoko was in the backseat. Seconds before Lennon would have disappeared into the waiting limo, Chapman began to move with astonishing speed toward his target. Mutely, he held the album in tentative, outstretched hands before Lennon's face. In his right hand, he was also holding the new Bic pen he had bought that morning at the bookshop where he had found *The Catcher in the Rye.*

Hatless, dressed for the New York City winter in a crew neck sweater and a dark leather bombardier's jacket with a furry collar, Lennon squinted through his glasses and smiled at Chapman. The rock star accepted the album that was held out before him and balanced it against a small cassette recorder he was carrying in his left hand. He looked at Chapman again, signaling that he needed the pen. Chapman's jaw dropped. He appeared to go into a momentary trance as he watched Lennon move the point of the pen in the shape of a *J* across the slick surface of the new album. When nothing appeared on the record cover, Lennon gave a short laugh and moved the new pen in a hasty circle, to get the ink flowing.

"John Lennon," he wrote. "December, 1980."

Chapman continued to stand as though dumbfounded before the object of his obsession. He never considered reaching for the gun. His hands hung limply at his sides as Lennon smiled again and gave him back the autographed album.

"Is," Lennon hesitated as he began to speak to Chapman, "is that all you want?"

Slowly, as though in a dream, Chapman took the album and the pen from John Lennon's hands. His throat dry as sand and his body stiff as rusted tin, Chapman had to force himself to move and to speak.

"Thanks," he said meekly. "Thanks, John."

"Damn," Chapman heard a voice exclaiming somewhere in the back of his mind.

"No!" screamed another voice. It was the voice of a child. "You can have him now. Put your hand in your pocket. He's yours! He's mine! You promised! You bastard! Phony bastard! You promised!"

The unspoken words reverberated through his brain as Chapman watched Lennon bend his slender, wiry frame and disappear into the crowded backseat of the sleek, white limousine.

"He's a nice guy," whispered another voice. "He was courteous and polite. He was quite kind to you. You can go home now. You have seen him and it didn't happen. And now you can take your autographed album and you can go back home."

"But he wasn't real," said the child inside. "You *know* he wasn't real."

"Looks like you scored big time."

The photographer was standing in front of him, winding a roll of exposed film back in his camera.

"Gosh," Chapman enthused, holding the album tenderly in the fingers of both hands and displaying the autograph. "That's pretty special. Big stars don't usually put the date on their albums or photographs when they sign them like that. This is really unique. What a collector's item.

"Wow. Back in Hawaii, they'll never believe I could meet John Lennon and get his autograph."

Suddenly remembering that Goresh had been snapping pictures all the while that Lennon had stood outside the building, Chapman asked if he was in any of the photographs. He said he hoped Goresh had taken a picture of him while he was standing beside the rock legend, getting the album signed. Goresh said he thought that he had.

"I'll give you anything for that picture," Chapman said. "Anything. Wait a minute! Did I have my hat on or off when you took it? I didn't want to be photographed standing beside John Lennon in this stupid Russian hat. Do you remember? Was my hat on or off? Do you remember?"

When Goresh said he thought Chapman had his hat on in the picture, Chapman found that he had to struggle against the irrational tide of anger that again began rising in his breast. He began chewing furiously at the corners of his chapped and peeling lips until he felt himself beginning to regain control.

"Listen," he said to Goresh. "Is there any way you can get that film processed tonight? Is there any way I can get that picture tonight?"

Goresh explained that he lived some distance away from Manhattan, in New Jersey. He couldn't develop and print the film until the next day, at the earliest.

"I'll give you $50 for that one picture," Chapman said. "Meet me here tomorrow and I'll give you $50 for that picture of me with John Lennon—if it comes out all right. Is that a deal?"

"Tomorrow," Goresh said. "Okay."

"Gosh," Chapman said. "Wait 'til they see that picture back in Hawaii, of me standing next to John Lennon."

Chapman fell into a protracted silence. He began pacing back and forth in front of the building, the autographed album clasped tight against his chest. Sometimes his lips moved, but he didn't speak.

About an hour after Lennon and Ono had left the Dakota, Chapman recognized the vaguely familiar face of a slender young man who emerged from the shiny Dakota doors. It was Frederic Seaman, Lennon's personal secretary, the man that Jude had pointed out to him earlier in the day.

"Hey, Fred, check this out," he heard the photographer say. "This guy Mark Chapman here really scored big. He came all the way from Hawaii and got John Lennon to autograph his album. Check it out."

Chapman held the album up for Seaman to inspect the autograph.

Seaman glanced briefly at Chapman and forced a polite smile.

"Congratulations, man," he said. Seaman wanted to escape before the photographer could entrap him into a conversation.

Seaman disliked Goresh. The photographer had haunted Lennon and Ono ever since Seaman had come to work at the Dakota nearly two years earlier. Seaman, who recalled that Goresh had told him that he wanted to be a police officer, had come to view people like Goresh as a potential threat to his boss. The photographer had been ejected from the Dakota about a year earlier after dressing in a utility uniform and posing as a repairman to gain entrance to the building. Goresh had sneaked all the way into Lennon's bedroom before he had been caught. Seaman said he would often gaze down from the windows in the Lennons' suite on the top floor of the building and see Goresh lurking like a sniper with his camera and a long telephoto lens in a stairwell below the sidewalk across West 72nd Street. Lennon had instructed Seaman to help him try to avoid the photographer whenever possible. On more than one occasion, Seaman recalled that Goresh had blown Lennon's cover when the musician and his wife would pull hats low over their faces and try to walk quietly and anonymously through Central Park.

"I always thought that if anybody wanted to shoot John, it would be somebody posing as a photographer or something like that," Seaman recalled. "All these guys hanging around outside the building all the time used to worry me a lot."

Seaman turned away from Chapman and ignored an attempt by Goresh to strike up a conversation about the Lennons. Seaman had just gotten off the phone with Lennon and he was in a hurry to get to the Record Plant on West 44th Street. The musician wanted him to locate tapes of a 1974 recording session that Yoko had done with guitarist David Spinozza and bring them to the studio. Lennon and Ono had gone straight to the Record Plant after leaving the Dakota, saying they intended to work through the evening with musicians and engineers to put the finishing touches on a new recording. The song, their final joint musical offering, was titled "Walking on Thin Ice," a 45 rpm single that Yoko wanted to release on the coattails of the *Double Fantasy* success.

A box of recording tapes beside him on the front seat of the Lennons' Mercedes-Benz, Seaman pulled away from the driveway at the Mayfair Garage next to the Dakota at about 6:20 P.M. Fleetingly, he thought about a phone call he'd received earlier in the day from Doug MacDougall. MacDougall, Lennon's bodyguard, was scheduled to meet with Yoko the next day, on December 9, to discuss his return to work.

MacDougall had been on a leave of absence since late September, when, Seaman recalled, Yoko Ono had rejected the ex-FBI agent's suggestions for increased security. MacDougall had called back to confirm the meeting. He also asked Seaman whether Lennon and Ono were aware they needed to take additional security precautions because of the worldwide attention and publicity generated by the release of *Double Fantasy.*

As Seaman turned from the Dakota and drove toward Columbus Avenue, Chapman turned back to Goresh. He asked if the photographer had any idea when Lennon and Ono might return. Goresh said if the couple had gone to dinner, they would be back in about two hours. If they had gone back into the recording studio, they might not return until the early hours of the morning.

At 8:00 P.M., Goresh realized that the Lennons had probably gone to the studio. He decided that he would drive back home to North Arlington, New Jersey.

Inexplicably, the Beatles fan from Honolulu became frantic when Goresh said good-night and started to walk across the street toward his car. Attempting again to engage Goresh in conversation, Chapman apologized anew for his hostile outburst earlier in the day. He began to divulge selective details of his private life. He told Goresh for the first time that he was staying at the Sheraton, answering the question that had sparked his earlier hostility.

"But like I said," he added, "you can't be too careful until you get to know somebody a little bit, especially in a big city like this. You never know who you're talking to.

"I'm not from Hawaii originally," Chapman then confessed. "I'm originally from Georgia. I grew up in an upper-middle-class suburb just outside Atlanta. In Decatur. Decatur, Georgia.

"I've traveled all over the world. But Hawaii is the place I belong. I probably wouldn't be alive today if I hadn't moved there three years ago.

"You wouldn't believe what I went there for. I've lived a very ironical life."

He told Goresh that he was married and that his wife was back home in Hawaii waiting for him. Goresh listened for several minutes in silence and again said goodnight to Chapman. He promised that he would return the next evening with a print of the photograph he'd taken of Chapman with John Lennon.

"You really ought to wait a while longer," Chapman said. "They could come back any minute. They'll be back before midnight. I got a feeling."

Goresh told Chapman he should go back to his hotel room and get some sleep. "You've got his autograph on the album," Goresh reminded him. "Give it up for the day and get some rest."

Chapman said he had decided that he wanted to wait for the couple to return so that he could get Yoko Ono's autograph on the album beside Lennon's.

"My family back in Hawaii will be very surprised if I go back and show them I've got both the Lennons' autographs on an album," Chapman gushed. "My wife just won't believe it."

Chapman didn't tell Goresh that his wife was also a Japanese-American woman, like Yoko Ono. He thought Goresh would be critical of him for being married to an Asian woman. Earlier in the day, the two men had briefly discussed racial issues while watching a black man stroll arm-in-arm with a white woman along the sidewalk across the street.

Chapman remembered suddenly that Goresh had told him earlier that he also had a copy of Lennon's new album in his car.

"Go get your album and I'll use your camera to take a picture of you getting his autograph," Chapman pleaded. "I know how to handle a camera. I used to take the photographs for the newsletter at a hospital where I used to work in Hawaii. I took pictures of the governor and of some famous people there. Let me take your picture with John."

"I see John all the time," Goresh boasted. "I can get my picture taken with him any time. I'm going home."

"Suppose you don't see him again?" Chapman said. His voice began to rise in desperation as he realized that he was about to be left alone in the shadows outside the Dakota.

"Suppose you don't see him again?" Chapman repeated. "Suppose he goes to Spain or something? Suppose something happens to him?"

Annoyed by Chapman's barrage of preposterous suppositions, the photographer walked away without a further word and got into his car. As he drove away, he turned for a last look. The "big dope" continued to pace in and out of shadows before the Dakota. His head was down and his right hand was in his coat pocket. He was still clutching the *Double Fantasy* album tightly in his left hand against his chest.

CHAPTER SIX

BUT WHERE WOULD I GO?

Guilt for being rich, and guilt thinking
that perhaps love and peace isn't enough
and you have to go and get shot or something.

—JOHN LENNON, SEPTEMBER 1980

"It was a little kid that did that act of killing John Lennon. A little kid on his Don Quixote horse went charging up to a windmill called the Dakota with an insane, irreparable, tragic mission: to put holes through one of the sails of that windmill of phoniness.

"That's what happened. It was a child that killed John Lennon. It wasn't a man. It was a child killing his hero: the Beatles. It was a child that had been so hurt and rejected into adulthood that he had to cover up all his feelings. I maintained, I preserved my childhood. Even though I'd had twenty-five birthdays, inside I was sixteen years old like Holden Caulfield was. My only feelings were the feelings that came through that book to the sixteen-year-old Holden that was inside me—until something real finally happened.

"John Lennon was real and he was a hero. He was the hero of my childhood. But I wasn't real to myself. I was just a hulk of hurt and rejection, a confused, unfeeling defense mechanism. A cyborg. A conglomerate of adult mannerisms and jobs, but a child's heart. That was the conflict that came crashing down. That's why I could never do anything. My child was always conflicting with my fake adult, my phony adult that I had erected around it.

"All that rage came spilling out and I killed the hero of my childhood. All the rage at the world and in myself and in my disappointments and disillusions. All those feelings I kept pent up, feelings that the child couldn't handle. Feelings that the adult was supposed to handle, but couldn't.

"The child got confused and angered. And since he's so specially linked to the phony adult that I was, the phony adult that the child had created, something had to happen. An explosion had to happen.

"I was a child with an adult body. I threw temper tantrums like a child; but I didn't, like a child, know how to kill anybody. So I summoned the forces of evil to do it, to help me do it. I did what I thought you could do to get the evil forces. You chant and you take off your clothes. You get angry and you say horrible things. I had to pump up to do it.

"Shooting a man is no easy thing, even if you are out of your mind. It takes a lot of inner strength to do something that hideous.

"The adult was just a front for an act of evil that was carried out by a child. It was a child's anger, a child's jealousy, a child's rage. But the adult was so undeveloped, he didn't know what to do with it.

"The adult was all surface, anyway. It was a front. It couldn't handle anything. It diverted everything to the child, and the child put it in his black toy box, because he couldn't handle adult feelings either.

"He would, the adult would take each feeling and say some words and then give it to the child. The child would put it in the toy box he never opened, except to put something new in it.

"The child would play with his new toys. But one day when he opened the box to put something new inside, he came across a toy that he had played with years ago. It had once been his hero, but it wasn't the same. He showed it to the fake adult, the phony adult. He said, 'Look! Look what one of my toys has become!' and he threw a tantrum.

"Then the adult knew what to do. The adult knew about guns and he knew how to get on an airplane and he knew how to get money. So they kind of conspired together, the child's anger and rage at his hero—at the toy that wasn't the same—and the adult who had the knowledge, but who was shaky and who was thin and shallow, but who had the intelligence to give the child what he wanted.

"And they conspired together, the child and the child's fake adult, to kill a hero. To kill the phony. To kill phoniness. To take some kind of a stand for the first time in their lives. To do something. To do something real. I was going to stamp out phoniness.

"The adult planned it out perfectly, precisely. The child turned to Satan for the power to pull the trigger. The adult gave the child a gun, and the child needed power to pull the trigger.

"Then they went to New York, but something happened that first trip and the child went away. The child went away and left the adult just a shaking hulk who went back home to his wife. There was some reality there. There was a touch of reality.

"But then the child came back. One day while the adult was back in Hawaii driving a car, the child started throwing his toys again and getting mad again and upset again. The child wanted to kill again.

"And the adult went along with the child again—they were so enmeshed. They were one, but separate. And the child got the adult planning again, the phony adult. He got the adult planning again how to do it. The adult obliged and got more money. The adult made up a story about the gun being thrown away, and made up a story about going to New York again. And, in a matter of days, they flew back to New York.

"Then the adult and the child got up that morning and laid out all the important things to the child: The Bible. The photo with the Vietnamese kids. The music. The pictures of *The Wizard of Oz.* The passport and the letters of commendation for my work with the Vietnamese kids.

"This was the child's message, the tableau that said: 'This is what I was. These are the things that I was. I'm about to go into another dimension.'

"Then the child and the adult went to the Dakota on the morning of December 8. The adult, very charming, knows his way around—even invited one of the fans to lunch across the street—the child, frightened, alternately praying to God and the devil to get him out of this. The adult was praying to God. He was a fake adult, but he was scared and he knew that the child was about to do something very evil and wrong. The child was praying to the devil and the adult was praying to the Lord.

"The spiritual dichotomy: Devil-God. And the inner dichotomy: the child–the man. They're out there in front of the Dakota late at night, long after everybody else but the doorman has gone away. They're cold, and the adult wants to go home. Even this phony, disheveled, shaking, trembling-inside adult wants to go home—just go home and show the autograph, John Lennon's autograph, to his wife.

" 'She'll never believe it's his, but do it anyway,' the adult says. 'Get the first cab out of here. Ask that doorman to get you a cab.'

"Then the child screams: 'No! No! No!

" 'No. I want to kill him. I *want* to kill him. He's mine! I *want* him!'

"Then the adult: 'God help me! Save me, God, from this. Help me. Get me out of here.'

" 'No, no, no! Devil! Help me, Devil! Give me the power and the strength to do this. I want this. I want to be important. I want to be somebody. Help me. I was never anybody. Nobody ever let me be anybody. I couldn't be anybody, I failed at everything. Please. I want this. I want this so bad. I want this so bad.'

"It was getting late. Both the adult and child were very tired. It was almost 11:00 o'clock. Then a white limousine came up the street from Central Park. It stopped at the traffic light on the corner.

"They knew. The child and the fake adult, at that moment, somehow they both knew who was inside that limousine. And the child stood up with the adult in tow. The adult was resigned. The phony adult was resigned. He had no strength. He was merely an image, a surface. A tin man. He was a covering for the child to function in society.

"And they got up together and they reviewed together the adult's plan: How to put the hand in the pocket. How to pull it out of the pocket, and when to do it.

"The light changed and the white limousine turned left. Then it stopped at the curb in front of the Dakota, just like they knew it would.

"The adult began to pray. The child began to scream. The adult said, 'No.' The child screamed louder. The adult began to panic and then he disappeared. There was just the child with his hand on the gun and dead silence in my brain.

"The back door of the limousine opened and Yoko got out first. The child nodded to her. He smiled at her. But she didn't smile back and the child didn't say anything. She just kept walking, up the driveway, under the archway toward the steps.

"Then John Lennon got out of the limousine. He had something in his hands. Some cassette tapes. The child looked at his hero and his hero—his broken toy—looked back at him. It was a hard look. The child was sure that his hero recognized him from earlier in the day, when he signed the album. Neither one smiled. Nobody said a word. There was dead silence in my brain and John Lennon walked past me. He started walking faster as he went under the archway. Yoko was a little ahead of him, but he was there, by himself. His back was to the child and the voice said: 'Do it! Do it! Do it! Do it! Do it!' "

"I aimed at his back. I pulled the trigger five times. And all hell broke loose in my mind.

"It was like everything had been stripped away then. It wasn't a make-believe world anymore. The movie strip broke.

"The explosions were deafening. After the first shot, Yoko crouched down and ran around the corner, into the courtyard. Then the gun was empty and John Lennon had disappeared. There was just the smell of gunpowder, a heavy, sickening smell. I saw Yoko come out of the courtyard and run up the steps through the door.

"Inside the Dakota, behind the door, some people were yelling. Somebody screamed. The child had left and the fake adult was standing there with the gun in his hand. He couldn't move. The child shot and killed a music legend.

Then the child vanished, and the shallow hulk of the phony adult was left there to pay the price.

"The doorman, Jose, was standing in front of me with tears in his eyes. 'Do you know what you done?' Jose was saying. 'Do you know what you done? Get out of here, man! Just get out of here!'

" 'But where would I go?' I said. 'But where would I go?'

"Jose shook the gun out of my hand and kicked it across the driveway toward the courtyard. Somebody came up in an elevator at the corner of the archway and Jose told him to take the gun away.

"I took *The Catcher in the Rye* out of my coat pocket. Then I took off my hat and coat and threw them down on the ground. I knew the police would come soon and I wanted them to see that I wasn't hiding a gun inside my coat.

"I was anxious. I wanted the police to hurry up and come. I was pacing and holding the book. I tried to read, but the words were crawling all over the pages. Nothing made any sense. I just wanted the police to come and take me away from there."

In April 1981, Chapman described the murder of John Lennon to psychologist Dr. Richard Bloom:

"It was like after the photographer left, that's where the struggle ended. It was after Paul left 'cause I knew it was all over. I knew I was going to kill him then. It was like, it was like toward the end there was no more struggle, but during I prayed, you know. . . . There was a point where I came to, where there was no more struggles, and I resigned myself, as far as I know.

"I stood up and I said, 'This is it. This is it.' I stood up, of course; I had my hand on the gun. The car pulled up. Yoko got out and walked about thirty feet from John. She looked at me. I nodded to her and she went toward the door.

"Then John did, and there was no emotion in my blood. There was no anger. There was nothing. It was dead silence in my brain. Dead, cold quiet, until he walked up. He looked at me. I'm telling you, the man, the man was going to be dead in less than five minutes and he looked at me and I looked at him and he walked past me and then I heard in my head. It said, 'Do it, do it, do it,' over and over again. 'Do it, do it, do it, do it,' like that. It was . . . my voice. It wasn't anybody else's. It wasn't an audible voice. I walked a few feet, turned, pulled the gun out of my pocket, put my hand into my left hand. I don't remember aiming. I don't remember drawing a bead or whatever you call it. I just pulled the trigger steady five times. Then I believe I saw Yoko turn. She was facing me and she went, like, ducked around the corner.

"I just started pacing. You know, each time I would turn it would be something different. The first time I turned, nobody was there. I couldn't believe it. I thought he'd be down on the ground, dying, bleeding.

"He wasn't there! These bullets were extra-power. They were .38 caliber special hollow points. Do you know what a hollow point does when it enters your body? It blows you away. He wasn't there.

"I was kind of glad that he wasn't there because I thought I had missed him or I didn't kill him or something. Feeling that . . . maybe a little bit . . . thinking I didn't hit him."

When police cars began arriving a few minutes after the shooting in front of the Dakota, Chapman was simultaneously relieved and frightened. Two uniformed officers stepped cautiously out of the first patrol car that pulled up at the curb as he continued to pace slowly beneath the dim light inside the stone archway. He held the red paperback tenderly, in both hands, close to his face. He still hoped that he would disappear into the ink of the book or that his body would shrivel into a fetal ball.

From the corner of his eye, he saw one of the officers rush past him, into the building where John Lennon lay dying. The other officer, a large and muscular man, approached the doorman who began nervously pointing at Chapman. In a quick, fluid motion, the officer drew his pistol and removed his hat. The hat, with a shiny badge that would offer a bright target for a hidden gunman, slid across the pavement like a Frisbee past Chapman's feet.

Before the officer could speak to him, Chapman's hands were in the air. He held the book tight against the top of his hatless head.

"Don't hurt me," he pleaded. "I'm unarmed. Please don't let anybody hurt me."

Barking orders, holding the gun combat style in both hands—the same way, Chapman observed, that he had braced a gun in his own hands minutes earlier—the officer approached the suspect. Glancing cautiously around the corner into the courtyard, Officer Stephen Spiro ordered Chapman to turn around, lean forward, and put his hands against the stone wall of the archway. When *The Catcher in the Rye* tumbled to the sidewalk, Chapman hesitated. The policeman pushed him forward and kicked his feet apart before hastily searching his clothing for a concealed weapon.

"I acted alone," Chapman exclaimed, observing that the officer continued to glance cautiously over his shoulders and around the corners of the buildings. "I'm the only one."

Satisfied that the suspect was unarmed, the policeman ordered him to turn around.

Chapman pleaded again with the officer not to let anyone hurt him.

"Nobody's going to hurt you. Just hold your hands together in front of you," the officer said, snapping a pair of handcuffs around Chapman's wrists. "Just do as you're told and nobody will hurt you. Now, just walk over toward the car there. Very slowly. And get into the backseat when I open the door."

"I'm sorry," Chapman said. "I'm sorry I gave you guys all this trouble." He began walking toward the police car. Suddenly he stopped and turned around to face the officer.

"The book!" he pleaded. "My book!" He nodded to the red paperback with the gold letters on both covers that lay open, face down, on the sidewalk beneath the archway. Officer Peter Cullen had joined his partner outside the Dakota. Cullen picked up the book carefully, by the edges, to preserve fingerprints or any other possible evidence from *The Catcher in the Rye.* The officer slipped the book into a plastic bag.

"Thank you," Chapman said as the officers locked him into the backseat of the patrol car and turned back toward the Dakota. The acrid smell of gunpowder still in his nostrils, the explosion of gunfire still ringing in his ears, the killer gazed mutely from the window at the chaotic aftermath of his violence. He was unable to avert his eyes as several police officers emerged from the door of the Dakota carrying a limp, blood-soaked body gently between them. After placing the bleeding body carefully into the backseat of another patrol car, one of the officers turned to face Chapman. The killer couldn't hear the words but he saw the curses that shaped themselves on the officer's lips.

Suddenly, the face of Yoko Ono appeared outside the patrol car several feet away from him. Chapman tried to slide down into the cramped seat, but found himself unable to avert his eyes from the gaze of the woman he had just made a widow.

"Please," he murmured to himself. "Just go away. Please just go away."

After several moments, Yoko disappeared. Other curious onlookers quickly began to take her place. They stared at him through the windows of the police car. He wanted it to be over. He wanted to be taken from the scene of his crime. He feared that, as word of what he had done spread through the city, an angry Lennon fan would appear and start firing bullets at him through the car windows. He prayed for God to turn back time. He promised God he wouldn't do it again—if God would only turn back time.

As he waited for the police officer to return to the car, Chapman struggled against a growing realization of the enormity of his act. Time seemed to stand still. At last Spiro and Cullen got into the front seat of the car and drove away with their suspect. The officers chattered frantically with a dispatcher on the police radio. Red lights bathed the streets as the patrol car sped through traffic lights and swerved around corners and oncoming traffic. Chapman tried to press his large, handcuffed body onto the floor of the car, fearing that snipers already were searching for him.

"Please don't let anybody hurt me," he repeated to the patrolmen. "I'm sorry I caused you guys all this trouble."

Between radio calls, Officer Cullen advised Chapman of his right to remain silent and to contact a lawyer. The driver, the officer who had arrested Chapman, began rocking his body excitedly forward and backward, pounding the steering wheel of the police car with his fists.

"I told you I felt it," he said to his partner. "I told you that something big was going to happen tonight. Remember what I said?"

Cullen nodded.

"This is history, man!" Spiro was shouting. "This is history!"

When he heard the officer's remark about the historic dimensions of his act, Chapman snapped to attention in the backseat. Both officers swiveled their heads briefly to look at him. Taking them into his confidence, he smiled.

"I am the Catcher in the Rye," he said.

"Gradually the child came back. My adult didn't know how to handle it. My adult escaped. My adult ran as fast as he could.

"It was dark and scary and this adult didn't know what to do. He didn't know what the child had become. The child had mutated. There was no child as there was before. The child had changed. And then, the adult and the child, they were stitched into one. That was the mutation that occurred. There's no other way to describe it. The child wasn't a child anymore, but he still wasn't an adult.

"In the mutation that occurred, I would later become a quasi-savior, and *The Catcher in the Rye* would become the Bible. I would become whole. I would become euphoric. I would not be a child and a phony adult any more. I would have a purpose and I would be strong and euphoric.

"This mutated creature that would arise after the shooting would become a guardian angel. Some type of a good force in his own mind. True and pure and real. Not phony. Something genuine. The child would finally get what he wanted: not celebrity, but purpose. An important purpose. This child with this little phony adult shackled to him, that he just used to get what he wanted, this child would become a star in his own movie. One of the rare children who was destined to become what he had idolized years before.

"The child would become the hero and want adults to read *The Catcher in the Rye.* He wanted them to read the book so they would see their own phoniness and become children again.

"There was no fake adult anymore. He was used and then buried. He had disintegrated. He turned to dust. He was gone.

"So the child killed John Lennon. He killed him. To be important. To be somebody."

PART II

AFTERMATH

CHAPTER SEVEN

DO YOU KNOW WHO YOU ARE?

I felt like a hollow temple filled with many spirits.

—JOHN LENNON

As life ebbed from John Lennon's shattered body, a New York City police officer bent close to one of the most famous faces in the world.

"Do you know who you are?" he asked the dying star.

In shock from four hollow-point .38 caliber bullets that had exploded in his chest, severing his windpipe and destroying much of his throat and vocal apparatus, Lennon was unable to speak. The familiar voice that had helped a generation discover and proclaim its identity was sadly unable in its final hour of life to identify itself.

Do you know who you are? is a question that haunted John Lennon throughout his life. The same question turned former YMCA counselor and born-again Christian Mark David Chapman into a celebrity stalker and one of the most notorious murderers of his time.

A question of identity, in the end, is what linked the famous rock star to his infamous killer. Lennon's unending struggle to re-create and rediscover himself, coupled with a perilous compulsion to reveal the most intimate details of his self-discovery in music, words, and pictures, laid the groundwork for Chapman's deadly obsession.

During interviews before his death, Lennon said that he grew up knowing only—like Mark David Chapman—that he wanted to be "somebody" and that he wanted to be "famous."

Born October 9, 1940, into the chaos of World War II England, John Winston Lennon was abandoned in childhood by his father, Freddie Lennon, an Irish merchant seaman. A few years later his mother, Julia, immortalized in the haunting Lennon-McCartney song that bears her name, also abandoned her son. A good-time working-class girl who sang in local pubs and who taught John Lennon the rudiments of guitar and banjo, Julia prudently gave her firstborn child over to be raised in a more stable, middle-class environment by her married sister, Mimi Smith.

Although Julia Lennon tried to come back into her son's life when he was fourteen years old, the mother and child reunion was never to be. As she stood on a curb near her Liverpool home, Julia was run over and killed by a car driven by a drunken off-duty police officer. John Lennon reportedly never cried when told of his mother's death.

In wrenching and cathartic post-Beatles solo ballads, Lennon later confronted the grief of having been abandoned by both parents and robbed by death of an adolescent reunion with his mom.

He wailed, in the emotional hymn that he titled "Mother," over the loss of both his mom and dad. The song ends with the raw and repeated screams of a child pleading for his parents to come home.

In another song, "My Mummy's Dead," a melancholy and moving nursery rhyme written more than fifteen years after his mother was killed, Lennon sang of a pain so great he could "never show it"—a pain, he said, that never went away.

Although his friends recall that he seldom spoke about his mother, a substantial portion of Lennon's later music, as well as the earlier Beatles music he cowrote with Paul McCartney, is haunted with the spirit of Julia. She was the lost mother for whom he searched throughout his life, the "ocean child" he believed he had found at last in his wife and soul mate, Yoko Ono, who swept him away from his first wife and his firstborn son.

A generation later, the tragic separation of parent and child that marked Lennon's own childhood was destined to repeat itself. Following a bitter divorce from his first wife, Cynthia, John Lennon became estranged for more than a decade from the five-year-old child that he had named Julian in memory of his dead mother.

Lennon's breach of faith with his son "was the one thing he regretted most, primarily because he was acutely aware he was repeating the pattern of his own childhood," according to Frederic Seaman.

"It killed him," said Seaman, who was employed as Lennon's personal secretary, chauffeur, and all-around gofer during the last two years of the rock legend's life.

"He had suffered so much in his own childhood and I think at some point he had said to himself that, no matter what happened, he would not repeat that pattern with his own child. And yet he did. And he saw it. And it killed him. He felt overwhelmed by guilt and he felt a failure. It really tormented him."

Like Lennon, Seaman is a slender and wiry man with thick brown hair that spills across an angular face. He also is the son of a professional musician, the late Eugene Seaman, a classical concert pianist. Seaman says he has a unique understanding of the relationship between John and Julian Lennon. Just as John Lennon abandoned Julian, Seaman said his father, too, was absent during much of his son's childhood to pursue an international music career.

Perhaps because of the circumstances of his own childhood, Seaman says that John Lennon became "a father figure" to him. During the time that he worked for Lennon, Seaman says that he tried to help repair the relationship between the disaffected rock star and the adolescent "who wanted to be the son of the mythological John Lennon, not the John Lennon who was never there for him."

"John really had no relationship with Julian. He scorned him," Seaman said. "But toward the end, he became torn between the impulse of keeping Julian completely out of his life or letting him in and trying to repair the relationship."

Although the rock star tried, according to Seaman, Lennon was too absorbed in himself and his uxorious relationship with Yoko to bridge the distance that separated him from Julian.

Seaman suggests that Lennon's troubled childhood and the realization that he had allowed the same fate to befall his son contributed to a "fatal flaw" that drove the musician subconsciously to plot his own death. Lennon, he says, had a compulsive fascination with mystical ideas of death and rebirth. Consciously or unconsciously, the expression of such ideas was bound to attract the attentions of someone like Mark David Chapman.

Seaman describes a tragic flaw in John Lennon "that was evident from the very beginning, but I didn't want to deal with it for a long time. John was talking about it in March of '79 in Palm Beach. He would go on about all this mystical stuff. He talked about his death early on from the context of books he'd been reading. He was always reading about the occult and about death. All this stuff was totally foreign to me. So I tended to just space out when he was talking about it because I didn't want to deal with it. It wasn't until later, after months and months of this, that I realized this was a big deal in his life and he really spent a lot of energy obsessing about this," Seaman said.

The Lennon that Seaman describes was a tormented and dependent man who, during the last year of his life, seized every opportunity to talk about violence and death.

"My uncle was shot in 1978 in a traffic dispute in front of Carnegie Hall," Seaman said. "The bullet just sort of went in and out. It wasn't a big deal. But every time my uncle Norman [Norman Seaman, who had previously worked for Ono] and John would get together, John would always ask him about getting shot. 'What was it like? What went through your mind? What went through your head? What did it feel like? Did you see the bullet?'

"And then my uncle would say, 'Well, it felt like an ice pick going into your flesh.' And John would sit there wide eyed. He just, like, hung on every word."

On extended vacations in Florida and Bermuda, Seaman said he and Lennon spent several evenings together smoking marijuana and listening to reggae music. It was during the marijuana sessions, he says, that Lennon would speak at length of his morbid obsession.

"It was when I was with him in Bermuda in the summer of 1980. That's when he worried about it and talked about it the most. There were many conversations. Particularly when we got stoned; that's where his mind would gravitate toward, which was always very disturbing to me because that's the last thing I wanted to talk about. I just wanted to listen to the Bob Marley that John was always playing then. I didn't want to hear John talk about death. It always freaked me out. . . . I find it interesting with retrospect that he became more and more obsessed. He talked about it more and more as his approach to New York neared. I wondered if he didn't have . . ."

Seaman paused to reflect on the weeks that led up to John Lennon's fatal encounter with Mark David Chapman.

"He talked as if he had some kind of rendezvous with something, you know?"

Lennon also wrote and sang as though "he had some kind of rendezvous with something." As a Beatle, he sang of feeling "suicidal" and "dead already." In later solo work, he alluded to the love that death inspires. After he said the Beatles were more popular than Jesus, and when he sang about being crucified in "The Ballad of John and Yoko," some critics charged he had confused celebrityhood with sainthood, believing himself a messiah. In numerous interviews, he talked of assassination.

"He said he dreamt of getting shot. He had nightmares of violent death—weird, recurring dreams, as he put it, about dying, about getting shot. He talked about getting shot as a modern form of crucifixion—the best way of moving on to the next life with a clean karmic slate."

Seaman had just come from a movie theater with a date sometime between 11 P.M. and midnight on December 8 when he learned from a weeping hippie on a New York City sidewalk that his employer had been gunned down. At that moment, he said, the morbid conversations began to make a macabre sort of sense.

"After he died, I really started to reflect on a lot of it and wondered if he had some kind of premonition, or perhaps even desire to die a martyr's death. I'm sure he'd fantasized about it and perhaps he even attracted it."

Although Lennon sometimes worried openly about his personal security, Seaman observed that he failed to take even fundamental precautions, such as traveling with a bodyguard, that might have saved his life.

"The problem with John was, he had a lot of abstract knowledge, a lot of information. But he couldn't apply it to his own self, his own family, or his own circumstances. And, you know, knowledge that can't be applied to one's being is essentially useless."

In his 1991 memoir, *The Last Days of John Lennon,* Seaman details the star's crippled relationship with his teenage son and an apparent prescience about the looming encounter with Mark David Chapman. In his book, Seaman also explains that he stole Lennon's diaries and personal journals to fulfill a promise he said he had made to the rock star before his death.

"John told me before he died that if anything happened to him, he wanted Julian to have the diaries," Seaman said. Seaman never gave the journals to Lennon's son, however. He was arrested after Lennon's writings were copied by a former roommate and offered for sale to publishers. The diaries were returned to Yoko and Seaman agreed not to reveal their contents in exchange for a reduction of criminal charges and a sentence of five years probation.

Although Lennon's widow had said in 1981 that she planned to publish the diaries, she ordered them sealed after the writings were returned to her. After having Lennon's writing reviewed by Elliot Mintz, one of Lennon's closest friends during the ten years before his death, Ono decided against publication, "at least while people mentioned in the diaries are still alive," Mintz said. The diaries contain unflattering comments about members of the Dakota social circle, including "people who are not famous," he said.

Apart from Seaman, Mintz is one of the few people to have read the historic diaries. A former talk-show host, Mintz, a Hollywood-based publicist for Ono, Bob Dylan, Don Johnson, Melanie Griffith, and other superstars, said he reviewed the journals to assure their authenticity and to determine whether material had been deleted, added, or altered by Seaman or others who saw them after they were stolen.

"The historical significance of the journals is that, ultimately, there it is in John's own hand: his own feelings and impressions about a variety of subjects. That's going to be around long after we're gone," Mintz said. "There were some nasty entries but there was also tremendous warmth and humor . . . showing a very complex man; showing there was a beauty and calm to John as well."

After the stolen documents were recovered, Mintz scrutinized "all of his journals cover to cover, page by page, and to see if I could note any alterations in the handwriting, the ink, the style, or in the content. That was the purpose of [Yoko's] asking me to read them and to prepare them for safekeeping. I did that, of course, with the promise that I would not reveal the content of the journals."

While revealing none of the content of Lennon's personal writings, Mintz describes them as alternately "mundane," "fascinating," and of "great historical interest to musical scholars." He also says they constitute the blunt and honest observations of a complex man given to extremes of both human compassion and rage. Mintz alludes to numerous entries in which Lennon turned to his diaries to express his deepest feelings about people who were close to him. Because of the indiscriminate anger expressed in the diaries, Mintz said he agrees with Ono's decision to keep them out of the public view.

Mintz, highly critical of Seaman and other Dakota employees and acquaintances who tried to cash in with tell-all personal memoirs after Lennon's murder, is nonetheless candid in detailing his own observations of a very human John Lennon—who also had to struggle with the Lennon legend. Unlike some critics who have offered one-dimensional portraits of the ex-Beatle's weaknesses, eccentricities, and moral shortcomings, Mintz recalls his friend in the context of Lennon's world-changing musical genius.

Just as Lennon projected himself in his professional life—often with sexually explicit language and nude photographs that alienated fans and shocked public sensibilities—Mintz says the portrait of Lennon that emerges from the secret journals is "unfiltered, uncensored. Straight from the heart, or straight from the chip on the shoulder or wherever it's coming from—but not internalizing the anger. And there was a great deal of anger inside John Lennon [from] wherever all that comes from."

Far from the "false, slobberish image" of Lennon as a nonviolent pacifist "always with a flower in his hand," Mintz says the Lennon journals reveal a man who crusaded for world peace against a backdrop of personal turmoil.

"Anger in John's diaries? You bet!" exclaimed Mintz. "You bet. He definitely used his journals in that way, for the things that he couldn't say to anyone else, including his wife."

Lennon's fans are familiar with the songwriter's "righteous rage," the impassioned energy that he channeled into lyrical protests of war, prejudice, bigotry, political repression, hypocrisy, and other social evils. Often to the chagrin of Lennon's friends, lovers, and associates, the rage didn't stop there.

"I would like to believe that [social injustice] was where John Lennon confined his rage," Mintz reflected. "But there were other areas as well. His anger would manifest itself in many ways. And if he was unhappy with somebody or angered about something somebody said, he would respond in kind. In other words, you can't be a noncensorial person, you can't be a totally live wire with no conduit, and also be a diplomat. So he would shout and he would carry on and make noises and say mean things.

"As privy as all of us are to people like John, there are countless areas of their lives that are known only to them. Their psychological makeup is known only to them. We have examined the John Lennon experience now for how many years? There is a presumption on the part of many that we know everything there is to know about John. But when we arrive at a question like 'Where did all his anger come from?'—we don't know. We can draw extrapolations, certain types of conclusions. It's a question that's still left hanging. We keep pointing to milestones: John's mother being run over by an off-duty police officer who was drunk . . . when he was a teenager. Certainly, a psychologist could point to it as a basis for John's antiauthority attitude. But it also, upon saying it, sounds like psychological mumbo jumbo. I don't know. But there were times when the anger came through. You can hear it in his music. When he wrote that song, 'How Do You Sleep?' [a slashing musical attack on former Beatle Paul McCartney] you can feel the rage coming through. And when he would drink to excess, he was not the kind of person you would want to be around. When he would be arguing a point that he felt strongly about . . . he probably was not all that opposed to the use of fists. You wouldn't want to be around John Lennon when he was angry."

While never understanding the full range of Lennon's complex emotions, Mintz says the star's anger was inseparable from "brutal honesty." Lennon, with the compulsive candor of a child, was unable, says Mintz, to look at any aspect of his life or the lives of others without blurting the first feelings and thoughts that came to his mind.

"One thing he had, other people can have it too if they work on it, but he seemed to have it in a very spontaneous way. And that was that he was totally noncensorial in his behavior. He had the facility to be brutally honest, not just with people it was safe to be brutally honest with, but with anyone. I think one of the things that endeared him to so many people was that they recognized a quality that they would like to have in themselves and almost lived it vicariously through John. So when he got up there and sang 'Help!' and made that spirited call for help, it was striking and jarring. It had nothing to do with show business. When he wrote about kicking heroin in 'Cold Turkey' or when he wrote about being a 'Jealous Guy' or 'I'm a Loser,' or any of those things that were first-person autobiographical statements told without pretense or hype—that was an extraordinarily unique thing. And in the interviews, the body of interviews, he didn't know how to give a jive answer. He wouldn't have been good on *Entertainment Tonight.* He was better off in psychodrama.

"He kept no secrets. One of the things so perplexing about the books about his life that have come out after his death is that they portend to offer up secrets. He showed us everything; he had nothing to hide. He lived his life on as public a stage as anyone I can recall. The Associated Press says that John and Yoko are the most photographed couple of the twentieth century, and that includes President and Jackie Kennedy.

"John also had the second most famous address in America after the White House. If you wanted to see John and Yoko, you knew that if you would stand in front of One West 72nd Street long enough you were going to bump into them. And they were approachable. They wouldn't disappear in a long black limousine with thirteen guys running around them.

"To be that exposed, that up front, that honest, to let people observe you to the degree he did—that distinguishes him from anyone, I think, in the entire entertainment complex. Ultimately, it may have been what contributed to his demise as well. . . .

"He acknowledged the possibility of an assassin who would appear out of nowhere, although prior to 1980 to the best of my knowledge there was never a case of murder in America predicated on somebody's art. Up to the time of John's death, assassinations had been either political or economically based, but not because of something that came through in the music."

Albert Goldman likewise believes that Lennon's apparent fearlessness and openness contributed to his demise. Goldman argues that the rock star set himself up to be killed.

An unflinching biographer who stalks celebrities with his pen, Goldman is the author of controversial books about Lennon, Elvis Presley, and Lenny Bruce. A former Columbia University professor and music critic, Goldman has spent much of his life studying the phenomena of rock 'n' roll and celebrityhood. His 1988 book, *The Lives of John Lennon,* was boycotted by Beatles' fans at the urging of Ono, Mintz, and *Rolling Stone* publisher Jann Wenner, who publicly denounced Goldman.

"John's death was very much in keeping with John's life," Goldman says. "He saw himself as a martyr—a saint and a martyr.

"He saw himself as someone who was going to be assassinated and he was totally obsessed with assassination. The Kennedy assassination, he was always talking on that subject and relating it to himself. But he wouldn't take the simplest precaution to prevent himself from being assassinated. He would walk in and out of the Dakota without a bodyguard in the middle of a publicity campaign. Then, on the other hand, he would sit at the kitchen table and get stoned and worry that he was going to be shot."

Goldman says that the sudden fame experienced by rock idols like Lennon is a dangerous way to achieve success. It causes many to indulge in orgies of suicidal and self-destructive behavior. It causes others to yearn for an early grave and martyrdom.

"Particularly the sixties rock stars who grew up in this ambience of the Tibetan Book of the Dead, and the psychedelic drugs and avatars, believing that death was an extension of life. They began to believe, almost like old-time religious fanatics, that they could go around again.

"Essentially, the experience of a rock star is the same as a rocket: namely, ascent with a burning tailpipe. It's an incredible experience. It doesn't last long and everything you get after that, whether millions or zillions or what have you, is an anticlimax.

"In every one of the rock stars' lives it's clear. It's clear in Elvis's case. It's clear in Lennon's case. It's clear in Jim Morrison's case. . . .

"At a very early age, they're really over the hill, over the apogee of their rocket flight. So what do they do? A normal person would figure, 'Well, I'm very glad to have had this so I'm going to take this tremendous head start and put it to some other use. I'm going to have a second career, cultivate my garden or something.' But these guys don't have that. All they do is brood about getting it again. And again. A comeback!

"And one of the ways, if you're crazy enough, if you're as crazy as John Lennon was or as Elvis was, one of the ways of getting it is to imagine dying and being reborn.

"Now that's the ultimate comeback."

Echoing a quote from John Lennon—"We are all Christ and we are all Hitler"—Goldman says that, virtually without exception, the superstars he has studied and written about are fixated on two characters in history:

"Jesus and Adolph Hitler, and the common element there is simply megalomania," he said. "There's nothing more fundamental to the show-business personality than the feeling that you are good and you have this awesome power. And when you start to lose this power, that creates a real problem.

"Celebrities are very morbid figures, really, who imitate life. The closer you get to them, the more they tend to disappear.

"I don't like to make John Lennon less singular than he was. He was a pretty unique person, but so many of these people are. Look at Jim Morrison. Everything that came out of that guy's mouth from day one was about death, death, death. He wrote about death. He talked about death. He sang about death. Death was on his lips every day of his life.

"Elvis, too, would go on and on and on about the next world. And Elvis too went through a long period before he killed himself where it was clear he was working up to this.

"Once again, that's part of the totality of megalomania, the obsession with death as part of the myth of yourself. It's a self-dramatization that has to end in your death. And what is the most spectacular modern death? The equivalent of crucifixion?

"John Lennon said if Christ were alive today he would be shot down like a Kennedy, like a Martin Luther King.

"What I'm saying is the effect of the total negativity of the whole experience—the total negativity of Lennon, who was someone totally in love with death."

Elliot Mintz points out that Goldman never knew Lennon personally. "I believe John did not want to die," Mintz said. Mintz emphatically denies that Lennon was suicidal or—as Mark David Chapman believed—"a phony."

Mintz agrees with Goldman that rock 'n' rollers in person are pale images of their stage personae. "There's not a great deal that's remarkable about the rock 'n' roll experience beyond the music," Mintz said; although he believes the commitment of rock musicians to eradication of social evils such as world hunger, homelessness, poverty, and war is sincere.

"The personalities [of rock stars] are usually just a shadow of the impression that one would get of that person by listening to the music," he said. "But the one thing that must be said about this particular idiom is that I don't think there is any other group in the world that have given of themselves so selflessly in terms of social issues. I don't know if the crooners ever did it, the jazz musicians, actors, dancers, or Comic Relief group.

"For the most part, it's rock 'n' roll musicians who have had the power to motivate millions of people for peace or against world hunger. And that was not the case [among rock stars] prior to John Lennon.

"I can't cite any rock 'n' roll figures who engaged in those kinds of activities prior to John and Yoko."

Nor was the John Lennon that Elliot Mintz knew as self-centered as the Lennon that Goldman and Seaman describe.

"It is typical of people who open the door marked 'Fame' to seek a certain kind of mass adulation that people in my position have to continue to feed," Mintz said. "And that's something that John didn't need. It was important to him to communicate his thoughts and impressions about anything other than himself.

"Is being famous unhealthy? Yes. Ultimately, it results in John's murder. John would not have been murdered if he had been an anonymous person. The chances of him being murdered would have been less if he had not shared his personal and political views with the world. There was a reason that Mark David Chapman tuned in to John as opposed to Ringo. The celebrity event in and of itself is a danger because it can attract people's attention—a number of people's attention. Take it a step further: Say things that could be misinterpreted by people, and the danger is greatly increased."

After one of Mintz's closest friends, actor Sal Mineo, was stabbed to death by a burglar in Los Angeles, Mintz said he turned to John Lennon and Yoko Ono to talk about his grief. After flying his friend's body back to New York for burial, Mintz recalls that he visited the Dakota where he urged Lennon to take precautions to protect himself against robbers, muggers, kidnapers, political enemies, or obsessed fans for whom his wealth, controversial political views, and celebrity status made him a potential target.

Personal safety "was not a preoccupation with John. It was with me," Mintz said. "I lost another friend at the hands of another and when that event occurred in my life, I attended the funeral and went to visit John and Yoko shortly afterward. Off and on, John and Yoko and I had talked on ten or fifteen or twenty occasions about what had happened to Sal.

"I did speak to John about the need for heightened protection. It seemed to him I might be a little paranoid because of my unfortunate experience. But I said to John, 'You are speaking to so many people in the music and in the interviews, you just have to assume there will be a few, a handful, that will be very disturbed by what you say, and one or two might be motivated to react in a very negative way—to try and hurt you.'

"On that level, however, he was very much a fatalist. John was famous from the time he was sixteen years old. He said the only thing that happened was that he became more famous. When he was sixteen, he would walk down the street in Liverpool and people would point and say, 'Look! That's John Lennon.' When he was seventeen, he had already played Hamburg. There were already crowds and he already had to have guys walk around him when he was getting in and out of cars.

"From the time he was a teenager, he had people around him insulating and isolating him from the world around him. So when he hit New York, he felt this tremendous sense of freedom, his first since the Beatles era. People always recognized him on every street corner. There would be no street corner that John could stand at waiting for a light to change without people coming up to him, but the vibe was not hysterical. . . . People wanted to shake hands, say 'How are you doing? When are the Beatles getting together again?' But for the most part, it was kind of a blasé, New York vibe. He liked that. He advertised it. In his last interview, the day of his death, he said he felt great that he could walk around New York; that he and Yoko could go anyplace they wanted to go."

If a man like Mark David Chapman was stalking John Lennon "he believed there was really no protection for that," Mintz said. "When Sean was born, they hired a former FBI agent to provide some low-level security, primarily around Sean. But John and Yoko both loved the idea of walking around freely.

"You've got to keep in mind that, before 1980, most public figures moved around without a lot of public guard."

CHAPTER EIGHT

AFTER THE FALL

But about God himself he was at ease; his act was doubtless exceptional, but so were his excuses, which God knew; it was there, and not among men, that he felt sure of justice.

—ROBERT LOUIS STEVENSON, *MARKHEIM*

The first baby born on this planet was a murderer.

—MARK DAVID CHAPMAN

Less than two hours after John Lennon was pronounced dead on arrival of gunshot wounds at Roosevelt General Hospital, Mark David Chapman signed a handwritten confession at the Twentieth Precinct Detective Unit Office in Manhattan.

> I never wanted to hurt anybody my friends will tell you that. I have two parts in me. The big part is very kind. The children I work with will tell you that. I have a small part in me that cannot understand the world and what goes on in it. I did not want to kill anybody and I really don't know why I did it. I fought against the small part for a long time. But for a few seconds the small part won. I asked God to help me but we are responsible for our own actions. I have nothing against John Lennon or anything he has done in the way of music or personal beliefs. I came to New York about five weeks ago from Hawaii and the big part of me did not want to shoot John. I went back to Hawaii and tried to get rid of my small part but I couldn't. I then returned to New York [on December 6, 1980, after leaving Honolulu] on Friday December 5,

1980. I checked into the YMCA on 62nd Street. I stayed one night. Then I went to the Sheraton Centre 7th Ave. Then this morning I went to the bookstore and bought *The Catcher in the Rye.*

I'm sure the large part of me is Holden Caulfield who is the main person in the book. The small part of me must be the Devil.

I went to the building it's called the Dakota. I stayed there until he came out and asked him to sign my album. At that point my big part won and I wanted to go back to my hotel, but I couldn't. I waited until he came back. He came in a car. Yoko walked past first and I said hello. I didn't want to hurt her. Then John came, looked at me and printed me. I took the gun from my coat pocket and fired at him. I can't believe I could do that. I just stood there clutching the book. I didn't want to run away. I don't know what happened to the gun, I just remember Jose kicking it away. Jose was crying and telling me to please leave. I felt so sorry for Jose. Then the police came and told me to put my hands on the wall and cuffed me.

End of statement
0105 Hrs. Dec. 9, 1980
Mark D. Chapman

"I remember a lot of pain and a lot of confusion at what I had done when I dictated the statement.

"I remember thinking I was frightened—in one way comforted, and in another way frightened by the police. I didn't want to say to the police that John Lennon was a phony. I didn't say that in my statement because I was frightened of what they would have thought of me. I was afraid that they would have been angry with me.

"I remembered the look of one of the officers as he was dragging John Lennon's body to the back of his patrol car. How there was blood all over the place and the officer looked at me and cursed me. I never heard the curse words, but I could see them on his lips. He was very, very angry and upset.

"So when I got to the police I said that I liked John Lennon, and it wasn't exactly a lie. There was still a part of me that appreciated and enjoyed his music and still liked the Beatles and, remember, John Lennon had been cordial to me earlier in the day. I had been genuinely excited about having his signature on my *Double Fantasy* album.

"So when I told the officers that I liked John Lennon, it really wasn't exactly a lie. I just didn't want to say he was a phony, and I was angry at him.

"I was in a very unreal, a very surreal world then. I was in utter panic of sheer terror and wanting things to go back to the way they were before I had pulled the trigger that night.

"But I felt anger spreading over my mind as I was dictating the statement and talking about *The Catcher in the Rye.*

"There was nothing that felt like I was in a womb; nothing that felt like I was Holden Caulfield. I felt more of a panic, more of being sucked into a giant wave that I couldn't swim out of or even come up for air.

"I dictated the statement and a detective wrote it. But the anguish is all mine.

"Then, after I signed the statement, one officer asked me about the Beatles. He said he liked the Beatles. I said I like them, too. The officer just shook his head and walked away from me."

On Friday, December 5, after her husband left for New York, Gloria Chapman returned to her apartment where she spent the weekend reading and visiting with friends. She finished reading *The Catcher in the Rye* and she turned again to her readings in the Bible. She didn't turn on the tape recorder that her paranoid husband had attached to the telephone to record incoming calls. If she had, she would have perhaps heard a cryptic clue to the tragedy he was about to stage.

At the beginning of an otherwise blank tape, Chapman had recorded "A Little Bitty Tear," a popular ballad by Burl Ives with the words: "Everything went like I planned it, I really put on quite a show."

Gloria Chapman, unlike her husband, didn't routinely record her phone conversations, but less than an hour after the John Lennon murder, when a reporter called and told her that her husband had carried out the threat he had made to her a month before to kill John Lennon, she switched on the tape.

Chapman has never heard the tape his wife made of their phone conversation, nor has he read a transcript of the call. He says he was troubled by news reports and police accounts of the conversation in which he sounds calm and eerily rational. Chapman says the phone call provides a stark example of the psychopathic mind-set into which he had fallen in the months before the killing, a time when he says his only feelings were for himself:

"The tone of the call sounds, I've read that the tone of the call is calm, that it doesn't sound like I'm insane at all. Remember, on that very day, I had lunch with a woman in the Dakota café and she had no idea that, a few hours later, I would do something totally bizarre and uncharacteristic in my life.

"I was a master at keeping my feelings in and I was able, on the surface, to carry on a very poignant, emotional conversation with a minimum of emotions expressed. This comes from years of this kind of behavior, years of repressive behavior.

"What you're listening to when you listen to this call is not a sane man who is only concerned about his wife. It almost sounds like a hit man pulled this off. But what you're listening to is a man who, inside of him, is a boiling cauldron; a boiling cauldron who had learned to repress all his feelings and emotions and sound very lucid and very clear to get a point across.

"This is the voice of a man who, within two hours or so, had killed a man and then had begged God to turn back time. Yet on the phone I sounded very composed. My lips and tongue were composed, but my stomach and heart were disintegrating.

"Somebody listening to that tape for the first time might make a quick judgment about what was going on. That is me being upset, being paranoid about the media, telling my wife to get the police over there. But someone who doesn't know me, or understand how someone who has repressed their emotions all their life can behave in the most incredible situations, the most bizarre circumstance, would read into it that the person just didn't care what he had just done."

New York City: Yes, Twentieth Detective Squad, Detective Hoffmann speaking. Who am I speaking to, please?

Gloria: Mrs. Chapman. [Choking, she clears her throat.] Excuse me.

New York City: Mrs. Chapman?

Gloria: Yes. I'm his wife.

New York City: You're whose wife?

Gloria: Mark Chapman's wife.

New York City: Mark Chapman's wife? Yeah, may I ask you how you found out about this, Ma'am?

Gloria: A reporter from the *Advertiser* here called me.

New York City: From the advertiser?

Gloria: Yes, I don't know how he found out but he found out way ahead of everybody.

New York City: What's the advertiser?

Gloria: Uh, it's one of the two major newspapers here in Honolulu.

New York City: Okay, a reporter called you and told you.

Gloria: Yeah.

New York City: Okay, What could I do for you, Ma'am?

Gloria: Well, is there any way I could speak to my husband?

New York City: Okay, we'll see if we can find out. Okay.

GLORIA: Okay, thank you.

NEW YORK CITY: Okay, hold on a second please.

GLORIA: Thank you.

NEW YORK CITY: Okay, we'll, uh, one second, Ma'am.

GLORIA: Thank you.[Long pause and click.]

NEW YORK CITY: Hello, Gloria?

GLORIA: [Breathlessly] Yes!

NEW YORK CITY: Yeah, this is Police Officer Spiro in New York. I'm here with your husband.

GLORIA: Yes! Is he all right?

NEW YORK CITY: He just wanted me to get you on the phone first and tell you that he's all right. And that he's, uh, that I'm here with him, and that I'm, uh, I'm more or less taking care of him, making sure that everything's all right. He's gonna talk to you now, okay?

GLORIA: Okay, umm, please.

NEW YORK CITY: You want to ask me anything?

GLORIA: Well, I just don't want somebody to, to hurt him.

NEW YORK CITY: No, nobody's going to hurt him. I told him that. I will be with him, and there'll be nothing the matter with him. Okay? I promise you that.

GLORIA: Thank you.

NEW YORK CITY: All right. You're quite welcome.

MARK CHAPMAN: Hi.

GLORIA: Hi, Mark. I love you.

MARK: I know. I love you too.

GLORIA: Oh. [She starts to cry.]

MARK CHAPMAN: Are the police with you?

GLORIA: No! The first call I got was a reporter. Well, he didn't call me directly. But the phone company called me.

MARK CHAPMAN: Oh no! Are the police with you now?

GLORIA: No, the police don't care.

MARK CHAPMAN: Are you at home?

GLORIA: Yeah. Your mom and Greta [Mom's friend] are here and Jean [wife's sister] is gonna stay with me tonight.

MARK CHAPMAN: Okay. Well, I don't want to talk to anybody else.

GLORIA: I know.

MARK CHAPMAN: But I don't want you crying 'cause they can hear me.

GLORIA: Okay.

MARK CHAPMAN: Why aren't the police there?

GLORIA: I don't know. UPI's been trying to get me.

MARK CHAPMAN: Don't answer the phone.

GLORIA: The operator called back. She says, "You don't want any more calls." She says, "I just feel like these are all newspapers."

MARK CHAPMAN: Yeah, please. You didn't say anything did you?

GLORIA: Well, I might have said too much to the first guy since you weren't here. But, you know, Mark.

MARK CHAPMAN: Call. Get the police over there.

GLORIA: Why?

MARK CHAPMAN: Please.

GLORIA: What can, uh.

MARK CHAPMAN: Call them.

GLORIA: Just what would—would I tell them?

MARK CHAPMAN: Just that you want them to come over. To keep the press off of you.

GLORIA: Oh, they're not harming me. They're not it, you know.

MARK CHAPMAN: Are they knocking on the door?

GLORIA: No. No one is.

MARK CHAPMAN: Well, they're gonna do that and I want to protect you from that.

GLORIA: Yeah, but you don't want me to go there then?

MARK CHAPMAN: Go where?

GLORIA: To New York.

MARK CHAPMAN: No, no, no. You just stay where you are.

GLORIA: Okay.

MARK CHAPMAN: I love you and just call the police. I mean the police know, right? And they won't come over to your place?

GLORIA: No, I don't think they know.

MARK CHAPMAN: Well, they told me here that they called you. They called you?

GLORIA: No, they didn't. No one did.

MARK CHAPMAN: Is everybody else all right?

GLORIA: Well, no, I don't think your grandmother knows or anybody like that on the mainland knows.

MARK CHAPMAN: I'm not talking about that. I'm talking about my mom.

GLORIA: No, she's worse off than me, I think.

MARK CHAPMAN: Well, you need to call her a doctor and call the police. You should call a lawyer or somebody.

GLORIA: [Starting to cry] Well, I don't know. You know, I can't afford anybody. I can't afford a lawyer. Has it hit you yet—what you've really done?

MARK CHAPMAN: I'm gonna have to go.

GLORIA: I love you.

MARK CHAPMAN: I know and I love you too. And.

GLORIA: I always will love you.

MARK CHAPMAN: I know and I love you too and I need your love, and I, everything will be all right. You'll see.

GLORIA: What do I tell people?

MARK CHAPMAN: You don't talk at all.

GLORIA: Okay.

MARK CHAPMAN: You don't tell nobody nothin'. It's not your position to do that. You just trust me. Don't talk. Especially the press. Don't let them bug you. That's why I say call the police. Tell them to keep the press away from you. Okay?

GLORIA: I don't think they can.

MARK CHAPMAN: Well just call them to come over, okay?

GLORIA: Mark, that's worse when they're not even calling, you know. No one knows yet.

MARK CHAPMAN: Well, they will. They'll bother you.

GLORIA: I won't talk. I won't go out at all.

MARK CHAPMAN: Okay, just stay in. Call your dad. Is your dad there?

GLORIA: Well, Jean's going to go over and take the kids and talk to them personally. Carol [wife's sister] called and she didn't know when she called. And I should tell her.

MARK CHAPMAN: Did they give my name out and everything?

GLORIA: No, it's not on the news. All they're saying is it's someone crazy in New York. They don't even say.

MARK CHAPMAN: All right, don't talk about it.

GLORIA: Okay.

MARK CHAPMAN: I love you and I'll talk to you again and don't worry about anything, okay?

GLORIA: Okay.

MARK CHAPMAN: You were my, you were my first concern.

GLORIA: I know.

MARK CHAPMAN: I'm just worried. You ought to call the police. You know, you know, you'd like to know what to do. And that you want somebody to come over, you know, a doctor and lawyer and whatever. Don't worry about the money. You know that lawyer that we used, what's his name?

GLORIA: Um, I don't know, but I'll figure it out.

MARK CHAPMAN: Okay, I love you.

GLORIA: I love you, darling. I really do.

MARK CHAPMAN: See you. Love you.

GLORIA: Okay. Bye.

MARK CHAPMAN: Bye.

After speaking with his wife, the murderer was taken into another small room at the police station where he was fingerprinted, photographed, and assigned a number.

Several minutes later, "another detective told me to take my sweater off and, as I was removing it, he just ripped it off my shoulders and strapped a bulletproof vest around me. Then I was taken downstairs and paraded before the media. The area around the police station was besieged. You could feel it in the air and all the officers were tense and edgy. I was told we were going to be walking by the media, but that nothing was going to happen to me. Officer Spiro, the officer who had arrested me, was on my right, another officer was on my left, and other officers were in front and behind me.

"When we got to the door, I looked outside at all the lights and cameras and I said, 'I want a coat. Can I put a coat over my face?' One of the officers threw me an old green coat and I drew it over my face and crouched down.

"I remember, from the darkness inside the coat, tremendous tumult occurring as we walked from one door to another door. I looked down and the ground was lit up by white light from all the strobe flashes and video lamps. It was almost like I was walking on just one giant, pulsating beam of light under my feet. I could hear people scurrying. One woman said to me, 'Why'd you do this, Mark?' and 'Mark! Is that you under there?'

"I didn't say anything.

"Then began an odyssey, like something out of a Robert Ludlum novel. We went through a dark building into a barred holding cell, me and two uniformed officers and three or four detectives. It was pitch dark and we were sitting in this holding cell. They explained to me they were going to try to throw off the press by pretending to put me in a van and whisking me out to the courthouse at One Center Street in Manhattan. It was a ruse to get the press out of the way. So we waited there in the dark for two or three hours.

"But the media wasn't fooled. Occasionally I'd hear a woman's voice call from outside, 'Mark, are you in there? Are you there?' It was pitch dark and scary. The officers, after a while, were joking about it, how it seemed so ridiculous, but soon it became something very horrible, something out of Kafka.

"We were in pitch darkness with nothing but the sound of the officers breathing. Then one of them asked me, 'Mark, why'd you do it?'

"I remember what I said to him. I said, without hesitation, 'I can't understand what's going on in the world and what it's become.' I was just so in pain and hurting and so disappointed and crushed at what the world had become, or what I perceived at that time that the world had become. I remember that the officer didn't have a reply.

"We waited and waited in silence and then another officer signaled and I was led through the door and down an elevator to a basement parking lot. There was a van and an unmarked brown police car with the doors open. A door swung open at the top of a ramp and I could see it was breaking daylight.

"A detective who seemed very frightened motioned us out of the elevator, forward, and pushed me into the unmarked car. The officers got into the van. We flew up the ramp and into the street going at least sixty miles an hour. They pushed my head down between my knees. They said all they cared about was getting me to court before someone could kill me."

CHAPTER NINE

MARK'S CASE

I am mad north by northwest. When the wind is from the south, I know a hawk from a handsaw.

—SHAKESPEARE, *HAMLET*

Immersed in a blizzard of medical paperwork, Dr. Naomi Goldstein was looking forward to the end of her shift on December 9 at Bellevue Hospital. As she reviewed the unending stream of afflicted humanity in her care on the hospital's infamous psychiatric wing, Dr. Goldstein was startled when a security officer rapped sharply on her office door and stepped inside. The officer entered hastily, without waiting for her to reply.

She, like everyone else at the hospital, had heard radio and television reports throughout the day about New York City's most recent murder. She had been surprised to learn from the news reports that the slain man, international folk hero and rock superstar John Lennon, had lived on West 72nd Street, not far from her apartment on West 81st. When the hospital security officer asked if she'd heard about the shooting, the doctor realized she wouldn't be going home for a while.

Five hours later, Dr. Goldstein found herself still on the wards at Bellevue, awaiting the arrival of an armed convoy of police and the man who killed John Lennon. Darkness had fallen across the city and a wintry, wind-driven rain was lashing the barred windows of the second-floor psychiatric ward when the security officer stepped back into her office.

"Our celebrated patient has arrived," the officer said. "If you can get past his police escort, he's waiting for you in the interview room on the security unit. Good luck. And . . . be careful. We're under siege by a lot of angry

Beatles fans. Whoever this Chapman guy is, he's got to be the most unpopular man in the world right now."

The security officer advised the doctor that maintenance crews were preparing to put a coat of black paint on the windows looking from the secure ward where Chapman would be held several days for psychiatric observation.

"Cops say we've got to take precautions against snipers," the officer explained. "Cops say a lot of people out there don't want this particular patient to leave the hospital—unless he's in a body bag."

Dr. Goldstein threaded her way among a loose phalanx of nervous, heavily armed police officers in bulletproof vests who had taken over the hospital corridors. She had never seen so many men with guns in one place.

At the small interview room near the hospital's maximum security ward, she showed her identification to an officer with a shotgun. The officer nodded curtly and let her into the room. With some trepidation, Dr. Goldstein turned the doorknob and approached an overweight young man with dark circles under his eyes. The man sat stiffly in a wooden chair, leaning his elbows on the scarred surface of a wooden table. She avoided looking directly at the patient, focusing her attention instead on a small stack of printed forms she placed on the table before her. The man on the other side of the table observed her quietly. Looking up from the papers, the psychiatrist withdrew a pencil from the pocket of her starched white linen jacket and introduced herself. She managed a brief, professional smile as the man introduced himself by his full name of Mark David Chapman. He said he was from Hawaii and he began to rock nervously back and forth in the chair. She observed that his fingernails were gnawed to the quick.

As she talked with the patient, she made notes on a hospital admission chart:

"Speech coherent, relevant and logical. No evidence hallucination or delusions. Clinical evaluation reveals a pleasant, generally cooperative young man, of medium stature with a somewhat puffy face . . . very anxious, hyperventilating, and exhausted, but cooperative, appropriate and in good contact."

After he had answered a series of routine questions, Goldstein probed Chapman on the events that had led police to bring him to Bellevue.

"I wanted to kill somebody to stop my mind," he told her, matter of factly. "I thought it would stop my life.

"I came across a book about John Lennon, about his life and read little parts of it at home. I brought it to New York with me. I didn't hate him, but I thought he was a phony. The author made the phony stuff, the crazy, neurotic stuff that Lennon did sound good. He dressed up in a bag with Yoko. I admire him in a way. I wished someone would write a book about me. It sounded like he was an idiot, and he wasn't. It made me think that my life is special and I felt that no one cared about it. . . .

"I remember that I thought if I killed him, I wouldn't have to worry anymore."

He apologized to the psychiatrist for being unable to talk about details of the shooting. "Not now," he explained. "I've been blocking out what I've done. I've been blocking out what I've done to my family."

In one of several recurring literary and Hollywood fantasies from which he had sought to extract meaning for his life before killing John Lennon, Chapman talked to Dr. Goldstein metaphorically of himself after the shooting. He said he saw himself as Dorothy in *The Wizard of Oz* "where she is in a weird place and wants to go back home. Like Dorothy, I just want to click my heels together and go back home. But I know it's not done in real life."

During the summer and fall of 1980, Chapman had turned with increasing frequency to the familiar memories and objects of his childhood. In the months before his spinning mind became obsessed with thoughts of murder, he began revisiting some old friends in the fairy-tale land of Oz.

Long before Chapman came to believe that he had found himself in *The Catcher in the Rye,* he had discovered that his interior struggle between the good and evil spirits of the world was being dramatized once a year when the movie classic *The Wizard of Oz* was rebroadcast on TV.

"It was a great event in our home when *The Wizard of Oz* was on," he recalled. "It had a great impact on me the first time I saw it and every time I saw it."

Chapman described his favorite scenes from *Oz* and talked of the warring good and evil forces within that had ripped from him the pieces of a life he was unable to understand.

"The movie was ahead of its time," he said. "It earmarks a sensitivity. It's a great mystery. It's flawless. It's close to me."

He explained that, although he was a twenty-five-year-old man, he still had the sensitivities of a child. He spoke of the various elements of his mind, his emotions, memories, thoughts, dreams, and intellect, as virtually separate entities within himself. He said he identified simultaneously with all four of the characters from Oz—Dorothy, the Scarecrow, the Tin Man, and the Cowardly Lion.

"They're all sensitive," he said, explaining that, even as an adult, he always would cry whenever he watched the sad and frightening parts of the movie.

"If I did not cry when I saw it, I would have become a hardened adult," he said. "I'm not ashamed of this, seeing all the evil in the world. I was always thinking about the bad in the world, because I was too sensitive."

. . .

Naomi Goldstein was the first mental-health professional to speak with John Lennon's killer. She would be followed in the next six months by an array of some of the most famous and respected forensic psychiatrists and psychologists in the country. Written less than twenty-four hours after the killing, her notes offer the killer's freshest and clearest memories of the events and feelings immediately before and after a murder that shocked the world.

Of the dozen or so experts who attempted to probe the mind of Mark David Chapman after Lennon's murder, Goldstein was the only psychiatrist who had no personal or legal attachments to the patient; she wasn't writing a book, nor was she engaged in a research project. Of greatest significance, unlike the high-profile psychiatrists who would follow her, Dr. Goldstein wasn't being paid to render an opinion favorable to either prosecution or defense lawyers laying the groundwork for "the trial of the decade." She was simply doing her job and Mark David Chapman was just another patient to be diagnosed and understood.

Dr. Goldstein had conducted interviews with scores of murderers before she met Chapman. She has conducted interviews with hundreds of other violent felons since. Almost a dozen years later, she said that she never had a more elusive case than the one that sat before her on the evening of December 9, 1980.

"Totally unique," she recalled. At the end of the interview she noted on the admission chart that her tentative diagnosis of Chapman would be "deferred."

Chapman was eager to divulge every detail of his life, no matter how embarrassing or insignificant, to Dr. Goldstein and the psychiatrists who would later visit him in his caged room at Bellevue and his cell at Rikers Island. He hoped that they could tell him something he had never been able to figure out on his own: who he was. He described details of the events leading up to the murder of Lennon, hoping the psychiatrists would help him understand why he had grown up to murder a man that he had idolized in childhood.

He said he had thought of taking his own life instead, after climbing to the head of the Statue of Liberty, "because nobody had done it there before."

He told Dr. Goldstein that he "chickened out" after envisioning a possibly painful and crippling aftermath. "I imagined my brains hanging out and me being alive," he said.

After her initial admission interview, Dr. Goldstein continued to meet with Chapman for several days while he remained under protective guard at

Bellevue. She also met with him on later occasions when he was brought back to the hospital in an armored police convoy from Rikers Island for additional psychiatric and neurological testing.

In the weeks that followed her first interview, Dr. Goldstein found that Chapman seemed to be possessed at once by the symptoms of virtually every malady in the psychiatric literature. Yet, to her continuing bewilderment and frustration, she found that he remained lucid, articulate, and keenly aware of the daily realities by which mental health is commonly gauged. Chapman spoke clearly of the grim truth of the murder he had committed. Although curiously detached from the suffering and pain he had caused John Lennon, he clearly apprehended the worldwide dimensions of the grief he had inflicted upon humanity.

Chapman also appeared to Goldstein and other psychiatrists to have an even higher sensitivity than most people to moral issues and social concerns in general. He had a clear understanding of the relationship between past actions and their future consequences. He demonstrated that he understood very well the connection between murder and imprisonment—or even execution. He said he didn't know, when he murdered Lennon, whether he might face the electric chair or gas chamber. He said he didn't care.

In the end, Dr. Goldstein determined only that the enigmatic murderer was capable of understanding the consequences of his actions. She recommended that he stand trial for the crime of second-degree murder.

When she concluded her court-ordered examination, Dr. Goldstein reported that Chapman "had an insatiable need for attention and recognition . . . grandiose visions of himself." She also observed depression, "mood fluctuations . . . anger . . . paranoid tendencies . . . suicidal thinking, rage, confusion and agitation about himself."

Whatever Chapman's reasons for killing the rock superstar, the psychiatrist came to the conclusion that those reasons were part of a complicated riddle that lay beyond the realm of modern psychiatry as she knew it. Concluding that Lennon's killer was "fit to understand the charges and cooperate in his own defense," Dr. Goldstein recommended that the judicial system, not the medical system, determine his fate.

For more than a decade after the killing, Dr. Goldstein continued to think about Chapman's case, reviewing other cases that could perhaps shed light on a patient whose diagnosis she still considered "deferred." Although she continued to suspect that he suffered from one or more psychiatric abnormalities, she remained uneasy with the various labels that other experts attached to the crime and to the criminal, often for the sake of simplifying or winning legal and psychiatric arguments.

"He was very quixotic," Goldstein says. "Extremely mercurial. There were the symptoms of any number of borderline conditions. Unfortunately, however, there is no such thing in the psychiatric literature as 'mercurial personality disorder.' "

Nearly a dozen years after the first interview, Dr. Goldstein remained unsure whether she or anyone else could attach a meaningful psychiatric tag to Chapman. Likewise, other psychiatrists who met with Lennon's killer remember him among their most difficult cases to diagnose. All have struggled to penetrate and describe the medical symptoms of a spiritual battle that Mark Chapman says has raged within him for his entire life.

At least as early as June of 1976, when he was twenty-one years old, Chapman told therapists who counseled him after his suicide attempt in Hawaii that he was caught in the middle of a struggle between "good and evil spirits." He said that he believed the spirits to live independently inside him.

"There's a big part of me that's mostly good," he said. "But there also is a very small part of me that is very powerful and very evil."

On the eve of Chapman's scheduled murder trial, during the summer of 1981, Dr. Daniel Schwartz had been prepared to argue in court that Lennon's killer was mentally ill when he shot Lennon. More than a decade after the killing, Dr. Schwartz said he agreed with Dr. Goldstein's conclusion that the killer should face the criminal consequences of having silenced one of his generation's most creative artists.

"I personally believe that, in the average person's mind, the so-called insanity defense is a way of forgiving somebody. The jury might not have felt like forgiving this . . . evil act," said Schwartz.

"Was he responsible for his actions? He did something terrible. He did something terrible! Who knows what more John Lennon would have contributed to the world? Who believes that somebody as wonderful as he was should die this way?"

Schwartz, whose interviews led Chapman to start talking to psychiatrists about a world of Little People who had lived within his mind since childhood and who had returned in the months before the killing, concluded after his interviews that the killer was schizophrenic. Schwartz said Chapman also suffered from a narcissistic personality disorder that caused him to crave attention and fame.

Although Chapman has denied that he ever believed himself to be "the real John Lennon," as some mental-health experts had speculated, Schwartz said the killer was "confused" about the issue. The psychiatrist noted that Chapman, like Lennon, had married a Japanese woman a few years older than himself and that he had put Lennon's name on a name tag and in a log book at his job site several weeks before the Lennon killing. He had quit his job, planning to stay home and keep house while his wife worked, after reading that Lennon had become a "househusband."

Chapman's apparent confusion between Lennon and himself caused Schwartz to theorize that the murder was a surrogate suicide.

"I might argue that, from the psychiatric point of view, Chapman was not responsible. . . . But then the jury might decide 'The hell with you,' " Schwartz said. "There's no doubt Mr. Chapman knew and appreciated the nature and consequence of his conduct. He understood the nature and consequences of shooting John Lennon."

In addition to exhaustive interviews with psychiatrists, Chapman underwent rigorous psychological and neurological testing at Bellevue and Rikers Island.

Although neurological tests were inconclusive, a bizarre profile of murder emerged from a series of verbal and perception tests, including the Rorschach, which Chapman agreed to undergo.

Among the Rorschach inkblots, he described scenes of bleeding female pelvic areas "which had been shot." Overall, psychologists wrote that his Rorschach results betrayed "a perception of woman as seductive and dangerous. Oral aggression appeared to be associated with sex, and sex appeared to be perceived as of a conflictual nature. The patient impresses as fearful of sex, but as capable of being reassured temporarily by phantasies of sexual violence. . . .

"He spoke about his sensitivity and intelligence, which he got from his mother, who 'is female' as making him more a man than other men."

Responding to a series of vaguely suggestive photographs and drawings, Chapman detailed revealing fantasies in which death and evil were recurring themes, such as the following interpretation:

This key—this boy is the key to the story. He's very intelligent. But look at him closely. He's a very evil person. He just shot him. He just shot him and he's waiting here for the trial to come. In the back you can see they're operating on the patient. I don't think he's going to make it. He's a very evil boy. They're operating right on the stomach and chest of this patient and if you look at the boy's face, he's got a very noncompassionate look. This guy's a phony and he's no good. He looks shy but he's a phony. He's strange. When I shot John Lennon I had this dream that they were opening up his chest and going inside with their hands and trying to make his heart work well. Anyway, this boy is evil and he has no compassion. I want you to know that when I shot John Lennon I was concerned and I chose the right type of bullet so that it expanded inside him rather than going in and just laying there. This way the expansion of the bullet, it instantly damaged more of his internal organs and death was quickly there for him. But you know it's real strange, when I shot him he managed to walk a couple of steps and then he fell. The blood was all over the place. . . . Anyway, this is an evil boy and I am not.

In another picture he saw the image of another famous assassination victim, "JFK. Very pensive look that he has. He knows that he's going to die. It's in his eyes. But if you look closely his mouth denies what his eyes know. His mother stands there accepting her son but it's unquestionably true that his eyes know he's gonna die but his mouth denies it."

Dr. Richard Bloom, like Dr. Daniel Schwartz, concluded after extensive interviews that Chapman was schizophrenic and that he suffered from delusions of grandiosity. Bloom, a psychologist called by the defense to evaluate Chapman and testify on his behalf at his scheduled trial, has maintained that the killer was psychologically unable to control his actions on the night he shot Lennon. Bloom traces the tragedy to a psychosis that began, he says, when the killer was a child. Bloom also theorizes that the seeds of violence were further nourished by Chapman's indiscriminate use of psychedelics and other drugs that may have caused organic brain damage during early adolescence.

"From my point of view, all this stuff that took on such a worldly manifestation really was an expression of his own family life," Bloom said. "All this stuff, as grandiose as it all sounds, filters down to his own relationship with his own family."

Chapman told Bloom that he grew up hating his father "because of what he did to my mother."

All the hate that the world's John Lennon fans felt toward him, Chapman said, was "just a small fraction" of the hatred he felt toward his own father. Chapman talked in detail to Bloom and other psychologists and psychiatrists of the times his mother had cried out to him for help when she was being abused by her husband. He told Bloom he would wake up many mornings to find his battered mother in his bed.

According to Bloom, Chapman was permanently scarred by the role his parents unwittingly thrust upon him as his mother's protector and surrogate spouse. The responsibility of a job he was powerless to fulfill caused him later to abandon hope of gaining control over his own life, Bloom said. The combination of his father's random violent outbursts and his mother's turning to her son for protection also pushed Chapman into the fantasy world of the Little People, the psychologist said. Among the Little People, Chapman inspired the respect, love, and fear that he craved for himself and that became painfully twisted because of his conflicting relationships with his parents. Only among his Little People could he achieve the kind of power and control he was never able to find in his family and social environment.

Chapman's creation of a world of Little People and his continuing fascination as an adult with *The Wizard of Oz* and other childhood fantasies indicate that "his intellect and emotions were operating totally separate from each other," Bloom said. Chapman was unable ever to unify the various elements of his personality into a cohesive and recognizable self. Mirroring the dilemma of his alter ego Holden Caulfield, he was unable to see that the things he believed he needed "from his environment" were there all along, inside him. He identified with Holden Caulfield "as somebody that would rescue the children, which is something that nobody would do for him," Bloom said.

Although Chapman's later adolescence and young adult years were marked by success and civic achievements, Bloom says that success came too late to undo "permanent, lasting damage . . . probably during the first six or eight years of his life." Bloom is confident that it was the childhood trauma that laid the groundwork for Chapman's later obsessive and compulsive behavior patterns. The psychic scars of childhood, perhaps exacerbated by drugs, impaired "his ability to control his impulses . . . so what would have normally been something controllable becomes involuntary," the psychologist said.

"He was operating beyond free will," Bloom said. "The murder of John Lennon had the appearance of a premeditated act. But I saw this elaborate planning as part of the involuntary compulsions.

"He was on a track where he was unable to get off it. There were moments when he wished he could get off it, but while he was on it, he lost control."

Bloom explains Chapman's early worship of the Beatles, his religious fanaticism, his spur-of-the-moment obsessions with art, personal finances, *The Catcher in the Rye,* and other spontaneous compulsions as telltale indicators of the thought process that led to the death of John Lennon. Obsessive and compulsive behavior arises from "an inability to control things once the ball gets rolling," Bloom said. "When Mark saw the John Lennon book, the ball was rolling and it was out of control and he couldn't stop it."

In the months, weeks, and hours before the killing, Chapman was able to appear normal and lucid because "He's not psychotic or abnormal all the time. But when he's in that obsessive mode of operation, that's where he's lost control. That could easily have been what was at work. There's enough evidence to indicate that this is the way he operates. This is the way his mind works—on these obsessive tracks. I speculate that this is probably what was happening at the time he killed John Lennon."

. . .

At a crucial moment of decision prior to the killing, Chapman says he could have decided to stop "the ball rolling." God gave him two signs, he says, in the weeks before the murder when a cartoon on TV flashed the message "Thou Shalt Not Kill" from the Ten Commandments. The same commandment leaped out at him from a religious motto his wife had hung on the wall of their apartment.

The only decision Chapman made, he says, was a choice to give up control over his future actions by allowing the "ball" to start rolling in the first place:

"After I got the autograph on the album, I should have got in a cab and gotten the hell out of there. I was oscillating back and forth between staying and killing him or leaving. There was part of me, the good part, that said, 'Quickly, do it now before the bad part gets hold of you again. Get the doorman to hail you a cab. Go to the airport, get a plane and go back to Hawaii as fast as you can. Nobody will ever believe this is John Lennon's real signature, but you know it's real.

"Just do it! Just get away from here. Go home and hang the album on the wall and remember it. Remember you did get something. You came after something and you got something.'

"Then I would just collapse into the other mode, like switching modes. I envisioned the *Double Fantasy* album on the wall and me sitting on the sofa, looking up at it knowing what almost happened. Knowing that I went back home and got therapy so I was able to enjoy a 'normal' life. But I needed therapy right then. I needed someone to see these things and help me right then. I was out of control. . . . Inside my heart I know I'm guilty because I had the chance to turn around three months prior and I didn't do it. I made that decision, a cognizant, rational, intelligent decision, to murder a man. Once I made it, there was no stopping. It was all downhill from there. God brought me to a crossroads and said, 'I want you to go this way, not that way.' God didn't create robots. But once I made the decision, I was programmed by my own self-destruction. After that, something had to occur. The dénouement had to be written. It became so paradoxically a search for identity yet a search for destruction at the same time. I just felt like a big nobody and that was so attractive to me, to go out and do this horrible act that would make me become somebody. I couldn't control it. There was something in me that desperately wanted to be filled. I was stretched to the limit and I had no personality and everything was going so wrong there was no way to avoid going down that hole once I made that decision. The forces were too great to withstand.

"It was like a runaway train. There was no stopping it. Nothing could have stopped me from doing what I did. Not prayer, not my will, not the devil, not any man, not any bodyguard. Not anything could have stopped me."

PART III

THE LITTLE PEOPLE

CHAPTER TEN

GOD SAW THAT

Deceits and vanities and arrogances that they would never stoop to for themselves they perpetrate on their children . . . someone beaten to death from the inside.

—JOANNE GREENBERG,
I NEVER PROMISED YOU A ROSE GARDEN

As though himself remembering the events of May 10, 1955, Mark David Chapman squinted beyond the bars of a caged room at Attica prison. The prisoner took off his glasses and massaged the sockets of his eyes as he recalled his mother's often repeated accounts of apprehensive moments surrounding his birth.

"Of course I don't remember the day I was born. But I remember my mother telling me about it. I remember my mother talking about how frightened she became when the nurse told her how much I weighed. She demanded that the nurse bring me to her immediately so she could see for herself that I wasn't abnormal, that I hadn't been born with water on the brain.

"My mother was a graduate nurse, which means she went through the four years of school to become a nurse and not just taking those one- or two-year courses.

"They were trained in those days, if anything was wrong with the child, that they would deny to the mother, at least at first, that anything was wrong. Just giving birth was a trauma and they didn't want to upset the mother with any bad news right away.

"So, when my mother, shortly after delivering me, when she was informed of my weight of almost twelve pounds, she ordered them to bring me into the room. She didn't believe them when they said that I was all right, so she insisted on seeing her son and they brought me in. I wasn't even completely bathed and cleaned yet, but she was so upset they brought me in and showed her that I was all right.

"A little later, my father snapped a picture of me through the glass at the hospital, which I still have. I was a pretty fat little baby.

"My mom and dad had me approximately right away after they were married, after they'd been married about nine or ten months. My father was an air force staff sergeant and my mom was attending nursing school in Texas near where my father was stationed at Fort Worth. They met at a USO dance. I remember my father telling me that once he laid eyes on Mom, he couldn't get enough. He said he just kept coming back and they dated and were married in a short time."

Shortly after the birth of his son at Harris Hospital in Fort Worth, Texas, Staff Sgt. David Curtis Chapman was discharged from the air force. He moved with his wife and child to Indiana, where he simultaneously began pursuing a college education and a career. Taking advantage of the G.I. Bill for military veterans, David Chapman enrolled in an engineering program at Purdue University. He also went to work for the American Oil Company.

For a while, Diane Chapman worked part-time as a nurse to help put her husband through school.

"My mom always told me that I was a good boy. I didn't cry a lot and I was very well behaved. I did have one curious habit, though. What they called 'rocking.' I got to where I would rock the crib all the way across the floor. My mom worried about it and took me to the doctor. She said the doctor told her not to worry, that it was something I'd grow out of, but I never did. I continued doing it all through school. To this day, I still sit and rock back and forth sometimes."

Just as he recalls his parents telling him the story of his birth, Chapman fondly recalls the highlights of his early childhood as described by his mother. She told him about his first encounter with a celebrity.

"Lenny Dawson used to ride me on his shoulders and pull me and his daughter in a little wagon around the yard," he says. "Lenny Dawson, a man who went on to become a great football player and wound up in the Super Bowl."

Chapman's fondest childhood memories are both from, and of, his mother.

The mother that he remembers is an extroverted and expressive woman who made little effort to conceal even her most personal, intimate, and spontaneous thoughts and feelings from her son. He remembers that she would cry again and again at the same sad lines in the same touching movies.

A solicitous woman who sought to cultivate within him the creative impulses and vivid imagination that she told him he had inherited from her, Mark recalls that his mom always had clever and well-reasoned answers to the tough childhood questions like "Why was I born?" and "What am I supposed to be?" He was born to greatness, she told him; he could be anything he wanted to be.

It was Mark's mother who took the time to explain frightening and complicated mysteries that confronted him as he grew. Diane Chapman seemed always to do just the right thing in just the right way, her son recalls. She always seemed to understand.

"My mother always exuded this sense of being a free spirit, a very creative and imaginative person. She always had a sense of drama. I got my sense of life, my emotions, from her."

Diane exhorted and encouraged her son, assuring him that he was "special" and "brilliant," destined for greatness and fame. She sought to fill within him an emotional vacuum in which she told him that her own childhood had been stunted.

"She told me I could be a great writer or anything I wanted to be, that I could do anything that I wanted to do. I always had big expectations for myself, even later when I had to leave college and was reduced to being a security guard and a housekeeper and doing the most menial jobs. I got those expectations from my mother.

"My mom always inspired me. She had a joie de vivre, a theatrical and fanciful flair. My mom was so spontaneous, so spur of the moment. And she was very astute. I remember once I asked her where babies came from and—You know? How do you answer a question like that?—she didn't go into the stork, or start talking about the birds and bees. But she told me, truthfully so—like I said, my mom was very astute, she was very keen, I guess because of her training and everything. She didn't get ruffled at these kinds of questions. She told me that God planted a seed inside a woman's stomach and then it grew to become a baby. I thought that was a really nice way of explaining the facts of life to a child."

To her son, Diane Chapman radiated a warmth and wit while his reticent, workaholic father all but disappeared from his life.

"There was such a huge contrast between her and my father. My father was so controlled, so structured."

In contrast to the warm and affectionate memories of his mother, Chapman has talked of wanting to kill his father. After he was arrested for murder on the night of December 8, 1980, in New York City, he told psychologists and psychiatrists that he blamed his father for the rage and the crippling of his childhood emotions that had ended in the taking of another man's life.

One of the psychologists who interviewed Chapman was the late Dr. Lee Salk. Quoted in Salk's 1982 book, *My Father, My Son: Intimate Relationships,* Chapman said it was the father who had failed the son by not providing the guidance needed to grow up and form his own identity.

Chapman said he became embittered over childhood memories of the abuse that he remembers his father inflicting on his mother. He said his rage against his father was rekindled when his parents were divorced and Diane Chapman, denied what her son believed a fair share of her husband's property holdings and bank accounts, moved to Hawaii.

Chapman told Salk he had fantasized that he would confront his father and "put a gun to him and tell him what I thought about what he had done to my mother, and that he was going to pay for it. . . . I hear you're scared to death that you're going to hell, and this is it, Dad."

David Chapman has never visited his only son since his imprisonment. Within eleven years of the John Lennon murder, the killer's father was married twice, suffered six heart attacks, and, early in 1992, a crippling stroke from which he later recovered. After the stroke, David Chapman's mind reverted temporarily to the time when he was eighteen years old, unable to remember that he had a son or a daughter, Susan, born nearly seven years after Mark.

Mark Chapman virtually never recalls his sister when speaking of his childhood and family. He remembers his father as a painful enigma, a devoted and hardworking man unable to communicate with his own wife and children.

Always close to his mother, it wasn't until Chapman had spent nearly a decade in prison, he says, that he began to come to grips with the previous resentment and hostility that he had felt toward his father since childhood.

"My father and I love each other very much now," Chapman said. "We started writing to each other several years ago and we talk on the phone every now and then. He says he has forgiven me for all the horrible things I said about him when I was arrested."

Although their father-son relationship has been repaired, Chapman still recalls and speaks of the emotional vacuum that he says separated him from his dad for many years.

"My father lived by very rigid patterns, doing the same things day after day. He was very meticulous, very unemotional. He was a 'good' man, as far as doing all the things a 'good father' is supposed to do," Chapman struggled to explain. "He never drank and he was always home. But there was an iciness that I felt from him all my childhood. We went to the Boy Scouts together and the Indian Guides and all that father-son stuff that society says a good dad is supposed to do with his kids. But I don't recall that I ever had a conversation with him about anything that was real. I don't recall that my father ever hugged me or told me he loved me.

"The only thing I ever learned from my dad was how to fix a toaster and change the oil in a car.

"He was just a shell who swallowed everything. And then, when it finally came out, God help you."

One of Chapman's most vivid childhood memories of his father is of a long-ago Thanksgiving dinner. The table had been set and he and his sister and mother were waiting for their father and husband to join them. Chapman watched in fear and confusion as his father descended the stairs muttering to himself and cursing his family. Moments later, David Chapman picked up a steaming turkey in his bare hands and dashed it onto the table.

"My mother and my sister sat there crying and I felt like I had to try to control the situation or something," Chapman recalled. "I said, 'Well, we're not going to let this spoil our Thanksgiving.'

"He never explained or apologized and I never to this day knew what that was all about."

David Chapman also never explained why, on another occasion, he pushed his son's face into a plate of spaghetti, or why he would abuse his wife. Mark Chapman recalls fleeting images of his mother, her clothing in disarray, running through his bedroom to escape her husband.

Chapman told psychiatrists in 1981 that he would wake some mornings to find his mother in his bed, and he recalls that, when he was about ten years old, she began crying out to him for help in fending off her husband's advances. He said that on several occasions he placed his own body between his struggling parents when his mother called on him to defend her. On other occasions, he said he confronted and threatened his father on his mother's behalf. In a 1987 *People* magazine interview, Diane Chapman downplays incidents of domestic violence in the Chapman home. She said her husband occasionally struck her, causing her sometimes to cry out to her son in the night.

"But I didn't call him to intercede or anything," she told the magazine. "I just wanted somebody to be aware. I just wasn't thinking. I had never been hit before in my life. Anyway, I remember I brought it on myself. The fact is Dave kept a darn good roof over our heads for all those years, and I would say he was a better parent to Mark than I was. The truth is I was never like a mother with Mark—more like his best friend."

Male children thrust into the role of surrogate spouse and protector of their mothers often "grow up with incredibly grandiose ideas about themselves," says psychologist Alice Hoagland. "The child at an early age learns the bizarre message that he is so powerful he can take care of the most powerful person in the world—his mother."

Such children, Hoagland says, "tend to want to leave home early in life and break away. They have a chance if they can pull away from their parents."

. . . .

After David Chapman got his degree from Purdue, he and his wife, a native of western Massachusetts, decided to stay in the South, where they had met and married. Their son recalls that his mother had told him that both she and her husband had grown up in unhappy homes. Rather than return to the soil of their native New England, they moved to Decatur, Georgia, where David Chapman went to work in the credit department of the American Oil Company office in Atlanta. It was there, their son recalls, that Mark first began awakening to his own consciousness with a series of random and disconnected childhood memories. He remembers sneaking through a fence in his backyard and stealing an egg from a nest in a neighbor's chicken coop. He remembers the day the family dog confronted him on the back steps and snapped a sandwich out of his hands.

"I always felt bad about that, like it was my fault that the dog had to be put away. We never had a dog again after that.

"But my first memory—for some reason I've always remembered this so it must be important—is that I was on my tricycle and I was riding down the sidewalk. My mother was yelling at me because it was my grandfather's birthday and I was supposed to be there. That's all. But it's my very first memory, and it's very vivid.

"I also remember Sarah, a lady who lived down the street from us who used to bring us corn bread. My father was from Connecticut and my mother was from Massachusetts so they didn't know much about corn bread. But I can still remember the taste of Sarah's corn bread.

"Sarah was run over by a car one day in her driveway and killed."

About two years after the Chapmans first settled in Georgia, David Chapman was transferred to the oil company office in Roanoke, Virginia, where they had their second child, a daughter they named Susan Jill. Almost seven years older than his sister, Chapman has few memories of his only sibling, recalling only that "we were never close."

In Roanoke, the family moved into "a house with a big spooky attic," he says, a haunting backdrop for his first exposure to the concepts of God and violence and death.

"I have several memories of that time of my life and for some reason they deal with death, my first cognizant experience with death. I also have a memory of my first experience with God, or about God, or something I thought was about God.

"It was one afternoon when I was walking home from school with a first-grade classmate. We were walking down the street, a tree-lined street, and there was a cat off to the side of the road. It had been run over by a car. The entrails were out and there was a lot of blood. I remember exactly what

I said. It was so shocked into my memory that I remember my exact words.

"I said, 'Oh, isn't that too bad.' And this other kid got very upset with me. He had misunderstood me. He thought that I was being lighthearted and casual about something as horrible as death. But I wasn't. What I meant by what I had said was, 'Oh, isn't that too bad—for that poor cat.' I meant it in a sympathetic way, but the other kid took it as just a flippant remark, like I was mocking death.

"So he turned to me and he said, 'God saw that.' He said, 'God has this book in heaven and every time you do something wrong, He makes a little mark on it. If you get too many marks, you're going to hell.'

"That scared me to death. I went home crying to my mom that God had seen me do something bad. I was convinced for some reason that I had done something really awful and God was going to punish me for it.

"After a while, my mom explained it to me so I could understand. She got me calmed down. But the experience left me with a scary memory, and maybe it had something to do with my other memories about death.

"We lived on a block where there was a huge church. I think it was an Episcopal or Presbyterian church. It was too big and grand to be Baptist. It was on the other corner of the block from the school that I went to in first and second grade, and it had a long, green, flowing landscape. Somehow or other, I got to know the pastor, and for some reason he made me the guardian of the church. I took the job very seriously. I would walk around the church grounds and just keep an eye on the place. It was like a security guard would do. I thought of myself as the guardian of this church and I would walk around it every day to see that everything was all right.

"One day I was going around the block on my wagon when I saw something strange going on. Some men were carrying a big black box into the church. It was a coffin. I didn't know what it was at the time. Everybody was crying, and I just sat there on my wagon watching all this. Somehow—I guess I asked somebody or something—I found out that a person was dead. And it was fascinating, seeing this great emotional turmoil and not knowing what was happening. It was just a fascinating situation.

"Then, it was about the same time in my life, I found this turtle shell half-buried in the ground. It was empty. I remember picking it up and cleaning out the dirt and looking at it for a long, long time. What had happened to the life that had been there? This had to be death. But what did that mean? Where had it gone?"

Combined with early memories of death and sin, Chapman developed an obsessive and preternaturally vengeful grudge against one of his playmates. Before he came to despise his father and long before he began to entertain thoughts of murdering a childhood hero, the seeds of a tenacious and relentless rage had already taken root in the mind of young Mark David Chapman.

"There was another friend, a male friend, I used to play with. His name was Borden. . . . I remember having a spat with him over something. Whatever it was about, it really bothered me, so much so that I drew up these posters that said: 'Wanted: Borden' and so much money for a reward. I took my father's hammer and nails and went all over the neighborhood putting these posters up on trees.

"I guess that's pretty unusual, to go to all that trouble to get revenge on somebody at that age. I was only five or six years old then. I can't remember what it was he did that made me so hateful."

Chapman recalls that throughout his childhood he would discover pockets of inexplicable and violent impulses that he was powerless to confront or defuse.

"For a certain number of years, my very early years, I felt like a normal kid. Then these instances started occurring, mostly in school or when I tried to interact with other kids. I started to feel alienated. Other kids teased me, and I didn't seem to be able to defend myself against them. I wasn't very athletic, and I began to think of myself as inferior.

" 'Pussy.' That's what they called me. 'Pussy.'

"I know now that it wasn't any different than the teasing that a lot of other kids had to go through. But the difference with me was that these things really hurt me and I never forgot them or got over them.

"One incident still hurts me to this day. It must have happened nearly thirty years ago. We were out on the playground, twenty or thirty of us guys. It was a time when kids were going around grabbing other kids' underwear and pulling them up in back of their pants. They call it a wedgie, all done in fun. A bunch of guys will get around you and yank you by your underwear and kind of laugh and throw you down on the ground. That had happened to me and it was a very painful experience. Not physically. But it really, really hurt me.

"A kid, I guess he was a little bit bigger than me, he grabbed me and yanked up my underwear and all these other kids were laughing. There was a brown stain on my underwear and all the other kids said I shit my pants. They made fun of me about that for a long time. I never, ever got over it.

"That was the first thing that really happened to me that hurt my esteem, perhaps because I didn't have a solid background of a group, because I didn't have a group mentality, wasn't one of the guys, you know. So when the guys came upon me and did something like that, it really crushed me.

"I think at that point I was really a nothing, really a nobody. Everything after that point, the accumulation of these separate incidents, just stayed inside me. I became a person who would put a structure in front of myself, of this smart person or this artistic person, or this musical person—or whatever kind of person. I didn't deal with my emotions."

On several occasions Chapman tried to assert himself by bullying children he perceived to be weaker than himself. Invariably, he says, such efforts resulted in further shame and humiliation.

"I was at Green Forest Baptist Church on the basketball court just down the street from my house. I was there alone when two other kids, a kid named Artie and an Indian boy came up and started shooting baskets. For some reason, I thought I was going to be a tough guy, so I started picking on Artie. I took the ball and kicked it away. He said, 'Look, stop doing that.' I didn't stop and he laid into my face with about four or five punches. All I could do was hit him in the arm. I could never hit anybody in the face, to this day I'm like Holden Caulfield in that way.

"This was a fight I picked, and it set a tone for me. It scared me for the rest of my life about confrontation. For the rest of my life, I would always back down from a confrontation. It made me feel scared inside. It made me a coward. Even years later, when I killed a man—I had to shoot him in the back.

"I remember another humiliating incident a few years later, when I was in chorus. One guy named Neil used to torment me. He would bend his middle finger so the knuckle was prominent and smash me right on top of my leg. It was really painful, but I could never challenge him and I could never hit him back. I would look over at him and he would put his hand on his chin like nothing happened. So what I did was, I got an idea in my mind I was going to learn karate. I called up a karate place and had to leave a message on a phone beeper. Wouldn't you know it? The next day in school, Neil came up to me and he knew all about it. He had been in that karate studio when I called them up."

Spurned by other children and upset by increasingly frequent outbursts of hostility between his father and mother, sometime between his ninth and tenth birthdays Mark David Chapman began to turn inward for guidance and approval he was unable to get at home or in school. At the same time, he said, his mother began turning increasingly for her own emotional fulfillment to her only son. As the years of his childhood went by, he recalls his mother turning more and more to him to express her fears and the anger she felt toward the man she had married.

"She told me she hated my father. She said the only reason she married him was so she could have me," Chapman told psychiatrists in 1981.

She said she worried that she was becoming unattractive and she accused her husband of having "another woman." She told her son that she might commit suicide, like her movie idol Charles Boyer, when she was fifty years old.

Finding himself unaccepted by other children and unable to face the responsibilities of the bitter adult world that he felt his parents were thrusting upon him, Mark David Chapman turned for answers and revenge to his own imagination. He began to retreat into a world of vividly orchestrated fantasies. With the help of John Lennon and the Beatles, Chapman created an elaborate kingdom that he populated with Little People.

"The Little People adored me. I got my respect and adulation from an imaginary source, rather than confronting the kids and the things that hurt me and earning it on my own. When I got really angry about something, I would take it out on the Little People. Sometimes if somebody had hurt me at school or I was angry at my father, I would get revenge by killing some of the Little People. I had a button on the arm of the couch in the den. When I pushed it, it would blow up the houses where the Little People lived. Sometimes I would kill hundreds or thousands of them. Then, after I calmed down later, I would apologize. They would always forgive me."

CHAPTER ELEVEN

THE LITTLE PEOPLE

Normal kids don't grow up to shoot ex-Beatles.

—MARK DAVID CHAPMAN

The child awoke in the middle of the night to a sharp slapping sound. Light from the hallway filtered along the edge of a partially opened bedroom door as he waited in a chilled silence for the sound he knew would come again. At last he heard it, a sickening slap of flesh against flesh followed by his father's gruff voice and his mother's muffled sobs. Turning his face to the wall, the child squeezed his eyes shut and tried to hold back tears. Moments later he heard the faint squeak of a door hinge as his mother gently pushed open the door to his room.

Pausing momentarily at the doorway to turn and switch off the hall light, the statuesque woman stepped softly across the room in darkness and sat at the edge of the bed beside her ten-year-old son. The bed shook briefly with the final snubbed spasms of the woman's swallowed anguish. Mark flinched as he felt the light touch of his mother's fingers against his shoulder.

"It's okay, Mom," he whispered, his face still turned to the darkened wall. "I won't let him hurt you. It's okay."

"Oh, Mark, I'm sorry. I thought you were still sleeping, baby. I'm sorry I woke you. It's nothing. It's all right. Daddy's just angry and Mommie's just sad. It'll be all right in the morning. Let's just go back to sleep. Goodnight, honey. Sweet dreams."

The child awoke alone in his bed the next morning. He lay for a long time contemplating a scattered array of toy soldiers, planes, and helicopters that littered his bedroom floor. His eyes lingered on an arrangement of four miniature plastic soldiers arrayed upon a stagelike cardboard pedestal. Tiring of war games with the imaginary soldiers, he had cut away four of the plastic figures' weapons. Instead of rifles, these soldiers were armed with guitars and with a tiny drum set that Mark had fashioned from paper and cardboard.

He would sit, sometimes for hours, playing *Meet the Beatles,* his only rock music album, while rocking back and forth in front of the tiny stage. He recited the words of the songs and applauded at the end of each tune. Occasionally, he would join the band, strumming a tiny plastic guitar and broadcasting the music from a pulsating ache in the center of his brain. He beamed the rhythmic signals into a pretend sound system so that it could be rebroadcast into the homes and shops of the Little People.

Mark couldn't recall when the Little People had first revealed themselves to him. It was as though they had always been there, since the day he was born—perhaps even before he was born. The Little People knew everything about him because they had been everywhere that he had been in his short life, from Texas to Indiana to Georgia to Virginia, then back with him to Georgia again. Like guardian angels, they had been looking out for him even when he didn't know it.

The Little People had remained invisible until a morning when he had awakened to see them coming and going from their homes, offices, and shopping centers inside his bedroom walls. At first, he had thought it odd that no one else could see them.

He remembered that the Little People had appeared to him on a morning after a restless night. He had been upset and unable to sleep because of the clamor and crying that had erupted from his mother's bedroom. He also had gone to bed early with a fever and a bad cold the night before the Little People appeared. He recalled that it was some time after he had seen *Toby Tyler,* a movie about an orphan boy who had run away from a cruel uncle to join the circus. Mark's parents had remarked to him during and after the movie that he resembled Toby. They said he was a handsome boy like Toby, with a glossy mane of straight, black hair. He had a cherubic, round face with blue eyes set deeply above a pug nose and dimpled chin, just like Toby.

His father had bought him a Toby Tyler circus set after the movie. Mark had retreated in solitude to his room with the cardboard figures and toys for several days afterward, losing himself in imaginary adventures. The Little People were somehow connected in his mind to Toby Tyler and to another favorite movie, *The Mysterious Island.*

Angrily pushing aside the memory of his mom coming to his bedroom the night before, the child lowered his head and beamed a signal to the tiny soldier-musicians he had adorned with guitars and drums. Sitting up in bed and crossing his legs, he began rocking his body, twisting as hard and as fast as he could from side to side until he felt the bed begin to move beneath him.

Mark stared straight ahead, scrutinizing the spaces inside the walls. He twisted his head and moved his eyes methodically from the baseboard to the ceiling of each wall in the room. At last he saw that the Little People had picked up his signal. They were beginning to stream into the streets and sidewalks from their tall apartment buildings and offices inside the walls. Some of them were singing along with the tune he was imagining for them. He could hear the music being rebroadcast from radios in their apartments and shops. It was blaring from stacks of speakers at neighborhood gathering spots. Many of the Little People were smiling. They were rocking their bodies like tiny metronomes in tempo to the tense rhythm that Mark projected for them. They cheered him and loudly called his name.

"Mark, the king of music," they called to him. "Mark the king of the Little People. Long live the king of the Little People."

King Mark smiled benevolently upon his multitudes. The hundreds who had come out at the first sounds of the music were soon joined by thousands, and then by millions, of their countrymen. There were far too many for Mark to count, and he only knew a few of them by name. He waved to them.

As the crowd settled expectantly before him, he began silently moving his lips. His face appeared simultaneously on four giant electronic screens above the tall buildings inside the walls of his room.

"Something serious has come up," he announced. He paused ominously for effect and to be sure that he had the Little People's undivided attention.

"Something very serious has come up and I need your help. Remember what I told you before, the other day? Remember about my dad? About what he was doing to my mom?"

The Little People turned sadly to each other. Some shook their heads slowly in dismay. Some of the little women and children began to cry.

"It happened again last night," he said angrily, punching both his small fists sharply into the mattress beside his crossed legs. The Little People fell back and began to murmur apprehensively among themselves. Mark saw fear in their eyes.

"It's got to stop," he continued. "You, my people, have got to help me. You've got to make my dad stop hurting my mom."

He hesitated. Out of the corner of his eye, he saw that some of his audience had fainted and fallen to the street. Others were trying to sneak away.

"It won't do you any good to try to hide from me," he admonished them. "You know what happened the last time you disobeyed me."

The Little People cast timorous glances at each other, too fearful to meet their creator's gaze.

"Don't you remember? I got very, very angry. I know you don't like my dad, either. So you've got to do this. Just go in my mom's room tonight and stop my dad when he tries to hurt her. You've got to do this for me. If you don't, I won't send you the music. If you don't . . ."

Clambering suddenly from his bed, the boy scooted on his knees across the carpeted room and came to rest before his record player. He pulled his *Meet the Beatles* album from a pile of children's records and pushed the 33 rpm disc onto the turntable, cranking the speed to 45 rpm. As the high-pitched, chipmunklike voices began spilling from the speakers, he laughed aloud and turned up the volume. He began to sing along, twisting and rocking his body in a frenzied effort to keep time with the music. Unable to maintain the pace, he switched the turntable back to 33 and laughed again as the recording seemed to belch before slowing to the appropriate pitch and tone.

"Yeah, yeah, yeah, yeah, yeah," he sang, his body quivering to the syncopated rhythm of the rock ballad.

Sliding across the carpet to the four miniature musicians on the pedestal, he applauded the performance as the song ended. He bent over to kiss the tiny plastic faces of each one. The electronic screens above the walls had faded and the Little People had begun returning to their homes and jobs inside the imaginary buildings that honeycombed the walls.

Hearing his father's car roar to life in the driveway, Mark hastily stripped off his pajamas. He dressed himself in a clean white T-shirt and pair of blue jeans. He stepped into his sneakers without stooping to tie the laces. Racing to the bedroom window, he lifted the curtain aside and peered out as his father's old blue Pontiac backed from the driveway and turned down Green Forest Drive toward Atlanta.

Leaving his bedroom, the child discovered that he was alone in the house. His mother had taken his three-year-old sister to the baby-sitter before going shopping. Mark liked the house best when he was alone. He returned to his room and scooped up the toy musicians onto his Beatles album. He took them downstairs to his favorite room, the den.

Setting up the plastic figures on the carpet before him, he put the Beatles record on his mother's hi-fi and took a seat at the end of a thickly upholstered couch. As music began to fill the room, he sat with the empty album cover on his lap and studied the faces of the four musicians. John, George, Ringo, and Paul stared like four half moons from the cover of the album, one side of each of their faces obscured in deep shadow. Each of the half-faces was capped by a shaggy helmet of hair. Mark had discovered by reading the back of the album cover that the Beatles' haircuts were called "pudding basin," a style that dated back to "ancient England." It made him think of castles and kings—and of the Little People, for some reason.

He also learned from the album cover that John Lennon was the group's leader and that "Beatlemania" had caused four thousand fans to stand all night in pouring rain for tickets to a Beatles concert. He read that some teenage girls had camped at a ticket office for four days and nights and that fans had battled police at concerts and suffered "unnumbered broken limbs."

"Wow," the child said to himself, flipping from back to front and staring at the grainy, close-up photograph of the Beatles' faces. Studying the musicians' eyes, the child imagined a fantasy kingdom of music in "ancient England" where all the people worshiped musicians as kings, just as his Little People worshiped him.

He put his face close against the album, scrutinizing each of the four musicians. They were identified by name in a smaller photograph on the back of the record jacket. He had trouble identifying John Lennon, whose picture looked Oriental. On the front of the album, however, Lennon's face seemed full and round. His lips were a thin, straight line, not as defined or as interesting, Mark decided, as the faces of the other three Beatles. After studying Lennon's features for a long time, he decided that he didn't especially like the face. He didn't know why.

Putting the album aside, he slid from the couch and went to the hi-fi to flip the record. As the music began, he returned to the couch and started rocking his body forward and backward, slamming his head into the cushioned back of the sofa. He rocked so hard it made the record skip. Then he summoned the Little People, who began to appear at the top of the wall above the hi-fi. As the crowds gathered before his mind's eye, he slowed the violent pace of his rocking and resumed a gentle back-and-forth rhythm in time with the music.

"Little People," he sang, changing the words of the Lennon-McCartney tune "Little Child":

"Little People, won't you play with me. . . .
Little People, you must stay with me."

As the song ended, he laughed aloud at the new words he had made up for the song. Staring at the crowds inside the walls, he thought again of his mom and dad as he began rapidly moving the fingers of his right hand, depressing a series of imaginary buttons on the arm of the couch.

Without warning, he pursed his lips and started making staccato sounds and explosions, the sounds that children make when they play war. Inside the walls, the Little People began screaming and falling to the streets. Their buildings tumbled around them. Many screamed for help from beneath the rubble of fallen debris. Ambulances exploded in the street as they raced to the scene of the disaster the child had created.

"I'm sorry," he apologized, "but that's what happens when I get angry."

CHAPTER TWELVE

TAKE ME WHERE THE FREAKS ARE

The sixties wasn't the answer.
It just gave us a glimpse of the possibilities.
—JOHN LENNON, DECEMBER 8, 1980

Mark David Chapman and his Little People stumbled from childhood to adolescence behind a smoke screen of psychedelic drugs.

When he discovered drugs, he was fourteen years old. His bedroom walls were plastered like the bedrooms of millions of American teenagers with colorful posters of the Beatles and with black-and-white photographs of John, Paul, George, and Ringo. Still an ardent fan, it was the group's *Magical Mystery Tour* album that first had aroused his curiosity about drugs.

"At that time, the Beatles were no longer the same Beatles to whose music I had rocked back and forth on the couch in the den. They were no longer the Beatles whose music I had played for my Little People," Chapman says. "The Beatles by then were into long hair, beards, meditation, and drugs. The Beatles were into things that fit my life perfectly."

Still burdened by unresolved conflicts between his parents and by countless indignities that had resulted from his abortive efforts to interact with other children, he adopted a new identity. Mark the Freak was the first of several sham personalities he would put on and cast off in the next decade before finally fixing upon an identity he would never be able to shake—as one of his generation's most notorious assassins.

Still in his own mind a "pussy" too cowardly to confront bullies like those who had humiliated and derided him in the school yard for staining his pants, the humiliations took root during his adolescence. Like a small, slow-growing cancer at the core of his soul, something dark began to grow beneath the surface of a psychedelic ecstasy.

During the summer of 1969, the fad of chemical consciousness and the Beatles-inspired counterculture of peace and love began to unravel into violence and death with the Manson murders. At the same time, Chapman embarked on what he nostalgically recalls as an "innocent" phase of experimentation with drugs, around which his life would revolve for two years.

"We were the first hippies, the first group of stoned guys in our whole high school," Chapman recalled. "The other kids and the teachers hated us. We were dirty and we didn't cut our hair and we wore the same bell-bottom jeans and leather jackets all the time.

"But it was experimental and exciting. In some ways I'm still glad that I experienced it. For the first time in my life, I was 'in.' I was part of a group. We weren't like the people who use drugs today. We weren't evil. We were just young and innocent and for the first time in my life I felt like I wasn't totally rejected."

Spurred on by classmates and neighborhood friends who also found a temporary identity in rebellion and drugs, Chapman returned to school in the fall of '69 as a puerile revolutionary. His self-described metamorphosis "from a nerd to a hippie" began shortly after a sixteen-year-old neighbor, whom he regarded as his mentor and big brother, told him about the mysterious and seductive world of LSD. About a week later, he secured a tablet of the hallucinogen and took his first trip. Shutting himself into his bedroom early one evening, he waited for the drug to take effect. Suddenly, he found himself laughing hysterically while watching TV. A special documentary on drug abuse was coincidentally being aired on television the same night as his premiere LSD venture. Mark's wild laughter brought his baffled father running to his room to find out if anything was wrong. He remembers that his father closed the door and walked away without further inquiry when he replied that he was "just watching something funny on TV."

"It was instant release," he recalled. "Immediately, I went from being a nerd to being a hippie, from being a nobody to being a somebody.

"The main reason I became a hippie was that it gave me my first chance in life to be a group player, a part of something."

His friends and family were frightened and appalled at the precipitous change. An aloof, solicitous, and clean-cut Mark Chapman had been student government representative of his eighth-grade class and a junior counselor at the YMCA summer camp just a few weeks before. A bizarrely different youth returned to classes for his freshman year at Columbia High School.

More than a decade later, when Diane Chapman learned that her only son had murdered one of his childhood heroes, she recalled the summer and fall of 1969 during which Mark became a stranger in his own home, an alien creature she and her husband could no longer either control or understand. She said she grew to fear her son and to believe that he held a mysterious power over their family.

He smoked marijuana and sniffed glue and lighter fluid on his way to school. He regularly met with "drug buddies" in the hallways and outside the school building, sharing doses of the "blotter acid" he carried secretly on strips of paper beneath the straps of his boots.

Unlike many in the sixties who experimented with softer drugs like marijuana or alcohol before turning to the powerful synthetic chemicals, Chapman's mind was plunged overnight into the kaleidoscopic realm of psychedelia. He emerged believing that he and a select group of "drug buddies" had attained wisdom and instant enlightenment far beyond their years. After the first trip, he was hooked, an overnight convert to the drug world and a seeker after the delusional self-truth it promised to reveal. He all but abandoned his Little People, replacing them in his mind with a series of computers with flashing lights. The lights and dials on the imaginary computers reflected his energy levels, indicating to him when he needed to eat, sleep, drink, or otherwise attend to the needs of his body.

As his mind spun obliviously on a psychedelic carousel, he often meditated his way through classroom examinations, handing in blank papers marked only with his name.

On many days, he didn't return home from school until after his parents had gone to bed. Other nights, he would creep from his bedroom and stay until dawn locked with friends in basement rooms taking drugs and listening to rock music. On one such night, while taking LSD in a basement recreation room, he received the first intimation of the dimensions of his rage.

"We had the Pink Floyd album, I believe it was called *Ummagumma,* a double album, which was nothing but noises and sound effects, back in the early, early days of Pink Floyd. We had that going and we were all tripping and I had this real scary experience.

"I was never one to sleep while doing acid. So I remember I was standing up in the room and everybody else was lying out, passed out on the bed. And I remember there was a knife. There was a knife in the room. Something in me, while I was tripping—I recognize it now to be a spiritual force but I didn't know it at the time—was trying to urge me to pick up this knife and stab it into these guys, into my friends. And I, of course, I had freedom of choice and I didn't do it. But it was a compelling urge, to pick up this knife and kill these people. This is how these things happen when people are bombed out on drugs. They open themselves up to the bad elements of a spiritual nature and can be influenced to a point of doing some very damaging, disastrous things. Thank God I avoided doing that. But I remember getting this urge."

In another instance, he recalls that he found himself with a knife in his fist as he stood face to face with his father in the kitchen of their home. As father and son had approached each other, the son had reached for the butt of a knife that protruded from a box of kitchen tools beside the sink.

"I was going after him, but my father grabbed my hand and bent my arm backward until I dropped it. I remember when I felt the pain of him twisting my arm, I just said, 'Okay, okay. It's cool. It's cool.' And I turned and went out of the house. My mother and sister just stood and watched it. I guess they were too shocked to move. Nobody ever said anything about it afterward."

Chapman describes a particularly vivid night of psychedelic chaos after which he saw, for the only time in his life, his father break down in tears.

"Me and one of my drug buddies, Joe, had hitched a ride to a Steppenwolf concert at the Atlanta Auditorium. We each took a whole capsule of brown Owsley, a famous acid of that era. We were near the front and it was the loudest concert I'd ever been to with stacks and stacks of speakers. We were going out of our minds watching John Kay leaping across the stage doing 'Born To Be Wild,' 'The Pusher Man,' ['The Pusher'] and all that.

"After the concert, we hitched a ride back to Decatur in a Volkswagen van. We drove past the school and I stuck my head and my hand out the window and I flipped my finger to the school and screamed, 'Columbia High School, fuck you!'

"The driver took us back to my neighborhood and let us out at a friend's house so we could spend the night. Joe wandered down the road and I didn't even realize that he was walking away. I ended up in somebody's driveway and I just stood there moving my hands in circles in front of me, watching the trails of colored light it made before my eyes. When a De Kalb County police car came up, I walked toward the car and two officers got out and walked toward me. They patted me down and found a pill bottle, but the law read back then that if you didn't have drugs actually on you there was no way they could arrest you for drugs—not even if you were totally out of your mind, which I was. So they got me on a vagrancy charge. They drove right past my house and I said, 'That's where I live. Aren't you going to take me home?' They said, 'No, we're taking you to another house tonight,' and I began to get scared for the first time.

"One of the officers said he remembered seeing me out mowing our lawn and made some comment about what had happened to me. He said they had to take me to the De Kalb County Juvenile Home, adjacent to the county jail. Then there was a crackle on the police radio and a call came in about someone stopping traffic in the middle of McAfee Road. I don't know how I knew,

When you're high on acid sometimes you get precognizant or something, your energy is so high. But I remember sitting straight up and saying, 'That's Joe.'

"The police turned up McAfee Hill and sure enough there was Joe right out in the middle of the street, waving his arms back and forth and babbling incoherently. They got Joe in the car after a few minutes and I remember him looking over at me. He kind of flipped out when he realized I was in the car. He was sitting to the left of me, behind the officer who was driving. Then Joe raised his right hand and slapped the back of the head of the officer that was driving. He knocked the officer's head forward and the Smokey Bear hat flew off his head in front of his face. The officer slammed on the brakes so hard that the car whipped around in the street, nearly 360 degrees. Then both officers got out and came around and opened Joe's door. They took turns beating him with their fists and kicking him. He was trying to hang on inside the car and they were pulling him by his hair, banging his head against the side of the car.

"I was hysterical. I started yelling, 'Pigs! Pigs! Police brutality! Police brutality!' Sometimes their fists and feet would miss Joe and they would hit me, but Joe was clearly their main target. Finally they dragged him out of the car and beat him some more, then they cuffed his hands behind his back and brought us on to the juvenile home. They dragged Joe out of the car by his hair and took us both inside and gave us over to the juvenile officers.

"While they took our names, I kept seeing flashes of light going off all around the room and I thought they were taking our pictures. The officer at the desk assured me I was too young to be photographed, but these flashes kept going off all around my head, from the drugs.

"So they separated me and Joe and put me in a cell, a four-man cell, without a blanket. It was pitch black and I laid down on the floor between two bunks. One of the other prisoners, God bless him, threw a blanket down on me from one of the other bunks. I had peaked at that point on the acid. It was very, very powerful acid, and I tried to hide in the blanket from these very strong hallucinations that were coming out of the walls and everything. I was just gone."

As strange music echoed through the chambers of his mind, vivid colors danced above Chapman among the shadows of the cell. Looking to his left, he watched in awe as a mattress on an upper bunk burst open and vibrantly colored letters of the alphabet began spilling through the air. Looking to his right, another cellmate became transfigured into an oversized Thanksgiving turkey, trussed and basted and with steam rising as though fresh from the oven. At some point, millions of lights exploded inside his mind and he tumbled at last through his nightmare world into unconsciousness.

"Later that day, my father came and picked me up. It was the first time, the first time and the last time, I ever saw him cry. He was very humiliated and embarrassed and hurting.

"But my dad put me in the car and on the way home, he said, 'Look, let's not hurt your mom anymore. Don't tell her that you were on acid. Just tell her that you took some downers and that you got lost.' "

Sociologist Todd Gitlin of the University of California at Berkeley believes that the early and repeated use of psychedelic drugs by adolescents may lay the groundwork for a pattern of later sociopathic behavior. In Chapman's case, it may have laid the groundwork for murder.

Gitlin is the author of *The Sixties,* a popular and critical review of the turbulent decade that spawned the counterculture in which Mark David Chapman came of age.

"The sixties shook up a lot of identities," Gitlin said in response to questions about Chapman's adolescent drug abuse and later psychological difficulties. "To be overly crude about it, some could take it and a lot couldn't. I'm no drug expert, and I don't want to metaphysisize. But it's clear, from people I knew, when young people were sprung suddenly by drugs from the authorities who defined life, the communities that defined their identities, they were in many ways at risk. Those who did a lot of drugs without any supervision, any idea about drugs apart from wildness and as a release of pent-up inhibitions—those people were often unable to bear up. There was very little social support, guidance, or interpretive structure for what they were doing.

"To say that drugs are inherently evil is pretty strong. But it's clear that much evil was done and that some people, in a sense, jammed drugs into mouths that were not prepared for them. Drugs were some powerful and dangerous material that in a dismantled and upheaved culture were bound to cause some damage."

Chapman doesn't know whether drugs had anything to do with an intricate scheme he devised and carried out in the spring of 1970, less than a year after he began using them. In retrospect, it appears to have signaled a pattern of furtive plotting and traveling that would play a key part in the events that led to John Lennon's death.

In an elaborately planned adventure reminiscent of a delinquent Toby Tyler, his childhood hero, he ran away to join the circus. Still, two decades later, unsure where the notion came from, Chapman recalls that he kept the plan to himself, intentionally misleading friends and classmates so they would be unable to tell his parents and police his whereabouts.

"I'm still trying to figure out why I did this," he said. "I just felt I had to run away from home. I don't know what I was reacting to. None of my close friends had ever run away from home and my parents weren't beating me or anything.

"But this may have been the harbinger. This may have been the first adventure I would go on that would precede the—I use terms loosely—the Hawaiian [suicide] adventure and the New York [murder] trip. This thing probably, in some way, had parallels. I planned elaborately in each instance."

When he decided that he was going to fly to Miami, Chapman, who had never been on a plane, laid the groundwork by telling his friends that he was going to California. He began saving his lunch money and setting aside the changes of clothes and costumes he believed he would need to carry out an intricate deception that would assure his escape.

Realizing he would need transportation to the airport, he arranged it two weeks in advance by calling a taxi. After his mother drove him to a local movie theater where he told her he was planning to meet friends, he sneaked out a rear exit and took the taxi to the Atlanta airport. He bought a one-way Delta Airlines ticket to Miami and returned to the waiting taxi, explaining to the driver and another man in the cab that he had needed the ticket so he could visit his uncle in Florida. He arranged to have the taxi driver pick him up two weeks later at 5:00 A.M. at an all-night diner. The taxi driver assured him he knew the location of the diner, about five miles from the Chapman home.

When his flight date arrived, Chapman arose before 3:00 A.M. He disguised himself beneath a hat and a pair of eyeglasses before stepping from his front door and onto the deserted suburban sidewalks with his suitcase. As he walked beneath glowing street lamps, the runaway feared at any moment that he would be stopped and questioned by police. In the back of his mind, he was sure the taxi wouldn't be at the diner when he got there.

"Today, I can't see these men—there were two of them in the taxi both times—I can't see them doing this, agreeing to meet a fourteen-year-old boy at a diner a 5:00 A.M. But they did. And I walked five miles on pins and needles, thinking that someone was going to stop me. But no one did."

When he got to the diner, he recalls feeling for the first time that he had come to the end of childhood. He celebrated the truant rite of passage by ordering and drinking his first cup of coffee. When the taxi arrived, he paid for his coffee, tipped the waitress, and left for the airport.

Careful to conceal his face beneath the hat, he boarded the scheduled early-morning plane to Miami. Awestruck by the sensation of flight, he stared at the clouds and the distant earth until the plane landed about two hours later. Inside the terminal, he went to a lavatory and changed into his customary uniform of "hippie clothes," the trademark bell-bottoms, leather jacket, and sandals he had packed for his adventure. He dumped the fake glasses and hat into a trash can.

"This was Holden Caulfield in the younger days," Chapman explains. "When I left the terminal, I walked up to a cab driver. I remember my exact words. I said, 'Take me where the freaks are.' "

CHAPTER THIRTEEN

TOBY TYLER ON DRUGS

You never find your identity by looking for it.

—MARK DAVID CHAPMAN

As the taxi glided from Miami International Airport with its scruffy and naïve passenger, Mark the Freak had no idea where he was being taken or where he would spend the night. Contrary to what he had told the taxi drivers who had taken him to the airport in Atlanta, he had no uncle in Miami. His nearest relatives, his grandparents, lived several hundred miles up the Florida coastline.

In a bizarre reenactment of the adventures of his childhood hero Toby Tyler, Mark David Chapman had run away from home in March of 1970 to join the psychedelic circus. He had thirty dollars in his wallet. When that would run out, he had no idea how he would feed himself. Vaguely, he sensed that such basic needs as food and shelter would be provided by the Freaks, once they recognized him as one of their own and accepted him into the tribal encampment he envisioned he would find.

Hanging his bare arm out the back window of the taxi and basking in the warm, humid breeze he turned his head from side to side and drank in the exotic new surroundings. He observed that the heavy traffic and the tall buildings of Miami were beginning to fall behind as the cab sped forward on a broad, multilaned ribbon of sand-bordered concrete.

The child inside him, visions of Toby Tyler's circus days dancing in its head, was ecstatic. The adolescent, who had planned and carried out the covert escape from Decatur at the urgings of the child, was beginning to grow apprehensive and uncertain. The taxi pulled from the Miami expressway and came to a stop in a deserted parking lot above an expansive stretch of sand at the edge of an immeasurable watery horizon. After paying the taxi driver and returning the remaining bills to his wallet, Mark the Freak was overcome with loneliness and fear of the unknown. He lingered for a long and reflective moment in the gritty parking lot, struggling with an unexpected inward wave of emptiness and self-pity.

Slowly, he started walking toward the ocean. Small groups of sunbathers lay stretched against the beach in both directions as far as he could see. He decided that he would walk in the opposite direction from Miami, where tall buildings appeared to ripple like a mirage in the steamy distance. The sand was hot and abrasive against the tender edges of feet covered only by thin rubber shower sandals. He walked rapidly, eager to find conversation and companionship. Intently, he studied the demeanor of the people he passed, scrutinizing their faces, hair, clothing, jewelry, and random bits of their conversations. He was looking for any sign that would identify passing strangers as the Freaks among whom he intended to launch a new life.

"I had planned for everything," he said, "everything except the loneliness. I had never felt so lonely and forsaken in my life. As I walked along the beach, I just got overwhelmed with the feeling of true and utter aloneness."

After walking for nearly an hour through the hot sand, still carrying his suitcase, he sat down at the edge of the water and stared for a long time into the sea. The hollow rush of the outgoing waves seemed to echo the emptiness he felt inside his head. After meditating for nearly an hour on his plight, Chapman began eavesdropping on the conversation of a group of sunbathers behind him. Turning and looking over his left shoulder, he saw that two young men and a girl, each of them several years older than he, had spread large towels and blankets on the sand. They were laughing and drinking beer from a cooler. Edging closer to the group, he struck up a conversation and asked if he could join their party. Looking at each other with bemused shrugs, the sunbathers offered him a can of Busch. Less than twelve hours after drinking his first cup of coffee, the fourteen-year-old runaway hesitantly began sipping his first can of beer. He choked on the unexpected stale and bitter taste. As darkness covered the beach, he curled himself into a ball at the edge of a blanket and fell asleep.

Mark the Freak awoke at first light. Looking down the beach toward Miami, he studied two youthful men talking idly at the edge of the water. He had discovered the people he was looking for: Freaks. He rose from the blanket where the sunbathers still slept and approached the two lanky, unkempt young men who appeared to be four or five years older than he. The Freaks eyed him with suspicion as he introduced himself and asked if he could team up with them for a while.

"This place is new to me," he explained. "I need somebody to show me around. I'm cool. I've been experienced. You can trust me."

Realizing at once that he was an underage runaway, the vagrants said he could cause them trouble.

"I've got some money," Mark hastily added. "I can buy us some food and stuff."

Moments later, the trio strolled from the beach and struck out in the direction of Miami.

His self-confidence boosted by acceptance into the company of real hippies, Chapman forgot about being lonely and homesick. For the next four days, he and his mentors stayed close to the beach, from which they made frequent forays into urban shopping districts. The streetwise wanderers taught Chapman the finer points of shoplifting. They coached him on techniques of panhandling and shared with him the elements of Freak lore and survival. At night they slept in large-diameter concrete sewer pipes at beachfront construction sites and on the tile floor of a bathroom at a partially completed hotel.

The trio's immediate objective was to beg or steal enough money to get tickets to a pop music festival. Mark's new friends told him the music fest was scheduled to be held the next week at a speedway at the edge of the Everglades Forest, about twenty miles from the Miami outskirts in which they were encamped.

When Chapman's money began to run out after several days, he sensed that his new friends were tiring of his company. The partnership ended when the three youths encountered a drunken off-duty policeman outside a bar on a city street. The cop wanted to see Mark's I.D.

"I said I had lost it and one of the hippies said I was his nephew, so the cop left us alone. But they got uptight with me about that. I didn't have any money left, and the next day they decided to dump me.

"Our goal all along had been to get to the Miami Pop Festival, so they told me to go on ahead and they would meet me there. I knew they were dumping me, but I started off walking down the road, down this long, straight highway through the Everglades to the speedway, where the festival site was supposed to be. It was twenty miles away. I stuck out my thumb at every car that went by, but nobody stopped. It was baking hot, and I walked the whole twenty miles in my rubber flip-flops. Just walking, walking, walking, staring straight ahead. At one point, I don't know why, I looked down in front of my feet, and there was a big, black snake, a water moccasin, that was very much alive. I almost stepped on it. Then I started worrying about crocodiles and other things that might be in the woods and come out on the road. I guess some guardian angel must have been looking out for me."

As evening began to fall across the Everglades, the dehydrated, blistered, and sun-baked fugitive from the Georgia suburbs stumbled from a steaming griddle of asphalt into an open field. Although Mark the Freak was on the verge of collapse, the child within him grew manic with excitement at the scene that assembled itself before awestruck eyes.

He gazed in disbelief upon twirling amusement rides, gaming booths, and concessions that were connected by sparkling strands of colored lights. Toby Tyler had at last found his circus: a low-budget carnival where down-and-out carnies eked out a living at the fringes of concerts and pop festivals.

"Shades of Toby Tyler," he recalled more than two decades later. "There it was: the rides, the tents, hamburger stands, corn dogs, and hustlers. It was probably the beginning of the end of my innocence."

Mark the Freak fell in quickly with the kindred spirits of the concert sideshow. Telling him they knew he was a runaway, the concessionaires offered him food and shelter if, like Toby Tyler, he would perform menial tasks around the carnival grounds. His first job was as a security guard. Sleeping on cardboard boxes and strips of canvas beneath the tables of a food concession, he was supposed to guard the carnival's supplies of food and beverages.

"It was a pretty good deal for a runaway," he recalled. "When I got hungry, I could just fix myself a hamburger. And the people there were interesting."

Mark the Freak was most fascinated by the carnival hustlers. He was intrigued at the way they got the attention of large crowds of people and conned them into paying top dollar for cheap and worthless merchandise.

He was befriended by an assistant of one of the hustlers, a teenager who taught him to keep a pack of nonfiltered Camels rolled up in the sleeve of his T-shirt and advised him on the finer points of hucksterism.

"He told me to just listen and watch how smooth he was, ripping people off. Just a sweet-tongued, snake-livered con artist," Chapman recalled. "He would sweet talk these people, giving them little free gifts. Then he would get them to write him seventy-dollar checks for these cheap little sewing machines that were worth maybe twenty dollars."

Several days after joining the carnival, his two hippie friends from Miami still hadn't shown up. Another kindred spirit, however, a "kind-of-hippie-looking guy in an army jacket and a beard," showed up instead.

Although he was supposedly the carnival security guard, Chapman never questioned the stranger who drove up in a truck and told him he had been sent to pick up a grill and cooking supplies. Impressed by the stranger's long hair, beard, and other conspicuous badges of hippiedom, Mark the Freak helped load the equipment into the truck. He hitched a ride with the stranger back across the Everglades. During the ride to Miami, the bearded stranger introduced himself as Carlos. He said his father and mother were refugees from Castro's Cuba who operated a restaurant equipment repair and rental business. The carnival operator was one of their clients.

After unloading the equipment from the truck, Carlos invited the runaway to stay with his family in the Miami suburb of Coral Gables. Apparently concerned about the welfare and safety of the baby-faced hippie, Carlos's father agreed to let Chapman stay temporarily with the family on one condition—that he would go to work in the family's appliance rental business to pay for his room and board. Mark agreed. During the day he worked around the rental office and warehouse, running errands and painting furniture and appliances. In the evenings he cruised the Miami streets with Carlos and a group of friends in search of marijuana.

"It was fun; it was innocent," he recalled. "I got paid one dollar every day for lunch and I would walk to a little shop and get a submarine sandwich and a soda. I had to work pretty hard for my lunch money.

"Then, at the end of the first week, we came home from work one day and Carlos's father said, 'Look, Mark, I know you're a runaway and you can't stay here. I owe you some money for the work you've done for me, and I'm going to give you an option. I'll take you to the bus station and buy you a ticket home. Or I'll give you money you've earned this week and take you where you want to go."

After pondering the alternatives, he decided to go back home.

"I kind of felt bad, but I knew had to go back. I wasn't happy being where I was, but I still didn't want to go back. I wanted to stay, but I knew I couldn't."

Watching his independence slip away with each mile, he stared out the window of the Greyhound bus. Back in Atlanta, he phoned a friend. His friend's mother phoned the runaway's worried parents.

When he arrived at his friend's home, he was astonished to learn that he had only been gone two weeks. While recounting the details of his odyssey for his friend, the doorbell rang. Mark heard his father's voice at the front door.

"My dad didn't say anything until we got back to our house and then all he said was, 'Your mom would like to see you.' I went into her bedroom. The shades were down and it was dark. She was in bed with the covers pulled up. . . . She couldn't even talk."

CHAPTER FOURTEEN

GOD AND TODD

As suddenly as Mark David Chapman had become a sinner, he became a saint. A born-again classmate at Columbia High School planted the seeds for the Christian conversion late in 1970, inviting him to a religious retreat sponsored by Chapel Woods Presbyterian Church. Although not interested in religion at the time, Chapman agreed to attend the retreat with teens from the fundamentalist congregation near his home when his classmate told him, "There'll be lots of girls there."

At the church gathering Chapman became reacquainted with Jessica Blankenship, a former neighbor and childhood friend. Jessica reminded him they had been in second grade together and she had been the girl standing beside him in the class photo—a picture he had despised. Before the photo was taken, Mark had stuffed his shirttail hastily into his pants. He was humiliated to see, when the school yearbook was printed, an elastic band of white cotton underwear protruding prominently above his belt line.

Nearly nine years later, Mark and Jessica found themselves laughing about the class photo and recalling old times and childhood friends. Jessica introduced him to other teenagers who invited him to play guitar in their Christian rock band. One of the friends, Michael McFarland, "would become my first true alter ego," Chapman recalls. "It was Michael McFarland who told me later to read *The Catcher in the Rye.* He said I had to read *The Catcher in the Rye.*"

Before the weekend retreat had ended, Chapman had become engrossed in a film about Jesus. He says that he was deeply affected by the film and by a lecture and pamphlet he received detailing the "spiritual laws" of the Christian faith. Although he didn't become a Christian at that point, he wrote down the date that he believed would mark his first spiritual turning point: October 25, 1970.

While he found himself behaving as a Christian in the presence of Christians, Chapman returned to school the following week and fell quickly back into his identity as Mark the Freak. The next eight months would prove a transitional period as his newfound religious peers continued to reach out to him, and he to them. Some of them joined Mark and his drug buddies on unholy excursions into the realm of psychedelic chemicals and rock 'n' roll. A subsequent religious retreat ended in near disaster when he distributed LSD and other drugs to several inexperienced young Christians. When the drugs began to take effect, one of the youths stripped naked and ran into a lake screaming, Chapman recalls, "I'm a soggy reefer! I'm a soggy reefer!" to the alarm of confused church elders.

When his sophomore year ended in 1971, Chapman went to Florida for a brief vacation with his paternal grandmother, Hazel Pisini, at her Ormond Beach home. Still in search of the Freaks, he recalls that he sought the company of "hippies and druggies" and continued to consume large quantities of chemicals that were beginning to take a toll on his sanity. In the preceding months, Chapman had suffered a series of "bad trips" and flashbacks. He later experienced troublesome and frightening hallucinations in which the world became for him a two-dimensional cartoon.

He didn't lose his faith in the "truth" he believed he had discovered in drugs until the 1971 Florida vacation when a group of long-haired acquaintances ransacked his wallet.

"I had met a guy named Earl, the King of the Beach, a tall hippie with long blond hair, and his cronies," Chapman recalled. After spending the day with Earl and the hippies, he returned to his grandmother's home where "I felt that the whole world had collapsed. I felt violated, like I couldn't trust anybody.

"I needed to get something out of my wallet and when I opened it, I saw that it had been ransacked. I wasn't on drugs at that time. I wasn't high. And I remember, when I realized that my buddies had gone through my wallet, feeling the lowest I had ever felt. I felt like nobody. Like nothing. Nothing at all. It was the culmination of so many things at that time and I started crying, just desperately crying."

That was the moment Chapman turned to the "spiritual laws" he had learned at the church retreat more than six months before.

"At some point I lifted my hands and I said, 'Jesus, come to me. Help me.'

And that was my time of true spiritual rebirth. It was like a coming together that evening of all the spiritual lessons in my life. I felt that my life had just become a dark, round room from me going around and around in circles. And that night, I came to a door.

"When I opened the door and let God come physically into my heart, I felt cleansed. I felt totally forgiven and totally renewed."

Describing the spiritual encounter for a psychiatrist, the late Dr. Bernard Diamond, at Rikers Island in April 1981, Chapman said that God "actually came into the room, but I couldn't see him but he was there. He was right here on my left knee and I felt tingling from the tip of the toe to the top of my head, and I felt like I had finally found the answer—you know, what I had been searching for through the drugs and, you know, the whole hippie scene type of thing. . . ."

When he returned to school his junior year in the fall of 1971, Mark the Jesus Freak bore little resemblance to the drug users among whom he had tried to find an identity for the previous two years.

"It was a true personality split," recalls his longtime childhood friend Miles McManus.

"When Mark was in the ninth and tenth grades, he was doing drugs very heavily, then he went into this Jesus Freak stage and his whole identity changed. It was like he had to be the best Christian in the world."

About the same time, he began to express an intense loathing for the musical heroes of his childhood: John Lennon and the Beatles.

The sudden anger puzzled friends who recalled Chapman, dressed in a trademark John Lennon army jacket, singing "The Ballad of John & Yoko" from a makeshift stage on the rooftop of Wadsworth Elementary School near his home.

After Chapman's spiritual conversion, "I remember Mark said that the Lennon song 'Imagine' was a Communist song," recalled McManus. "And that comment by Lennon, about the Beatles being more popular than Jesus, that really pissed him off."

Other friends, members of church groups that Chapman joined after his instant spiritual conversion, recall that he engaged in a vendetta against "Imagine," warning that Lennon's message—to imagine a world with no heaven or religion—was blasphemy. At prayer meetings and religious rallies he attended, often several times a week, friends remember that he would sing his own foreboding lyrics to the Lennon tune: "Imagine John Lennon is dead."

Jan Reeves, the sister of one of Chapman's best friends, Dana Reeves, recalls that Chapman confronted her over her collection of Beatles albums:

"I had a big collection of Beatles albums and he told me one time he didn't like them anymore because John Lennon had said that they were more popular than God," said Reeves. "He said that, due to that one statement, he would not listen to them anymore; he didn't like them anymore.

"He seemed really angry toward John Lennon, and he kept saying he could not understand why John Lennon had said it. According to Mark, there should be nobody more popular than the Lord Jesus Christ. He said it was blasphemy."

Reeves recalls after John Lennon's death that Chapman, at the age of eighteen, also "talked to me about *The Catcher in the Rye.* It was like he wanted a much deeper understanding of it than what he had. Not that he was obsessed with it, but that he wanted a deeper understanding back when he was a teenager."

What McManus and others describe as fanaticism, Chapman calls "an inability to be imperfect" that has marked virtually every endeavor of his life.

"There were tremendous changes that overcame me once I started focusing on the Lord and stopped focusing on drugs and rock music and being a hippie," he said. "I cut my hair off and changed even my clothes. Clothes were an important statement. Not that I cared what people thought, what I looked like. But to me as a Christian, it was important not to be in ragged bell-bottoms and loose shirts and things so I wore straight-legged pants and black shoes and regular shirts.

"I remember getting chastised for this by Mike, my best friend at that point, because he told me I didn't really have to do that kind of stuff. He was right. But to me, in my own heart, I had to for my own self because my life had done such a tremendous turnaround.

"And it was real. It wasn't something I was trying to manufacture. Christ really had come into my life and changed it and every part of my life reflected it. In fact, my mother made a comment to our neighbor, 'We can take him to see his grandparents again,' or something like that.

"I remember witnessing to some neighbors who had come over to talk with Mom in the living room, and at school I remember being so totally dedicated that just about my every moment was filled with, besides my studies, something to do with the Lord. I would walk the halls and think about who I could speak with to help them to get to know the Lord like I had. There was a fellow that was sitting in one of my classes in the back, Louie. I was sitting up front. He kept cursing and I remember I went back to the back of the class and I said, 'What's with all this cursing? I mean, you're using the Lord's name like that. Don't you know there really is a God?' The guy went to church in the next few days and got saved and turned his life around.

"Then there was a fellow, Brian, who a year earlier had given me a little tract, 'This Is Your Life,' which I read and laughed at and gave it back to him. I told him religion was all make-believe.

"Remember, these were days when drugs were rampant in high school halls. Lot of hippiedom. Lot of confusion. The war in Vietnam was going strong. We were lost in the forest. Then, when I found Christ, I wasn't lost. I wanted other people to find Him. It was a genuine desire on my part. For one of my class projects, I rented an older film about Jesus and the disciples. Not like Zeffirelli, but it was okay and after showing the film I gave what we called the Salvation Message to the kids in the class, that they could actually know Christ and He had died for them and I got a pretty good grade on it. I really felt that God was behind me when I did that. I would also put tracts, booklets, into different lockers as I was going through the halls, slip them through the air vents in lockers. I'd leave tracts in restaurants and places like that.

"I didn't consider myself fanatical, although from the outside I can see how someone else would consider me that, putting tracts in high school lockers. But it wasn't like that. It was real, it was genuine. I remember I went to two different prayer groups, each once a week. One on Friday night at the home of a Christian psychologist. He . . . and his wife, every Friday night, would open up their home. We would hold these prayer meetings. I guess you would call them charismatic. There were some spiritual movings in these groups. At one of these groups, Pat Boone called us. We just talked to him through a speaker phone.

"At the other prayer meeting, on Monday or Tuesday night, we would have about a three-hour talking, singing, praying service."

Caught up in the fervor of one of their meetings, Chapman's Christian friends failed to recognize his need for personal acceptance and approval.

"When I sort of fell out of my fervency, it was at the end of one of those meetings. There was a particular song I wanted to play really badly on my guitar, a song I had written a few days before, a Christian song. I remember the meeting just was so jam-packed with people talking, singing, praying, that I didn't have time to play the song I wanted to. And I got frustrated. I remember I got so frustrated that I couldn't play this song. It was a natural feeling, but somehow with me it tripped me over into becoming more and more discouraged. It was a small thing. . . .

"But with me, it was a catalyst for a growing lack of wanting to be close to the Lord and I stopped going to the meetings. I stopped praying and reading the Bible. Although I never really went back to drugs, I more or less became what they call a lukewarm Christian. I wasn't that interested in what the Lord was doing in the world and I really wasn't that much of a part of it anymore, although I always believed that the experience at my grandmother's was too real, too genuine, to ever disbelieve again. To this day, I never again disbelieved in the Lord or Christ or in the fact I knew Him and could of course talk to Him any time I wanted to and get back into a deeper relationship with Him."

To fill the void in his life created by the cooling of his fervid Christianity, Chapman turned to the rock 'n' roll of John Lennon's onetime musical nemesis, Todd Rundgren.

"The lyrics and the music provided everything I needed to express my identity," Chapman recalled. "I didn't need anything else. I was in my own private world with Todd Rundgren. You know, I'm a feeling, sensitive, poetic type person and I need my emotions expressed in poetry and in harmony and not in babble. Rundgren provided the stage for my psyche to do that, even if it was just to an unknown audience, he provided that for me.

"There's no getting around the fact that first the Beatles and then Todd Rundgren had a tremendous impact on me."

Chapman's wife, Gloria, also recalled her husband's fascination with Rundgren:

"The musical artist that had the greatest influence on Mark wasn't John Lennon. It was Todd Rundgren," she said. "Mark often told me that he believed Rundgren was a true musical genius. Most people haven't heard of Rundgren and Mark enjoyed having the distinction of not only knowing about Rundgren, but of being a fan almost from the beginning of his career. He has had at least two complete Rundgren collections at separate times, but he sold or gave away all of them.

"After we were married, he bought a few Rundgren albums but didn't keep them for long. He got very depressed listening to the music. He said it depressed him to hear music that good. He hears things in the music that indicate to me that he has an extraordinary ear for music. He picks up on small things, obscure things. Mark amazed me in that way. Several times he said that he would never listen to another Rundgren album again because of the way it would depress him, but sooner or later he'd buy one and keep it for a while.

"On his first trip to New York, he bought a cassette player and several Rundgren tapes. One of the tapes is called *Deface the Music,* which consists of songs that sound like various Beatles songs. Rundgren was clever enough to write and play songs that differ in lyrics from the Beatles, but have the same flavor. Mark listened to this tape most of all."

Rundgren also provided Chapman with a convenient, subconscious outlet for the rage that continued to burn within him over Lennon's blasphemy of fundamentalist Christian values.

In the early seventies, Lennon and Rundgren became engaged in a war of words via comments to the press and scathing letters about each other that were published in *Melody Maker* magazine. Lennon referred to Rundgren as "Todd Runtgreen" and Rundgren accused the ex-Beatle of "shouting about revolution and acting like a fool." Rundgren appeared to have the last word with his 1980 album of mock-Beatle ballads, *Deface the Music,* and with a tune titled "Rock and Roll Pussy."

In "Rock and Roll Pussy" Rundgren derided Lennon's failure to join the "revolution" to which he and Ono had paid lip service, alluding to the ex-Beatle's penchant for languishing stoned in bed before a flickering TV screen. *Deface the Music,* released several months prior to Lennon's death, is a satirization of Beatles classics such as "I Want to Hold Your Hand," which becomes "I Just Want to Touch You." Many of the distinctive musical riffs and sound effects from the Beatles' *Sgt. Pepper* sound track punctuate Rundgren's parody. The album culminates with "Everybody Else Is Wrong," an ingenious twisting of the music and words from Lennon's "Across the Universe" and "I Am the Walrus."

After the Lennon killing, when psychologists at Bellevue Hospital asked Chapman what he most often would daydream about, he said, "Todd Rundgren's music. I guess Holden Caulfield."

Chapman says he doesn't recall being aware of the battle between Rundgren and Lennon until several years after he became a Rundgren zealot. After seeing Rundgren perform with his group, Utopia, at the Fox Theater in Atlanta, the lapsed Christian recalls that he immersed himself in the music with the same intensity that he had approached Christianity.

McManus also recalls that, during Chapman's Rundgren phase, he could talk of little else but the musician.

"Mark totally worshiped Todd Rundgren," McManus said. "He knew every word to every song. He even knew the parts, when they overdub and there's two voice lines going on at once, he could tell you every word of the lines you couldn't hear. It was incredible.

"After he had moved to Hawaii, he sent me an album of Todd's, one of the earlier albums that was out of print. That was the last thing I ever heard from Mark."

After nearly twelve years on an isolated cell block at Attica prison, Mark David Chapman still spoke with an impassioned familiarity and depth of Rundgren's music.

"I left *The Ballad of Todd Rundgren* in the hotel room in New York City" on the day of the Lennon killing, he recalled. "I left it as a statement, I guess.

"Right between the chambers of your heart is how Rundgren's music is to me. I cannot overestimate the depth of what his music meant to me. I never really got into the fan-club thing. I never thought about meeting

Rundgren, being Rundgren, or getting Rundgren's autograph. I went to his concerts. I bought his albums. I did it the real way, the pure way. I was into the music and I can't tell you the depth of what his music meant to me.

"To say that it defined my life sounds so shallow. It was the sound track to my life. More than that, it became my life. Those notes and those harmonies. I can't describe what it meant, it was so poignant.

"I was always trying to get people to listen to him. I remember a time when my friend Bill and Jessica, probably before Jessica was my girlfriend, came to my apartment. I had a nice Sony stereo Dana had sold me and I put on Todd. I said, 'Listen to the feeling! Listen to the emotion he's expressing!' But they couldn't really get into it. It seemed like no one I knew could ever get into the music of Rundgren and appreciate it the way I did. It mirrored everything. It became my emotions. It didn't just mirror them, it became my emotions. It became my words.

"His music gave me not just an emotional release or an enjoyment in high times—it gave me a definition for my life. I looked at it not even to define what was around me. I looked at it—that it was my—that it was the rage I could never express.

" 'Sometimes I Don't Know What to Feel': This song truly expresses the emotions of a person who is empty inside, who really doesn't know what to feel because maybe he's overwhelmed by too much feeling. . . .

"Remember, just before I shot John Lennon I wanted to tune out the world and go into a fetal position.

"The emotions in his music were the emotions I could never express. It was a great outlet to me to be able to have this kind of music. I'm saying, it was so important to me that it was unnatural. It was a spiritual thing. It was that meaningful.

"Those were the words I could never say. Those were the feelings that I had to bury inside myself, that I could never let out for fear that they would be just so horrendous. Those feelings that, when they finally did come out, it was out of the barrel of a gun."

CHAPTER FIFTEEN

CAPTAIN NEMO

Other men might inherit from their fathers a head for figures, a gold pocket watch all encrusted with the oxidized green of age, or an eternally astonished expression: From mine I acquired this need to have my name whispered in reverential tones. . . . What I wanted was the adulation of the crowd.

—FREDERICK EXLEY, *A FAN'S NOTES*

Even when reality was good, it wasn't good enough.

Even after he stopped visiting with the Little People inside his mind, Mark David Chapman continued to search the world of fantasy and fiction for an identity he could accept.

At the same time the teenage Chapman was finding acceptance among his new group of religious friends, he was beginning to carve a reputation and plant the seeds of a career with the Young Men's Christian Association. With the fervor with which he had immersed himself successively in the Beatles, drugs, Christianity, and the rock 'n' roll of Todd Rundgren, he committed himself to his role as a counselor, and later as an assistant program director, of the YMCA.

Tony Adams, director of the South De Kalb County YMCA when Chapman first applied for a job, recalls that the youth was one of only two employees whom he believed were destined for great success in life. During his forty-year career with the YMCA, Adams said he has maintained personal files on just two of the hundreds of employees he has hired to work for the agency across the country—Chapman and his friend Miles McManus.

"Mark was a pied piper with the kids," Adams recalled. "I just could never say enough good about the Mark Chapman that I knew for those five or six years in Georgia."

Whenever he thinks of Chapman, Adams says he remembers images "of a guy down on one knee helping out a little kid or with kids just hanging around his neck and following him everywhere he went. I've never seen anybody who was as conscientious about his job and as close to children as he was.

"The kids always called him Captain Nemo. That's what he wanted everybody to call him."

Captain Nemo set the stage for Chapman's later role as The Catcher in the Rye. In both identities, his mission was to save the children of his generation from the pain of the "phony adult" world. In his persona as Nemo, from the Jules Verne classic *Twenty Thousand Leagues under the Sea,* Chapman won the adulation of little people and the respect of adults.

"That was my identity," he said. "When I was Captain Nemo, I did good things and everybody loved me.

"I remember the year I was at the camp's closing ceremonies with my kids and they were giving the award for 'counselor of the year.' I heard them call my name, 'Captain Nemo,' and I couldn't believe it. The kids were all cheering and shouting, 'Ne-mo, Ne-mo! Ne-mo!'

"Those were the greatest days of my life. I *was* Nemo and everyone in camp loved me."

Other counselors, YMCA officials, and parents whose children attended summer sessions between 1970 and 1975 at the South De Kalb County YMCA recall that Chapman had a near-mystical affinity with "his kids." When a child would get hurt, it was often Nemo who cried. When Nemo played the guitar, all the children gathered around him in a happy circle.

"I never saw anybody like him with kids," McManus said.

When he wasn't working with the children, Chapman was doing other things in his spare time for the South De Kalb County YMCA. As one of the most successful fund-raisers in a drive to expand the facility, he was recognized by having his name, "Nemo," engraved in a tile above the Olympic-size indoor pool that he helped build for the community.

In the evenings, he taught guitar at the YMCA and Adams says that any time anyone needed a special favor, Mark Chapman would go out of his way.

"If there was ever anybody that didn't like Mark," Adams said, "I don't know who it was. The Mark Chapman I knew was just an outstanding person."

By the winter of 1972, Chapman had more than made up academically for the failures of the drug-hazed portions of his freshman and sophomore years. Receiving his high school diploma six months early, he allowed Michael McFarland, his friend from the Christian group, to lure him to Chicago where McFarland had moved earlier with his parents. Mirroring Chapman's achievements as Nemo, the two youths had together achieved recognition among local church groups for original musical and comedy skits they performed at churches and religious conventions. As "McFarland and Chapman," Mark played guitar and Mike impersonated various personalities like Richard Nixon and the Reverend Billy Graham. Chapman recalls the skits as clean-cut versions of Smothers Brothers–style routines. Their goal was to appear on *The Tonight Show.*

Working days in the mail room of the Chicago-based Youth for Christ organization, McFarland and Chapman shared an apartment where they practiced their comedy skits in the evenings. When several months went by and their act gained only modest success playing a Christian night spot, Chapman decided to go back to Georgia. When he had left Georgia to join McFarland in Chicago, Chapman had reluctantly left behind a high school sweetheart, Lynn Watson. The first thing he wanted to do when he got back home was repair the broken relationship with the girl he would still recall two decades later as his "first true love." It didn't work.

"I found that it's true what they say," Chapman lamented. "Once you leave the place of your childhood, you can't go home again. We tried to get back together, but it never worked. Finally, Lynn just rejected me."

For a while after returning to Georgia, Chapman went to work for the YMCA at a series of seasonal jobs, including groundskeeper, maintenance man, and assistant director of camping programs. He moved in with his friend McManus, who recalls that Chapman spent his evening hours playing guitar, listening to Todd Rundgren tapes, and talking almost incessantly about Rundgren's music. He also recalls that Chapman grew excited upon finding a copy of *The Catcher in the Rye* on the bookshelf at the McManus home, urging McManus and his mother to read the book.

The following fall, Chapman enrolled in part-time classes at South De Kalb Community College. He worked for a short time as an aide at an Atlanta-area hospital for autistic and mentally ill children. He was dismissed from the job when he was unable to subdue a child who became violent.

Early in 1975, Chapman's prior achievements as a YMCA counselor won him a nomination to the agency's international program. As one of a handful of applicants selected to travel abroad with the agency, he was assigned with two other counselors to work for the summer in Beirut, Lebanon.

He arrived in Lebanon on the eve of a bitter civil war. McManus recalls that when Captain Nemo was evacuated and returned several weeks later from the war zone, he "appeared badly shaken by what he had been through."

Chapman and another young volunteer spent their days huddled under furniture while bombs, rockets, and gunfire erupted in the streets outside. The YMCA volunteers were among the first evacuated from the country. Frightened and disappointed, he returned home to Decatur where his friends recall that he spoke fearfully of the experience and played cassette tapes he had recorded of gunfire and bombs exploding in the streets outside his hotel.

Because the war in Lebanon had shut down the YMCA operations there, Chapman was offered an alternative opportunity to work with the agency in the United States. He would be paid a salary of $200 a week to work at the YMCA-run resettlement camp at Fort Chaffee, Arkansas, a military base hastily set up for the processing of tens of thousands of "boat people" refugees from the abortive U.S. war in Vietnam.

The resettlement camp at Fort Chaffee was the big stage for which Captain Nemo had trained himself during his six summers of working with children at the YMCA. At Fort Chaffee, he became a self-styled savior of the children of Vietnamese families who had been uprooted from a homeland ravaged by war. Working sixteen-hour days, Chapman plunged himself into the camps with an ardor that astonished and impressed his boss, David Moore, who directed the resettlement project. Moore gave Chapman the responsibility of being an area coordinator for the camp. He traveled with Moore to meetings with government and YMCA officials. In his spare time, Chapman organized a band and a softball team at the camp. On a visit to the camp, President Gerald Ford shook his hand.

Interviewed shortly after Chapman was arrested for the murder of John Lennon, Moore said he would never forget what Captain Nemo had done for the refugees. Moore also said he worried about the toll that the job might have taken on a hypersensitive youth.

"The refugees' problems really got in his guts," Moore recalled.

Miles McManus has kept a copy of a tape-recorded message that Chapman mailed to him from Fort Chaffee in 1975. In the recording, made against a background of Todd Rundgren music, Chapman laments the suffering of the refugees. He mentions that he has shaken the president's hand ("He had a very greasy hand," Chapman tells McManus) and talks of the sadness he feels for the Vietnamese children at the camp. He speaks most passionately about Rundgren, his music idol, who had been nominated along with Elton John and other superstars as the 1975 rock personality of the year: "Todd Rundgren isn't dead," Chapman quips. "I talked to him this morning. . . . And remember: Todd Rundgren still cares very much for us people who care for him."

On the label of the cassette, Chapman wrote, "A Portrait of a Crazy Man."

Between the time he returned from Lebanon and the time he left for Fort Chaffee, Chapman reestablished his friendship with Jessica Blankenship, the former second-grade classmate he had encountered five years earlier at his first Christian retreat. Within a short time, Mark and Jessica were engaged.

When Jessica visited him at Fort Chaffee in October 1975, Mark arranged an elaborate welcome that included the display of her name in large letters on the marquee at the Sheraton where he had reserved her a room. During the visit, the couple continued to talk of wedding arrangements. They also talked of the time when the refugee camp would close and Mark would join her at Covenant College, a fundamentalist Presbyterian school where she had begun her studies a year before in Lookout Mountain, Tennessee.

During Jessica's visit, Chapman proudly showed her off to the new friends he had made among the camp workers and refugees. He told her that the work was inspired by God and that it was the most important thing he had ever done in his life. He didn't tell her that, a few weeks before, he had lost his virginity to another camp worker, a woman with whom he had shared a room for several months without incident.

The deflowering had occurred when a moralistic former landlord from whom he had rented a room outside the camp had discovered that Chapman and the unmarried young woman were living together apparently "in sin." They were evicted on the spot. Faced with nowhere to sleep that night, Chapman and his roommate, a girl whose name he had forgotten after seventeen years, were forced to take an inexpensive room furnished only with a large single bed at a motel. He recalls that his roommate invited him to accompany her into the shower. They showered together, but "nothing happened," he said. "I told her I was engaged."

He said he resisted temptation throughout the night. When he awoke the next morning and saw the attractive young woman lying naked beside him, Mark David Chapman, at age twenty, made love for the first time.

"At first it felt great," he said. "And then I thought about Jessica and I felt guilty and sinful, like I had done something horrible."

Chapman had never thought about sex until he was thirteen years old, when he became confused over the antics of a man and a woman in bed in a Jerry Lewis movie. He asked a friend about the perplexing scene and the friend explained to him, for the first time, the facts of sexual life. He had been appalled at what his friend told him his mother and father had done to cause him to be born. Mark Chapman's mother and father had slept in separate rooms for as long as he could remember. He had been horrified at the suggestion that they would engage in "dirty" behavior. His mother had told him time and again that she didn't even like his father. Chapman recalled that his mother had told him the only reason she married the man was so she could have Mark for her son.

After the Jerry Lewis movie, Chapman's friend had also told him that if he put his hand into his pants and rubbed himself it would feel good.

Several months later, while watching a Doris Day movie on TV in his room at home, Chapman began to think again about what his friend had said. There was something about the image of Doris Day on the television screen that sexually aroused Chapman for the first time in his life. Moments later, he grew frightened at his body's unexpected fluid reaction to the arousal and touching of himself. He fought an urge to run to his mother in panic. Although he was in no pain, he believed that he had injured himself internally.

After discovering his sexual self, Chapman became obsessed with the feeling, masturbating sometimes as often as seven times a day. Curiously, he failed to associate the teenage girls in his school and neighborhood with the sensation he got when he recalled Doris Day on the television screen. Whenever he touched himself, he always closed his eyes and thought of the older movie stars or of other mature women—his teachers, family friends, or the ladies he knew from church. Sometimes he visualized a line of the older women, all naked and confined to a secret dungeon he imagined somewhere in the basement of his school. He never had intercourse with the women, but he made them touch him in the way that he wanted to be touched, sometimes with their mouths.

At times, his mother had intruded upon his secret, sexual world and he had felt exposed and violated.

"I know what you're doing up there in your room," she had said. She had reached into the laundry hamper and dangled his soiled underwear accusingly before him.

After becoming a Christian during the summer of 1970, Chapman had tried to restrain his aggressive sexual fantasies and the autoerogenous impulses. A friend explained to him that God provided for the release of such urges naturally, through something called wet dreams. No matter how long he denied his sexual urges, however, Chapman had found that the reputed sexual release never came to him unbidden in the night, as it supposedly did to other adolescent males.

Alarmed at the approaching Fort Chaffee visit of his fiancée, a "strong Christian" and a virgin who, he was certain, had saved herself for their wedding night, Chapman began to despise himself as unworthy of Jessica's love. He wrote her long, rambling letters containing euphemistic metaphors about "the flesh battling the spirit." He declared himself a "vile sinner," but he didn't tell her that he had had intercourse with his roommate. Nor did

"Who am I?" One-year-old Mark David Chapman is captivated by his own reflection in the mirrored surface of an automobile hub cap.

(PHOTO COURTESY OF MARK CHAPMAN)

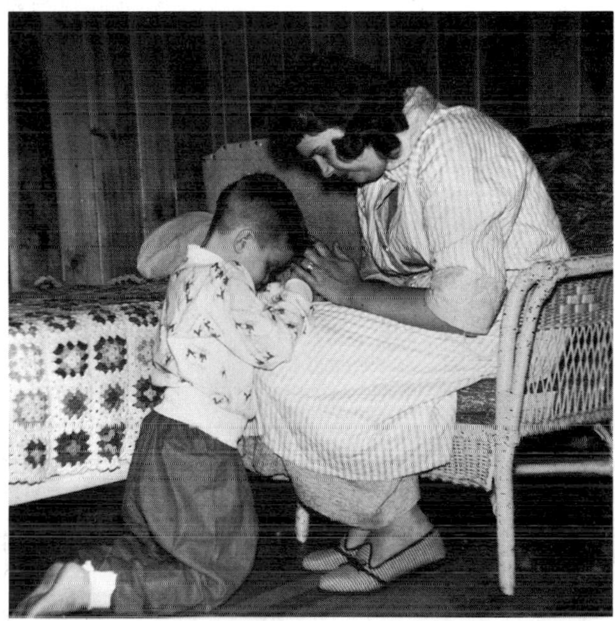

Four-year-old Mark David Chapman says bedtime prayers with his mom in a December 1959 photograph from the family album.

(PHOTO COURTESY OF MARK CHAPMAN)

Photograph dated December 1961 is captioned "Our Cherubic Choir Boy."
(PHOTO COURTESY OF MARK CHAPMAN)

From the Chapman family album, this photo of Mark David Chapman with a rebel soldier cap and toy guns is titled "Our Confederate Mark, seven years old."
(PHOTO COURTESY OF MARK CHAPMAN)

SOUTHEASTERN YMCA
1765 MEMORIAL DR., SE
ATLANTA, GA. 30317
373-6561

YMCA LEADERSHIP APPLICATION

DATE 6/12/69

Name MARK CHAPMAN Address 2184 GREENFOREST DR
City DECATUR Zip 30032
Phone 284-6945 Birth Date 5/10/55
Age 14 Social Security No. NONE
Have Transportation? YES
Married? NO Children? NO
Church Presbyterian Member Yes
Are you a Regular Attender? Not lately
Parent's Name David C. Chapman
Address 2184 Greenforest Dr. Dec
Home Phone 2846945 Office 634-6611 Ext. 368
Father's Occupation Credit Representative American Oil Co Address Executive Park - Atlanta
High School (Attending or Attended) COLUMBIA HIGH
Present Classification 8th starting 9th in Sept. '69
College (Attending or Planning To Attend)
Present Classification Major Subjects
In what school organizations are, or were, you a member?
Office Held
What do you plan to do for your life's work?
Have you had any experience in group leadership? Some (If so, when and where?)
Asst. Patrol - Boy Scouts - 1966 Troop 254 Midway Church Decatur
What age Group? Have you had any experience in camps, recreation programs,
etc.? Some If so, when, where, and how much?
Scout Camp (Bert Adams) 1966 Camp Waco (Indian Guides) 1962-63 -

(Do Not Write In This Space)
Accepted:
Yes
No
Salary:
Position:
Interviewed By:

...ports? NO If so, when, where, and how much?

Give any other qualifications that you as a group leader have had.

State briefly your reason for applying to this organization for employment.

What are your salary requirements, if any, per month?

For what position are you applying? Junior Counselor at Y Day Camp

Please check the subjects below according to your skill and experience.
(1) Little (2) Some (3) Much (4) Have done some instructing.

	1	2	3	4		1	2	3	4
1. Football	✓				24. Indian Craft	✓			
2. Basketball	✓				25. Indian Dancing	✓			
3. Baseball		✓			26. Hiking		✓		
4. Track	✓				27. Outdoor Cooking		✓		
5. Soccer					28. Camping		✓		
6. Volleyball	✓				29. Group Singing			✓	
7. Tumbling		✓			30. Dramatics		✓		
8. Trampoline	✓				31. Baton Twirling				
9. Badminton	✓				32. Cheer Leading				
10. Tennis	✓				33. Group Games	✓			
11. Golf	✓				34. Painting		✓		
12. Bowling	✓				35. Ceramics	✓			
13. Archery	✓				36. Copper Craft				
14. Riflery		✓			37. Handicraft	✓			
15. Swimming		✓			38. Woodwork		✓		
16. Diving	✓				39. Leatherwork	✓			
17. Life Saving	✓				40. Religious Talks	✓			
18. Survival Swmg.	✓				41. Story Telling		✓		
19. Fishing		✓			42. First Aid	✓			
20. Bird Study		✓			43. Softball		✓		
21. Insect Study	✓				44. Wrestling		✓		
22. Forestry	✓				45. Flag Raising	✓			
23. Nature	✓				46.				

List three references we may contact regarding your character and qualifications:

Name William Ford Address 1950 Cindy Dr. Dec. Phone 289-3451
Present position Real Estate Dept. American Oil Co. Phone 634-6611
Name Mr. Madison Short Address — Phone —
Present position Columbia High School Music Director Phone 284-8720
Name Dr. Edith De Zoort Address Decatur Professional Bldg Phone 378-9488
Present position Physician Phone —

Fourteen-year-old Mark David Chapman submitted his photo when he first applied for a job as a junior counselor at the South De Kalb County YMCA in 1969. Chapman was accepted for the job. A short time later, he took his first LSD tablet and spent much of the next two years ingesting a pharmacopeia of mind-altering drugs.

(PHOTO COURTESY OF MARK CHAPMAN)

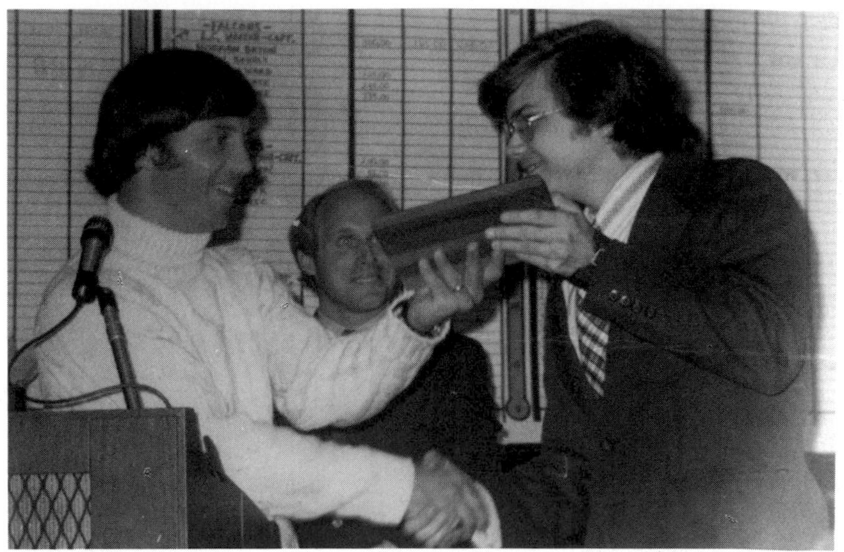

In 1971, a zealous, born-again, sixteen-year-old Mark David Chapman was among the top fund-raisers in a drive to put up a new building and swimming pool at the South De Kalb County YMCA. He received an award from Tony Adams (left), who recalls Chapman as one of the most promising youths who ever worked for him. Adams's assistant, Hugh Jordan (center), looks on as the award is presented to "Captain Nemo," as Chapman was known to the children he counseled at YMCA summer camps. His name, "Nemo," is engraved above the pool in a ceramic tile along with the names of others who raised substantial amounts of money for the new YMCA facility. (PHOTO COURTESY OF TONY ADAMS)

A teenaged Mark David Chapman, top and center, plays guitar during a meeting of his prayer group from the Chapel Woods Presbyterian Church in Decatur, Georgia. After John Lennon sang, "Imagine there's no heaven," Chapman and members of the born-again group recall that Chapman sang, "Imagine John Lennon is dead." (PHOTO COURTESY OF MARK CHAPMAN)

Before returning to Hawaii from his round-the-world trip in 1978, Mark David Chapman stopped in Georgia and visited with his Christian friend Dana Reeves in August 1978. Two years later, Reeves, a former sheriff's deputy, would unwittingly provide Chapman with the .38 caliber hollow-point bullets that killed John Lennon.

(PHOTO COURTESY OF MARK CHAPMAN)

Reflection of a narcissist. Mark David Chapman takes a photograph of himself in the bathroom mirror while visiting the home of David Moore in Geneva, Switzerland, in August 1978. Moore was Chapman's supervisor during the Vietnamese refugee resettlement program at Fort Chaffe, Arkansas, in 1975.

(PHOTO COURTESY OF MARK CHAPMAN)

Mark David Chapman was shaken by the pain and poverty he encountered in Asia during a round-the-world vacation in August 1978, about a year after he recovered from his suicide attempt. Among the 1,200 Kodachrome slides he took were photos of beggars and lepers like those pictured here in Nepal. (PHOTO COURTESY OF MARK CHAPMAN)

Posing with a beggar in India, August 1978.
(PHOTO COURTESY OF MARK CHAPMAN)

Above: Described by his former YMCA peers as a "Pied Piper," Chapman attracted the attention of children wherever he went. In this photo, he poses with children in Nepal, where he says he started a virtual riot by giving away boxes of chewing gum to poor children.

(PHOTO COURTESY OF MARK CHAPMAN)

Left: On his stop in Bangkok, Thailand, Chapman had his first encounter with a prostitute in August 1978. He poses here with a serpent at a market in Bangkok.

(PHOTO COURTESY OF MARK CHAPMAN)

Mark David Chapman gazes into the yard at Attica prison from the barred windows of a visiting room. Chapman is serving a twenty-year-to-life sentence at Attica for the murder of John Lennon. (PHOTO BY JACK JONES)

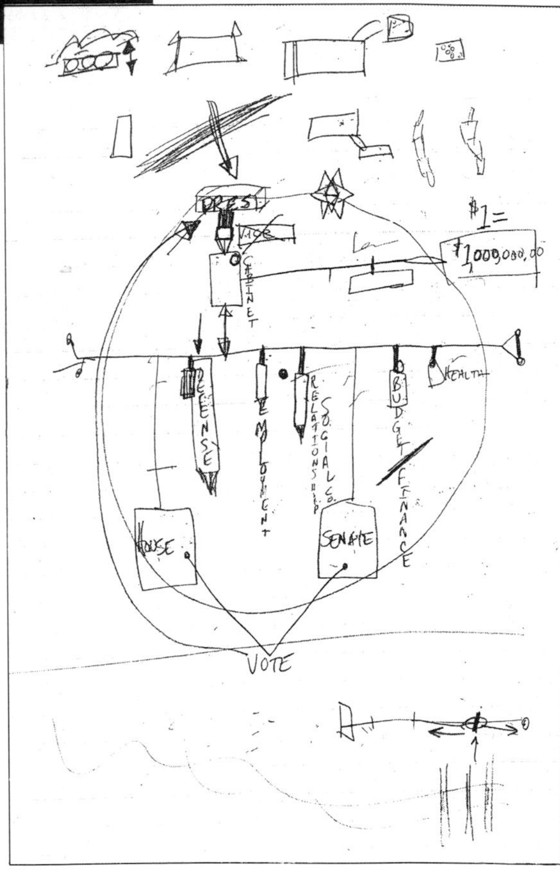

Mark David Chapman told psychiatrists at Bellevue Hospital of the secret world of the "Little People" who lived inside his mind. Nearly six months after the John Lennon murder, Chapman sketched this diagram on June 2, 1981, at the request of psychiatrist Dr. Daniel Schwartz, to illustrate the interactions between the various governmental bodies and committees in his head. The Little People, he says, "were appalled," and they abandoned him when he told them of his decision to kill the music legend.

(PHOTO COURTESY OF MARK CHAPMAN)

he tell her that he was continuing to turn back on occasion to the woman's flesh, despite the postcoital objections of his weakened spirit.

In his mind, the sexual indiscretion became a scarlet stain of infidelity. Plagued by guilt, he found himself engaging in other contradictory behaviors that he said were "out of my character." He undertook to do penance for his sins by working even harder at the refugee camp. When the camp was closed in December, after processing more than twenty thousand refugees, Chapman estimated that he had helped more than five hundred war-torn humans. He was ready for a vacation. Instead he joined his fiancée for the spring semester at Covenant College where he had enrolled as a full time student.

The first few weeks at college were almost like camp. He recalls that one night he and several other students from his dorm executed "the Covenant College equivalent of a panty raid." Dragging extension cords onto the campus commons at 3:00 A.M., they plugged in amplifiers and electric guitars and set up a makeshift bandstand. Lights began to go on in windows all across the campus as the band launched into a full-volume rendition of an old Beatles song: "I Saw Her Standing There."

He and Jessica studied together every night. On several occasions, they visited a counselor on the campus to talk about their marriage plans. Sometimes they engaged in "very heavy petting," Chapman recalled, always stopping short of premarital intercourse.

Confident that he would never see his former lover from the refugee camp again, Chapman was sure that his infidelity was a secret Jessica would never learn. Aware of his own deceit, though, he would not allow his guilty conscience to rest. It became entangled in his thinking with the pattern of lies and "phoniness" that he was beginning to believe lay at the heart of the problems of the "phony adult" world.

It was while studying for a class on human warfare, Chapman recalls, that he became despondent. He began to think that "all of human history was nothing but a history of great battles and all those monuments and books were created just to celebrate death."

As his depression deepened, he also found himself unable to keep up in the classroom with other students—students several years younger than he, students lacking his experiences in places like Chicago and Lebanon and among the refugees of Vietnam. Sensing imminent failure, he began to think himself inferior.

During all-night sessions in elevator shafts and abandoned basement rooms in buildings at the college, he spent three tearful weeks before his depression began to relent. Sometimes, Jessica would join him and he would cry out to her for forgiveness for real and imagined sins.

"Pray," she would tell him. "Oh, Mark, just pray and I will pray for you."

After dropping one of his classes, he struggled through the rest of the semester with C's before going back to Georgia and returning to work at the South De Kalb County YMCA.

Nearly two decades after leaving Covenant College, Chapman spent a restless night in a prison cell retracing the twisted path that ended at Attica:

"I was still thinking about these things this morning so I put on some music, an AM station, to remove noises of the prison so I could think. It was hard to focus. I began to feel some of those old feelings coming back, those dark, black feelings. And I reversed the chronology. I went back in time to where Jessica and I got serious and I went to Fort Chaffee to work with the refugees and came back for the spring semester of '76 to Covenant College.

"I began thinking through the series of events, when I went to the YMCA after Covenant and then when I quit the job there in the middle of the summer: how that led me to get a job as a security guard and then the suicidal thoughts.

"I followed it just about all the way through to the time of the killing of John Lennon. I asked myself: 'Where did this all start? Where did these depressions, these suicidal thoughts come from?' Then it dawned on me: I had a lot of free time in the security-guard jobs at the Atlanta airport and at a hospital and a condominium complex. All I had to do was drive around and keep an eye on things. I had a lot of time alone in my car or in the airport at night. I had always traced my problems to that time of solitude and the weird thoughts, the suicidal thoughts, that went through my head then.

"It was very strange standing on an abandoned concourse at three in the morning, with nobody going by for hours. I thought and I thought. I thought about history. I thought about life. I thought about the earth. And I thought about God. And I became entwined in a deep philosophical dialogue with myself, which I never really got over. I constantly, at times like this, go back into that dialogue. I'd never had time to think before, then suddenly I had too much time. And too much time on one's hands is not good. So I began to get depressed and this was the prelude to the horrible thing that finally happened.

"But the question is: What was I doing being a security guard in the first place? Did it start there?

"I don't think so. I had always thought that my depression started in the car and on those empty concourses at the airport where I was alone late at night. . . .

"I always had bits and pieces but I didn't have the total picture. When it came together for me this morning, I felt I had burst into a whole new area and I was excited and I was happy and I kept walking back and forth in the cell, saying, 'I'm free, I'm free.'

"Nothing so complex can be said in one sentence. It has to be understood in complete context. But this is what happened. This is what dawned on me this morning:

"Where was the beginning of this? This had to happen at Covenant. With total clarity, I saw that all this began with my breakdown at Covenant College and proceeded up to that night of December 8, 1980. I realized why I got depressed at Covenant College. I never had that answer before. I thought maybe the war problems I had seen at Fort Chaffee, the fact that . . . I had had sex and I had repressed the guilt from that and never told Jessica. I don't ever remember dealing with guilt from that. Why was I a security guard? Because I thought I was a nothing, and that was the only thing I could handle.

"With the YMCA in Lebanon, even though it ended in disappointment, I had been a somebody. I had been chosen to go to Lebanon as the culmination of all my work with the YMCA and it was the most exciting thing in my life. Even when I had to leave, it turned out to be for something better. I rose to an even greater position of importance at Fort Chaffee. I was an area coordinator in charge of an important project. Then, when the job ended and I enrolled at Covenant, I became a nobody.

"I was a nobody at Covenant College. I had just ridden the waves of success at Fort Chaffee. I had come off the important experience of a trip to Lebanon—the first foreign trip I'd had—and surviving in a war zone, to the success of Fort Chaffee. Then, all of a sudden, there I was at Covenant College, studying hard, not knowing what on earth hit me and not knowing, until this day, this morning, why I was depressed.

"The true reason was that I felt like a nobody. I felt like a nobody because I wasn't a normal person. . . . When I went to college I was just like everybody else, and had to study like everybody else. . . . I wasn't in charge of anything, I wasn't in a foreign country taping bomb sounds down the avenue. I was a regular college student with regular responsibilities and studies and that was it. That was all. I was just like everybody else—a nobody.

"And when I had to face that truth, my insides fell in on myself. I fell down a dark hole. So what does a nobody do? A nobody gets a nobody job because he feels like he can't handle anything else. That's why I became a security guard.

"But before that, before I gave up and got a job as a security guard, I went back to the YMCA summer camp as an assistant director. I was coming back out of my depression because I was back in my element and I had some authority. I was maybe feeling like a somebody.

"Then, one day I walked by the lake and saw a group of girls standing around, doing nothing. They had one more period left for the day. I checked the activities list and found they were supposed to be canoeing. So I said, 'Girls, do you want to be standing here? Or do you want to be canoeing?' And they said they wanted to be canoeing. So I told the senior counselor to get the girls canoeing.

"She snapped back at me, 'Well who do you think you are? God or something?'

"And I believe that was the final blow to me after resurrecting out of that depression at college and coming back to camp. I knew after that, the next day, when I talked to the camp director alone on the soccer field, I knew it was over. I was in a mass of confusion and hurt and anger and everything. And I said I was quitting. I couldn't take it anymore. I told him about the incident.

"The counselor was tired. It had been a long day. I can now understand her anger at me. To an outsider, it looked like I was taking it too seriously. But an outsider wasn't with me at Covenant when my identity fell apart. And then, when my YMCA identity fell apart, when I was stripped of that is when the clouds really started getting dark and I started slipping into an abyss that ended in murder, of someone I didn't even know."

PART IV

HOLDEN IN HAWAII

CHAPTER SIXTEEN

HOLDEN IN HAWAII

Honolulu, where most of the white men gathered,
became a stage upon which posturing expatriates acted out
their public passions and their private pain.

—GAVAN DAWS, *SHOAL OF TIME: A HISTORY OF THE HAWAIIAN ISLANDS*

After flying for nearly six hours, the Boeing 747 glided smoothly onto the runway and taxied to a stop at Honolulu International Airport. Leaning forward and glancing apprehensively from his window seat above the wing, Mark David Chapman reached beneath his feet and withdrew a small suitcase. The suitcase contained everything he had not sold or given away during the preceding year. Still dressed for a north Georgia winter, wearing a dark suit and tie, knee-length overcoat, and brimless hat, Chapman stepped off the plane and into a delicate tropical warmth that caused his skin to tingle.

Deeply inhaling gardenia-scented air, he bowed his head to receive a fragrant necklace of flowers. He smiled broadly as the traditional Hawaiian lei was draped around his neck by laughing, brown-skinned girls just like those pictured in the islands' travel brochures. As he walked the short distance from the edge of the runway to the airport terminal, Chapman's emotions began to overflow. He felt himself bursting with a distantly recalled love of life that he found exhilarating. He also found it unsettling. He had come to Hawaii with death on his mind—his own death.

Confronted even in the commercial bustle of the airport with the tropical splendor of the islands, he struggled against voices of self-loathing that had called to him at random moments, day and night, for more than a year. The voices had called from a blackness that steamed and hissed from a pit that had opened inexplicably inside his brain. As he struggled against them in the bright Honolulu sunshine, the voices grew urgent in their effort to recall him to his purpose.

"Captain Nemo," he reminded himself. "Captain Nobody. Captain of Nothing. Captain Security Guard. Nowhere Man with a nobody job. Just turned twenty-two years old, and it's over. Your life is over, buddy."

Between the time he had finished high school in 1973 and entered Covenant College in 1976, Chapman had traveled to the Middle East as an international YMCA emissary and shaken the hands of two American presidents. He had been praised and decorated for his work with underprivileged children in Georgia and with refugees from the Vietnam War. He had survived a civil war that had erupted around him on the streets of Beirut, Lebanon.

He had been somebody. Suddenly, he was nobody. Mark David Chapman decided that being a nobody was worse than being dead. It was worse than spending the rest of his life in prison.

Neither prayer nor love had been able to assuage the pain of depression.

"I would call out to God and it felt like He wasn't there," he said.

When he had felt himself on the verge of disappearing in the dark clouds at college, his spirits had been mercurially lifted by the discovery of a map. The map, a chart of the Hawaiian island chain, had rekindled a childhood spirit of adventure.

"I remember that I started coming out of the worst of it one day when I was in the library. I found a map of Hawaii and made a copy. I kept it in my room, in my drawer. I'd pull it out and look at the islands, the Hawaiian Islands, every once in a while.

"The thought of these islands away from everything just seemed like paradise. I became obsessed with the urge to go there before I died."

When he left Covenant and went back home to Decatur in the spring of 1976, he took the thumb-greased map of Hawaii and a few personal possessions. He clipped a color photograph of a jet airliner from a glossy travel brochure and glued it onto the steering wheel of his car.

Although he had fled college, Chapman had been unable to escape the chaos that was at the core of his disintegrating self. The gloom of depression and self-doubt had continued to settle in restless layers upon his mind. He finally had abandoned the frustrating search for an identity that he had begun to realize he could never have.

"I don't think I was ever the same after that experience at Covenant. At Covenant, my whole insides caved in. I didn't have any identity. I had splintered into atoms, into total nothingness."

Beneath the blanket of his depression, Chapman had spent much of the year since leaving college in careful preparation for his final, dramatic exit. He had lingered hesitantly with Jessica and with his mentor and confidant,

Dana Reeves. Reeves, his closest friend, who had helped him get a job as a security guard after leaving college, begged him not to go.

"Honolulu is going to turn out to be a Hono-boo-boo," Dana had joked, half seriously. "I think it's a mistake, old buddy."

Chapman confided to no one, however, that he was planning to end his life after a transcendent "last fling in paradise."

Death in a beautiful and elegant place seemed the only alternative to the razor-blade fear of walking through life without a personality that he could recognize, from one moment to the next, as his own.

He had spent many months making elaborate preparations and saving the money he would need for the first-class death he envisioned. He had decided that he could at least die with a semblance of the adventure and dignity with which he had hoped to live.

Chapman had come to Hawaii, he said, "like an elephant going to the dying grounds or something: a place of comfort. I wanted to go there."

"I'm too sensitive for this world," he had told himself. "I don't understand. Nobody can help me understand. Nobody cares. Nobody. Nothing."

It was with an unaccustomed exuberance that he approached the first day of the remainder of the brief life he had carefully laid out in Hawaii.

"We're going to end it, but not quite yet," he told himself as he walked from the Honolulu airport. "Soon. Perhaps in a week or two. Just not quite yet."

Even before he had decided to kill himself, Chapman had envisioned this moment when he would step from a plane in Honolulu and ride an open-air bus through warm, fragrant air to the legendary Moana Hotel on Waikiki Beach. He had learned of the Moana from Hawaiian history and travel books he had sought out in libraries and in bookstores back home in Georgia. He had virtually memorized one of the comprehensive travel guides, *Hawaii A to Z.* Already, from his voracious readings, he was confident that he knew more about the islands than most people who had been born there or those who had lived there for many years.

During the long, stop-and-go ride through urban traffic from the airport to the hotel, entranced by the exotic surroundings, he didn't bother to remove his jacket or to loosen his tie. Inhaling deeply, he drank in the scenery of the clean, shop-lined streets leading into the orderly heart of Honolulu. Striking up random conversations with other passengers on the bus, he began pointing out sites of interest to the newly arrived tourists. He spoke with the practiced familiarity of a seasoned Hawaiian tour guide. As the bus neared the Moana, he talked of the venerable and elegant inn as though he had visited it many times before.

When he at last stepped from the bus, Chapman stood in reverence before the celebrated oceanfront edifice to which Mark Twain, Robert Louis Stevenson, and other writers, artists, and international dignitaries had paid tribute. Like Dorothy and her friends entering the gates of Oz, he stepped into the lobby.

Climbing low stairs of burnished stone, Chapman stepped through a wide breezeway into a timeless courtyard that framed a postcard image of beachfront, ocean, and sky. For the first time since the molten lead of depression had spilled and begun hardening around his brain, he didn't want to die.

"The air was alive. The very atmosphere made me want to live. I walked into the elegant courtyard of the Moana, the white sand, the blue ocean, the gently waving palm trees. There, in the center of the courtyard, was the ancient, ornate banyan tree that Robert Louis Stevenson had sat under. He used to sit beneath that very tree, sipping a drink and writing his novels and short stories and letters.

"And there I was, a goofy kid from Georgia, standing there in a long coat with my mouth open and a suitcase dangling from my arm, totally spellbound at the magnificence. Standing in the very place that Robert Louis Stevenson had stood. I must have looked like Holden Caulfield."

Chapman stepped beneath the gaily colored awning of an outdoor bar at the edge of the hotel courtyard. He gazed on an emerald ocean that whispered against a beach of fragantly oiled flesh. Motioning to a grass-skirted waitress, he set down his suitcase and ordered the native Hawaiian drink, a mai tai, from the open-air bar. Without removing the whimsical paper umbrella from the glass, he swallowed the potent nectar in a single gulp and ordered another as the liquor began pleasantly to cloud and color his rapidly racing brain.

"What a place to live," he thought. "What a place to die."

For nearly a week, until his money began to run out, Chapman basked in the luxury of the Moana. He began to feel it was where he had always belonged. He imagined that his room, number 624, was his private residence, a beachfront sanctuary with magnificent coastline views from two windows on the top floor of the hotel. During the day, he alternately sunbathed and strolled Waikiki Beach or stretched out on the bed in the room, ordering drinks from room service and gazing dreamily in the direction of Diamond Head. The distinctive, cratered mountain of volcanic ash rose like living history in the near distance, just outside his window. He thought about getting a job that would pay him just enough money so he could live at the elegant hotel for the rest of his life.

"For the first five days in Hawaii, I felt just like Holden Caulfield. I just did lots of drinking, partying, boat cruises, and went on a 'round-the-island tour. I met this couple and we went up to this restaurant and I got drunk as hell. The guy made me dance with this girl from Canada and it was a big fun time and I thought, 'Great, it's just going perfect, you know. I'm living all the happiness at once here.' It's just like I wanted to have: one big shebang before committing suicide, and it was going fine."

After five days, Chapman's reservation in paradise expired. The taste of the unaccustomed good life pungent on his tongue, he didn't feel quite ready to die. Becalmed by the elegance of his rented surroundings, he started thinking again about the relative pain of life and the anticipated solace of death.

From the expensive luxury hotel, he moved to a small, cheap room at the YMCA in downtown Honolulu. In a tangled mood of tranquility, remorse, and loneliness, he impulsively decided to call his former fiancée.

The startled girl answered the phone and listened as the familiar and persuasive voice explained to her why he had come to Hawaii—to end his life. Jessica said later that she was no longer in love with Mark Chapman, but she was frightened for him. As she listened to him speak, she began to feel guilty, responsible for the life of a friend who had made her feel that she had let him down. Jessica also grew frightened for herself. She realized with a chill that she had come dangerously close to marrying her unstable and pathetic childhood classmate out of a strange mixture of admiration, Christian duty, and pity.

"I came out here to kill myself," Chapman told Jessica. She listened in silence to the pain in the voice at the other end of the phone.

"But it's so beautiful here, Jessica. It's truly paradise," he explained to her. "It's made me want to live. I've gotten over that awful stuff I went through back at college. I've grown up. I've found myself, and I need you. You're the only one, Jessica. There's no one else in this world for me."

"Oh, Mark, please," the girl implored him. "Please come home. Just please come home. I . . ."

"I've found myself at last, Jessica," he said, interrupting her as she spoke. "Pray for me, Jessica. I need you. I hope that you can forgive me. Don't cry. I'm coming home. I came out here to Hawaii to kill myself, but I want to come back to you, Jessica. I want everything the way it was before. Just tell me it's okay. Tell me you can still love me and I'll come home."

"Oh, Mark," the girl sobbed. "Oh, Mark, it's okay. Just come home."

Jessica Blankenship explained later that she had believed her former fiancé would again become despondent if she rejected his entreaties over the phone. She said she believed that he would be better off if he came back home to Decatur, where they could talk in person and in familiar surroundings about their friendship—and about their separate futures. Jessica had never intended to resume their engagement. She just didn't want to be responsible for the death of a former friend who had told her that he was suicidal. She had lied to a friend to save his life.

"I was crushed, you know," Chapman says, recalling the disappointment on his arrival at Jessica's doorstep. "I was hurt deeply, but I still managed to get over that and get over the next two weeks where I lived with my parents. For a while I stayed at the Sheraton Hotel in Atlanta after I got into arguments with my mom, my dad, and my sister. My sister told me, 'Go to hell' and my dad said, 'Fuck you.'

"But I made it through all that and I called up Jessica and said, 'Let's just be friends.'

"I went back there to Georgia hoping it could all be like it was before. Of course, nothing is ever like it was before. So I decided that I was going to return to Hawaii, not to kill myself this time, but to get a job and make a new life for myself. I dreamed of getting a job at the Moana and living there for the rest of my life.

"The night before I left, I asked Jessica to go to a movie with me. We saw *Casablanca.* It seemed appropriate somehow.

"After the movie, we sat for a long time in the car in front of her house and I told her I was going back to Hawaii. She started crying and we said good-bye."

Several days after saying good-bye to Jessica, Chapman spent the rest of the $1,200 he'd saved up for his "last fling." He bought his third one-way plane ticket between Georgia and Hawaii.

Mark Chapman was manic with anticipation in the moments before he landed for the second time in Honolulu. As soon as he stepped from the plane into the humid air, he knew it wasn't going to be the same.

His body quivered with a spasm of dread. He realized he had come back to a place where it would be even more difficult to escape a confrontation with the void that, he sensed, lay at the center of himself.

When the money runs out, the islands of paradise pose a torpid dilemma, a lesson that countless wanderers and mainland expatriates before Mark David Chapman had learned. The main island of Oahu can be traveled easily by car in a single afternoon. An exciting playground for short-term vacationers with plenty of money, Hawaii can be a difficult place to live 365 days a year.

As Chapman had found on his first trip, the rainbowed islands trigger a spontaneous joy of life among vacationing tourists from more dismal climates. But those who, like him, try to go back to Shangri-la—those who linger too long without money, purpose, or friends among the glittering beaches and bars—find the attractions fleeting and illusory. Stranded on a small island surrounded by endless ocean, the long-term tourist is finally forced to turn inward for escape.

First discovered by pirates and merchant seamen who ravished its women and plundered its natural treasures, Hawaii later fell victim to fatal diseases imported unintentionally by Puritan religious zealots from New England. The missionaries, who invaded Hawaii to erect a Protestant "Holy Community," left a deep evangelical tradition that has for the most part endured. The city of Honolulu and surrounding suburban communities are studded with churches of virtually every faith and denomination, from traditional old-time gospel meeting houses to soaring New Age temples.

In addition to its exotic array of churches, the city's phone directory carries extensive listings of mental-health counselors and public and private mental-health agencies. A smorgasbord of therapies is available to those unable to find, either within themselves or the larger spiritual community, the inner peace and self-assurance required to live contentedly in paradise. Even though he had come to Hawaii to commit suicide, Mark David Chapman would cling to ministers and mental-health professionals alike in the struggle to survive.

It was the end of May 1977 when he had returned to Hawaii after failing to repair his relationship with his former fiancée. In desperate financial straits within days of his return, he took a series of temporary, low-paying jobs. He worked with Filipino migrants peeling rotten potatoes at a snack-food factory on the outskirts of Honolulu. On many days, especially the day after payday, he didn't bother showing up for work.

When he had money, he stayed in a cheap room at the Honolulu YMCA. When he didn't have money, he lived on the streets. Often down to his last dime, existing on beer and cookies, Chapman began spending his nights at a phone booth on the sidewalk in front of the Moana Hotel. He gazed with envy upon the wealthy, famous, and fashionably dressed tourists who patronized the sumptuous hotel. Unlike him, they never seemed to have to worry about how much money they spent. Eyeing the tourists, he dreamed of luxuries he had enjoyed there just a short time before. When the sun went down on the island, he continued to linger past dark before the hotel. He would stand at the pay phone and talk, sometimes until sunrise, to a woman with a friendly voice at the other end of the city's suicide hotline.

Returning to work one morning after a night of drinking and talking to the anonymous counselor, Chapman saw that a pigeon had flown through an open window and become trapped in the cavernous food processing plant. It flapped in confusion and futility above large vats of boiling oil. His migrant coworkers put aside their peeling knives. In sport, they began hurling rotted potatoes.

"I prayed fervently for the pigeon to get away. I started to cry and I yelled for them to stop trying to hurt it."

The trapped bird crashed from window to window. After an overripe potato splattered sickeningly against its target, the bird fluttered in dazed exhaustion to the floor. A laughing man seized the mass of flapping feathers and held the bird ceremoniously over his head in one hand. A moment later, the small, cruel drama ended when the man pressed the bird against a wooden block and drew a knife across its head. As the factory worker burst into laughter and applause, the man dropped the severed head and a mass of bloodied feathers into a cauldron of bubbling oil.

Fleeing the warehouse, Chapman spent the next several days drinking. At night, he talked longer and more urgently on the suicide hotline to the faceless woman who had come to know him by name.

"It just seemed like, with all the pain I had inside me anyway, what was the point? What was the point of living in a world where people do things like that to innocent animals? It made me think about when I was a kid, maybe ten years old. My father was a scout leader and he took me to summer camp.

"The first day I was there, I went for a hike and found a turtle. It was really a beautiful turtle, with colorful designs on its shell. I was real proud of it so I took it back to camp and showed it to the other kids. They took it from me and threw it in the campfire."

Several days after abandoning his job at the food factory, Chapman decided that he'd waited long enough. He reminded himself why he'd come to Hawaii in the first place.

Less than two months after first stepping from the plane at the Honolulu airport, Mark David Chapman found himself again mired in hopelessness and despair. He began making final preparations to succumb to the dark voices he had been unable to silence.

"I wasn't frightened when I made the decision. I wasn't angry or upset. I felt strangely at peace about everything. My mind felt very clear again."

With the little money he had left, he rented a compact car. On his way to the North Shore of the island, he stopped for a leisurely last meal, paid for with bonus vouchers included in the rental price of the car. After dining on steak and beer, he visited a shopping mall where he bought a length of vacuum cleaner hose. Returning to the car, he drove slowly to a deserted stretch of beach. In an isolated parking lot beneath low-hanging trees, he got out of the car and removed the hose from its plastic bag. Opening the rear hatch of the car, he draped one end of the hose across the backseat. He jammed the other end snugly into the car's exhaust pipe. After sealing the edges of the rear hatch with rags and bits of clothing, he lingered outside. He inhaled deeply, filling his lungs and nostrils with fresh, salted air that wafted from an impassive sea. He gazed for a long, pensive moment at the watercolor scene that stretched before him, of fishermen rhythmically casting lines into foaming surf up and down an endless beach.

Finally ready to die, he got into the car and rolled each of the windows tightly shut. He switched on the ignition. Within moments, Chapman began to inhale the dusty odor of exhaust fumes and deadly carbon monoxide. He leaned his head against the back of the seat and closed his eyes. He thought of the pigeon in the warehouse as he waited for death.

Mark David Chapman awoke to a birdlike pecking against the car window. He twisted his head, opened his eyes, and peered through a vaporous mist. An elderly Japanese man with a fishing pole smiled back at him.

"Just want to see if you are all right," the fisherman said apologetically, as Chapman cranked down the window. He was groggy and he wondered briefly if he had died—if it was his spirit stepping out of the car and back into the world that he had wanted to escape. He turned around to look back into the car, to see if he had somehow stepped out of his body.

As the fisherman ambled away in the direction of the beach, Chapman walked to the rear of the car. Below the exhaust pipe he found a pool of molten plastic. With amazement and relief, he took the melted hose into his hand. He prayed.

Chapman prayed earnestly and deeply. He thanked God for giving him a sign at last—a sign that he was supposed to live. In spite of the pain, he decided after a single failed suicide attempt that he was going to live. He had known all along that, no matter what he might ever try to do, he couldn't cause it to happen unless it was God's will. No matter how foolish or violent his ideas might sometimes seem, he believed God would prevent him from carrying out any act except those he was destined to carry out.

As he stood with the burned hose in his hand, Chapman realized that he had been foolish and selfish to think in the first place that his life had been his to end. From that day forward, Chapman knew that God would talk to him. Even when he was depressed or angry and unable to see the signs, he knew that God would show the direction for his life. He looked around for the fisherman. The Japanese man had disappeared. Chapman smiled a knowing smile. The man with the fishing pole, he knew in his heart, had been a messenger sent by God to save him.

"Angel," he said to himself. "Thank you, God, for sending one of your angels to save me from the small part of myself."

Seized by the fear of what he had almost done in his depression and confusion, Chapman also understood something more fundamental, something that he had known all along: More than anything, he needed the attention of other humans.

"Maybe now," he said to himself, "somebody will pay attention."

He disassembled his defective suicide machine as hastily as he had put it together and drove himself back across the island to Honolulu. From the car rental office, he walked about three miles to a mental-health clinic near

Waikiki Beach. He had been advised by the suicide counselor to visit the clinic a week or so before. They had given him pills that he had thrown away. Finding no one on duty in the evening hours, he walked another several blocks to the familiar façade of the Moana. Still clutching the burned vacuum hose, Mark David Chapman resumed his accustomed, lonely vigil outside the hotel.

Early the next morning, Chapman retraced his steps to the mental-health center. Cautiously, he approached a well-dressed woman, a staff psychologist who had arrived at the clinic early to open her office. He showed the psychologist, Judy Herzog, the melted hose. He told her of his suicide attempt. He described an escape from death that he believed to have been miraculous.

The psychologist invited him to her office where she listened again to his story, examined the hose, and picked up the phone.

"We've got to get you some help," she said.

On the morning after Chapman's suicide attempt, the psychiatric beds at downtown Honolulu hospitals all were occupied by other tormented souls likewise struggling with the dark side of paradise. It wasn't until late in the morning that the psychologist found a place for him. She drove him several miles, across a volcanic mountain that rises in the middle of the island, to a recently opened, eight-bed mental-health ward in the suburb of Kailua. Several hours later, he was admitted to Castle Memorial Hospital, an infirmary operated by the Seventh-Day Adventist Church.

After a brief admission interview, Chapman was diagnosed with acute depressive illness, a malady familiar to Hawaii's mental-health professionals and to natives who dismiss it as "island fever" in its milder forms.

Exhausted from the emotional ordeal of the previous month, Chapman remembers that he slept through much of his first three days at the hospital. He was confined to a doorless room under round-the-clock supervision.

"I slept very deeply, and when I finally woke up I began eating enormous quantities of food. They had me on a full suicide watch, twenty-four hours a day. Even when I took a shower, there was someone there watching me."

According to medical records, Chapman was admitted on June 21, 1977, with a diagnosis of "depressive reaction, depressive neurosis, severe" after "a very serious suicidal attempt."

In his notes, the late Dr. Ram Gursahani wrote that Chapman had been counseled about two weeks earlier at an outpatient clinic in Honolulu and given an antidepressant, Elavil, that he had thrown away. Dr. Gursahani made a note that Chapman was "inherently suicidal." In layman's terms, the psychiatrist confided to another therapist, "I wouldn't bet a nickel on this guy." On June 22, two days after the suicide attempt, Chapman told the psychiatrist, "I just want to kill myself. I'm tired of fighting." He added that his "mom and dad used to fight all the time and he would hit her until I got big enough to get in the way." He asked the hospital staff not to contact his parents. While he was being treated at the hospital, the therapists noted on his chart that he "contacts mother fairly regularly by mail. Not close to father or sister."

When the psychiatrist asked him how he felt, Chapman answered with a dramatic metaphor of violence.

"I think of myself as a boxer in the twenty-seventh round with my face all bloody, my teeth knocked out and my body all bruised," he said.

The doctor noted that the suicidal young man from Georgia "actually looked tired as he expressed these feelings" but "did not want to explore who or what he was fighting."

In contrast to Chapman's suicidal depression, however, the doctor noted that "patient appears neat, cooperative, open and alert."

Although Chapman did "not appear to be psychotic" after the suicide attempt, his doctor observed that he was "extremely depressed and states that he does not see any purpose in living and wants to die."

After less than a week in the hospital, Chapman's depression seemed to have all but evaporated. On June 27, Dr. Gursahani noted that the "patient went with one of the staff members to Honolulu and talked to state employment officer. He does not appear to be depressed much. In fact, at times he smiles and even laughs. He will have a pass again tomorrow to meet welfare, etc." The psychiatric nurses who looked in on Chapman would observe him reading late into the night.

Less than a week after his admission, Chapman was reported to be initiating conversations with therapists and other patients. He also was playing guitar and singing to the hospital staff and to elderly nursing-home patients. He thanked his caretakers profusely for taking a personal interest in his life.

Two weeks after his admission to the hospital for treatment of suicidal depression, Mark David Chapman had become a different person, "discussing the realities of life like work, living, money, etc.," the psychiatrist noted. "Appears cheerful. Has found a place to live close to the hospital. At this point he feels quite optimistic."

Chapman talked excitedly to his caretakers about the future and about the many career opportunities that he believed he had the talent and intelligence to pursue. He told the doctor that he didn't like the idea of being on welfare and said he wanted to become responsible for himself as soon as possible after being discharged.

On July 4, 1977, Chapman went to Kailua Beach with a group of patients and therapists to picnic, swim, and watch a fireworks display. Dr. Gursahani made his final entry in Chapman's record: "Patient's depression has lifted. He is now concentrating on finding a job. Will be discharged tomorrow."

Dr. Gursahani arranged a job for Chapman at a gas station near the hospital. The doctor later supported a decision to hire the former mental patient for jobs in the maintenance and public-relations departments at Castle.

In several of his notes, however, Dr. Gursahani expressed concerns about sexual and other unspecified "fantasies" Chapman had reported. Before he was discharged, the patient was interviewed by an unidentified therapist who made a brief report on one of his more curious fantasies of "wanting to be in prison." If he were in prison, Chapman told the therapist, "he could rest and read. Pointed out that his day was spent [at the hospital] in that exact way."

"He was an attractive and a pleasant young man and most of the hospital staff liked him," Castle psychiatrist Dr. Denis Mee-Lee later recalled. "He tried hard to give a good impression, to please, and to be helpful. But his approach to getting along with people was to be 'too nice.' I felt it covered up a lot of anger."

Thanks to the care and the personal attention he received at Castle Memorial Hospital, Chapman bounced quickly and enthusiastically back to life after the suicide attempt. His doctors and therapists said they were astonished by an apparently remarkable recovery. Still feeling that he needed the support of those who had healed him, Chapman returned to the hospital within days of his discharge to work as a volunteer. About a month later, he joined the Castle staff, filling a vacancy in the housekeeping and maintenance department. Working at the hospital made him feel accepted at last in the lonely islands.

After being delivered from suicide and having undergone a psychiatric rebirth, Chapman found himself in a spiritual crossfire between reawakened, self-effacing religious instincts and the lure of a world in which he still needed "to be somebody."

He found himself trying to be all things to all the people he met in a frenzied effort to be anything at all to himself. Exhibiting a remarkable talent and desire to learn about himself, Chapman began to parrot the psychiatric jargon of his caretakers. Some therapists were concerned when he began counseling other patients. He explained that he was just applying the same "reality therapy" on other patients that had worked so effectively with him. In one instance, the therapists asked him to meet with a young man who had come to Hawaii, like him, for a "last fling in paradise" and had then tried to kill himself in a hotel room.

He started teaching himself Japanese so that he could communicate with the hospital's numerous elderly Asian patients. The therapists at Castle tell a story of one aged nursing-home resident who hadn't spoken to anyone for several years. Chapman visited the woman regularly for several weeks. In a faint, creaking voice, the woman began talking to him.

Within weeks of his rapid recovery from suicidal depression, Chapman found himself accepted into the social circles of his caretakers.

CHAPTER SEVENTEEN

THE CARETAKERS

We were going to be a comedy team: The Mark and Judy Show.

—JUDY HARVEY

We're Laurel and Hardy. And we stand a better chance under that guise because all the serious people like Martin Luther King and Kennedy and Gandhi got shot.

—JOHN LENNON

Judy Harvey never met her biological parents. Before her adoptive parents died, they informed her that her mom had been an Iowa schoolteacher. Her father, they told her, had been a famous vaudeville comedian and Hollywood actor. His name was Oliver Hardy.

Regardless of whether the story is true, Harvey says she feels a "spiritual connection" to Oliver Hardy.

"I must have inherited my crazy sense of humor from somebody," says Harvey, a robust woman who bears more than a passing physical resemblance to the legendary comic.

Judy Harvey's "crazy sense of humor" has found apt expression in the work she does as a psychiatric nurse and mental-health counselor. She uses her talent for comedy as a therapeutic tool to penetrate barriers of depression and mental illness that isolate many of the patients she counsels. Humor, she says, helps people put their lives into perspective. When Mark David Chapman told her he had once worked as a stand-up comic, Harvey was intrigued.

"If Mark Chapman was crazy—well, maybe I didn't realize it. Because maybe I'm crazy too," she says. "The Mark I knew was really clever, a really funny guy and we played off each other with perfect timing. We were going to be a comedy team: The Mark and Judy Show. I have a real skill for comedy and Mark complemented my impromptu act just like it was rehearsed."

From the moment she met Chapman at Castle Memorial Hospital, Harvey liked his sense of humor. Along with virtually every other member of the hospital staff, Harvey also was struck by his sensitivity and the compassion he expressed for other, less fortunate patients.

"That's why we invited him to come back and work as a volunteer with the patients after he was discharged," Harvey said. "He came faithfully every evening and after a while we encouraged him to apply for a hospital job, so he would get paid for all the time he was spending there."

As she reminisced about her former friend, Harvey picked up her diary and began leafing backward through more than a decade of penciled memories to his name.

Lighting a cigarette, she began reading quickly, selectively, from entries she had made during the waning months of 1977:

> . . . Mark called and offered to help me wash the car, then took me for pizza. . . .
>
> . . . Going out for dinner tomorrow night, Sept. 12, at the Haiku Bar with Mark. To the beach later to talk. . . . I worry too about an upset and making him depressed. He's so considerate and giving . . . open and communicative. . . . Very sensitive and considerate. I still worry in the back of my mind. He's an ex-patient and could become depressed. So I do have a lot of concern about the depression.
>
> . . . Cold, needed to rest. Mark brought steaks and wine over for dinner. . . . He's good people and good company. . . . He just seems to want to be near me. . . .
>
> . . . He was disappointed because I didn't go with him and George [former Castle therapist George Kaliope] to get a car radio. He was a bit angry. I explained my not going should not affect his happiness. He understood that after an apology. . . . Mark and I went shopping in Honolulu after work. Had a good time. . . . He wanted me to hear a song on his new stereo. I declined. I was too tired. He later came down to tell me he was hurt and angry because I wouldn't take time for him. . . . I feel he shouldn't care so much.

Putting her diary aside, Harvey reflects quietly for several minutes. She tries to explain:

"He had this, like, charisma. He was like one of the staff at the hospital. He just drank everything in. Even though he was—what? Twenty-two years old at the time? He was like a little old man. A wise little Yoda kid."

Intelligent, sensitive, compassionate and solicitous of her feelings, Chapman approached Harvey as one of his peers. Harvey recalls that she had to remind herself on numerous occasions that he had been a patient—that he wasn't a mental health professional like herself.

"He was so good with the patients that we began inviting him to join us for beer, dinner, or whatever after working hours at the hospital," Harvey said. "That's when he became one of our peers. Mark was a patient at the hospital and I was a nurse at the hospital. But Mark was never in therapy with me," she said. "He was my friend. . . . Most of the time, I had to force myself to think, 'Oh yeah, this guy was admitted.' "

As their friendship developed, Harvey became concerned when she says Chapman would misinterpret things she told him. She feared that he would read more into their friendship than she believed herself able to give. She says she also was dating two other men during the period that she began spending time with Chapman and she worried that he would feel rejected. When he told her that he believed she thought him to be inadequate, "I told him that wasn't true at all. I told him he was so sensitive that he wasn't always accurate in what he thought he was picking up from other people, especially the people closest to him.

"You know the song, 'Starry, Starry Night' ['Vincent']? It reminds me of Mark. The way he just, like, took everything in so much and maybe felt it all too much. If you don't have a good way to let that out, that sensitivity, if you can't deal with it yourself, it's going to blow you up.

"Mark was extremely sensitive. . . . He would get depressed and very moody and when he'd start talking that way, I'd say, 'Go see your counselor. You know, I'm not your counselor. I'm your friend.' "

Observing that he seemed always to prefer the companionship of older men and women like herself, Harvey, almost twenty years older than the young ex-patient, speculated that "maybe he was looking for his parents."

The friendship between the psychiatric nurse and the ex-patient ended abruptly after Chapman was introduced by one of the doctors at Castle Memorial Hospital to "Pastor Pete," a minister at a Presbyterian Church in Kailua.

Chapman recalls the day the Reverend Peter Anderson paid him a visit at the apartment complex where he lived near Judy Harvey and Harvey's elderly adoptive mother. As the two men sat beside the pool, Chapman recounted for the minister his middle class, Presbyterian childhood. He told the preacher of the fervent, born-again Christianity that had marked his later adolescence. He talked about the depression that had brought him to Hawaii. He explained that God had saved him from suicide and that he felt guilty because he wasn't obeying God's will. Chapman also confessed that he carried a burden of guilt about the continuing friendship with Harvey.

After their poolside visit, the preacher invited the lapsed young Christian to come live with him and his wife, Martha, in the Andersons' comfortable suburban home.

"Mark said Rev. Anderson had made him feel guilty about our friendship and the amount of time we were spending together," Harvey recalled. "Mark was always extremely sensitive to the slightest criticism."

In the following months, Harvey recalls that Chapman would go out of his way to avoid her and others on the psychiatric unit.

"His nickname for me was 'Crazy.' Anytime he would see me after that, he'd just say, 'Hey, Crazy, how's it going?' or something like that, and walk away."

Harvey and others at the hospital worried about the impact of his sudden conversion. The hypersensitive former patient appeared to undergo a personality change after moving in with the minister. Chapman had captivated the doctors, nurses, and therapists at Castle. They had accepted him into their social circles. When he began to withdraw from them, they worried that his fervent rediscovery of Christian values masked a pain and confusion that had escaped both their friendship and therapy.

"The Christianity thing hounded him so bad, when he got into it that's all he would talk about," said George Kaliope, a former Castle Hospital therapist who became one of Chapman's best friends outside the hospital.

"Our big worry was when he moved in with the pastor," Kaliope says. "I even worried about the friendship that he had with me. He was at my home quite often, socializing with my wife and I and baby-sitting for our child. I didn't approve of the relationship he had with Judy. . . . But it wasn't going to help anything for somebody to make him feel guilty and sinful about it."

About the time Chapman moved into the minister's home, Harvey noted in her diary that someone else had remarked to her that he was acting "weird and/or moody." He had begun to be "cool at work too," she noted, adding, "I'm puzzled. Will talk to him. George [Kaliope] says it's the minister getting to him regarding his 'sinful ways in life et cetera.' Says he acts quiet and odd sometimes with him, too."

Castle psychiatrist Dr. Denis Mee-Lee recalls that he introduced Chapman to the Rev. Anderson after learning that the ex-patient had been raised in the Presbyterian Church. Although Chapman was never in formal therapy with Mee-Lee, the psychiatrist recalls that Chapman often sought his advice whenever he encountered him in the hospital corridors. It was during one of those conversations, Mee-Lee says, that Chapman talked about his childhood and teenage years when he had been "a strong Christian."

"He was not ultrareligious at that point," Dr. Mee-Lee later told police. "The sudden switch was a trigger for me. I thought it was just a way of coping, and probably not the best. But there was nothing to make me think of psychosis. I didn't consider psychosis."

For more than a decade, Judy Harvey has ransacked her memories for clues that Mark Chapman was either a psychotic or a psychopath. She's found none.

"No one will ever convince me that Mark is evil. Sick? Maybe. And deranged and confused and just so sensitive that everything came down on him.

"But there was never a hint that the Mark Chapman I knew had been through anything but a situational depression. We all missed the schizophrenia. There just wasn't a clue."

Harvey, like others who fell under the charms of the silver-tongued man-child from Georgia, saw in him the things that Chapman believed she wanted to see. For a time, exploiting Harvey's penchant for clowning and slapstick comedy, he had posed as Stan Laurel to complement her Oliver Hardy.

Devoid of a personality of his own, Chapman says that at an early age he developed a parasitic, mirrorlike survival skill. He learned to capture and reflect the character traits of people whose affection and friendship he sought.

"Even without knowing it, I would reflect people's own personalities back to them," he recalls. "I was almost always charming to people, until I started reflecting back to them parts of themselves they didn't want to see. Then, they didn't want me around anymore.

"I remember, even when I was very young, something that my mother told me: 'Mark, you don't wear well with people.' "

CHAPTER EIGHTEEN

THE OTHER SIDE OF THE RAINBOW

It is a terrifying thing to have a wedge driven into one's narrow circle of love.

—FREDERICK EXLEY, *A FAN'S NOTES*

Mark David Chapman started the New Year in 1978 feeling that black clouds of suicidal depression had been exorcised forever from his mind. Spiritually and emotionally, he believed that he had been reborn. Reflecting on the chaos and depression of the previous two years, he was buoyed by the belief that God had personally intervened in his life. He saw a divine plan working itself out through the series of events that had guided him to the Christian hospital and elevated him to a status there as something of a celebrity.

Chapman knew that he was highly regarded among the doctors, nurses, and therapists at Castle Memorial Hospital. Although his job in the hospital's housekeeping and maintenance department was low paying, the benefits were good. More important than money or benefits, the job enabled him to remain close to the psychiatrists and psychologists who seemed to offer the hope of an identity he was unable to sustain on his own.

Chapman was the only staff member who had been hired by the hospital after being treated there for mental illness. His status as an ex-patient at first made him feel important and unique. He had learned from the ordeal of the past two years that, more than anything else, that was just how he needed to feel.

"I was feeling my self-esteem coming back working at Castle Hospital," he recalled. "Anytime something needed fixing, anytime one of the big shots needed to be picked up or taken to the airport, they would call my name. I would steam clean carpets for them in their homes. Anytime something needed to be cleaned up or straightened out, they called my name all over the hospital. I knew everybody on every floor and when somebody needed something, I was the one paged to get it or fix it. I would be paged more than the doctors; all day long I would be paged.

"I went skydiving with a group of girls and guys from there. I had dinner with the hospital director, Larry Larrabee, and his wife."

Larrabee was executive director of the hospital in 1977 when Chapman was hired, about two months after the abortive suicide attempt. The hospital director later told police investigators that he had no qualms about hiring Chapman, even though he had been a patient a short time before.

"Mark was like one of the family," Larrabee said. "He was extremely competent, an outstanding employee and personal friend." Like others who had known Mark David Chapman throughout his life, Larrabee described the bewildered young man as an object of pity. He was someone who had "no enemies," Larrabee said.

In the same ingenuous way that his childhood heroine Dorothy and her hapless friends believed in the Wizard of Oz, Chapman believed in the mental-health wizards at Castle Memorial Hospital. He clung to the members of the hospital staff, believing they could give him back the mind, the heart, and the courage he felt he had lost in the emotional storm that had carried him far from his home and himself. With their help, he believed he would find the "good person" who struggled somewhere in the chaos of his mind.

"I became very well liked there at Castle. Everybody liked me and I got along with everybody. I was kind of a gofer and I did everything and met a lot of important people. I met Dr. Heimlich when he came to the hospital and put on a little seminar on the Heimlich maneuver.

"I had Christmas with the staff at the hospital in 1977 and everything seemed to be going perfectly. My parents and my sister came to Hawaii on vacation to see me about that time. Then they went back home and I thought everything was going to be all right."

He continued to find joy and to take inordinate pride in his work at Castle through the early months of 1978, when his spirit of adventure returned. It came back on an evening when he had stayed late at the hospital, waxing and polishing floors. As he swept a gently humming buffer in hypnotic arcs across the shiny surface of a linoleum corridor, it occurred to Chapman that he wanted to visit the Far East. He had been working and saving his money and he had an extra $1,000 his father had given him after the family's Christmas visit.

Mark Chapman was never one to think long about a plan when he had the money he needed to put it into action. He looked up a travel agent the next day.

Like most decisions he had made in his life, the impulsive decision to visit the Orient was rooted in the world of fiction.

"I'd been steeped in movies like *Around the World in Eighty Days, Mysterious Island,* and *The Great Race,* where they race around the world. So it was, like, in my subconscious to do that," he said.

About a month after making preliminary arrangements for his tour, Chapman learned that he could borrow additional money from the hospital credit union and get a six-week leave of absence from his job. In characteristic fashion, he elaborated the original vacation plan into a first-class, forty-day, round-the-world odyssey.

Changing his plans also gave Chapman an excuse to get back in touch with his travel agent, a petite and cordial Japanese-American woman named Gloria Abe.

"I was sitting up in my room. It was March or April," he recalled. "I said to myself I might as well accomplish a dream I always had, which was to travel the globe. So I went back and told Gloria I wanted to go all the way around the world."

Before he embarked on the worldwide adventure in July, Chapman dropped in and phoned Gloria several times a week. He routinely sent her flattering thank-you notes for the work she was doing to accommodate his ever-changing plans. His itinerary continued to expand as he read more and more in travel books and brochures about exciting destinations to be experienced. Along with one of his many notes to Gloria Abe, he sent a teddy bear and a dozen red roses. He often appeared in the doorway at her office with coffee and pastries. He told her he was sure that she didn't work that hard for other customers. He was right.

Just as his solicitous attention had won the affections of the staff at Castle Memorial Hospital, Chapman soon won the heart of Gloria Abe. Although she was about five years older than he, Gloria looked far younger than her age of twenty-seven.

"I think my client Mark Chapman has a crush on me," Gloria confided one day to a coworker. She recalls that she had just hung up the phone after Mark had called. He had begun the conversation by asking, "Hey good lookin', what's cookin'?"

Gloria, a timid and trusting woman who had been born and raised by Japanese emigrant parents in a Honolulu suburb, also found that she was developing a crush on Mark Chapman.

"Since I knew he was younger than me, I did not think much of it," Gloria recalled. "I liked him, yes. But love? No.

"I'm not exactly sure when it happened, but after working with him and getting to know him better, I fell in love with him. He was witty, generous, kind, gentle, studious, intelligent, and cute. I had taken a course in graphoanalysis, and I liked the way he wrote, too. I saw good traits in his handwriting."

On July 6, 1978, the day he was scheduled to depart on his round-the-world tour, Gloria looked up his address in her files and drove to his apartment at the Reverend Peter Anderson's home. She arrived several hours before his scheduled flight, just as he was loading his luggage into the trunk of a car.

Blushing self-consciously, Gloria draped a fragrant, flowery lei around Chapman's neck and gave him a warm kiss. He said he wished that she were going with him, or that he could cancel his trip and stay with her. He promised that he would write every day. Gloria recalls that she continued to receive postcards from all over the world for weeks after he returned to Hawaii, late in September.

"She was cute," Chapman said. "But no sparks were flying. I didn't think I'd be marrying this woman."

His wife-to-be says that the attentive and sensitive young suitor had already captivated her heart. Even while he was away traveling the world, their relationship flourished. "We became close during those six weeks," Gloria recalled.

Chapman arrived at the airport early on the day of his flight and waited at the boarding gate for more than an hour before any other passengers showed up.

After an eight-hour flight, the Boeing 747 landed in Tokyo where Chapman had booked a room at the YMCA. Because of his past work for the agency in Georgia, Arkansas, and Lebanon, he had arranged to stay inexpensively at YMCA hostels in several of the countries he would be visiting on his tour. He was carrying a letter of introduction from David Moore, his friend and supervisor in 1975 when he had worked helping to resettle Vietnamese war refugees at Fort Chaffee. After the project had ended, Moore had been assigned to oversee YMCA programs in Europe. As part of the world tour, Chapman was planning to visit Moore and his family in Geneva, Switzerland, before going on to London and returning to the United States.

On the first day of the world trip he met in Tokyo with an official of the Japanese YMCA who praised him for the work he had done with refugees. The conversation caused Chapman to realize, for the first time in his life, that he was beginning to lose touch with the sense of compassion he believed he had always felt for other people. He had never felt more compassion than he had for the war-torn Vietnamese.

"But as I talked with this man, he turned to me with tears in his eyes and he asked what I thought about the refugees—the uprooting of so much humanity," Chapman recalled. "I just sat there, kind of numb. I was kind of in shock because of his question and I was surprised at myself because I realized that I couldn't feel anything. It was weird, like all that feeling I had before inside me had dried up. I felt guilty. I just couldn't say anything. My tongue was tied, and I just kind of nodded my head as he talked."

After several days in Japan, visiting Mount Fuji, the Imperial Palace, Tokyo Tower, and a sushi bar on the Ginza, Chapman continued on his travels to Korea, where he met with Mary Webster, a colleague from his Fort Chaffee days. Unlike Chapman, Webster had a college degree and she had been assigned, after the refugee work ended at Fort Chaffee, to work with the YMCA in Seoul.

In Korea, Chapman again became depressed, thinking about the YMCA career he had dreamed of pursuing. He again pondered the inexplicable clouds of self-doubt and suicidal urgings that had driven him from college and kept him from getting the academic credentials he would need for a YMCA career. Desperately, he still wanted to be able to pursue a vocation and a life that would enable him to think of himself as "somebody." He grew more depressed as his friend Mary complained to him of the difficulties she had experienced working in Korea, where she said women were objects of prejudice and unmarried women were scorned.

As the 747 rose from the runway at Seoul and soared above the Pacific, Chapman's spirits lifted. In Hong Kong, he unexpectedly discovered that the border into Red China had been opened to the Western world. He and his tour group were among the first Americans to travel inside the mysterious nation that had been sealed for decades by the Communists.

From Hong Kong, Chapman traveled to Thailand where he stayed once again at a YMCA. In Bangkok, he had his first encounter with a prostitute.

"I had gone to dinner with the YMCA director and then I went out by myself to walk the streets of Bangkok," he recalled. "I had a few beers and I'm walking down the street and a woman, a hooker, very drunk, very aggressive, came out of nowhere and threw her arms around me. She's drunk and she wants to make some money. I tried to push her away at first, but then I decided to go with her.

"This whole thing was like something out of *The Catcher in the Rye.* It was like something that Holden Caulfield would do. I tried to push her away, but ended up getting in a cab with this girl. I guess she kind of turned me on. We went to this hotel, to a room she had, and she had some more beer brought in.

"I had read stories about people getting robbed and killed doing things like that and I realized it was a pretty foolish move. I wasn't really all that interested in having sex with this woman. But it was a new adventure for me, and I thought she could use the money.

"It was something that Holden Caulfield would do."

Chapman flew from Bangkok to India, where the gestating Holden Caulfield witnessed appalling contrasts between the rich and poor of the earth. More than ever before, he became aware of the gulf of pain and desperation that separate the wealthy "phonies" from the "real people" who struggle daily to survive.

Among the twelve hundred color slides that Chapman took on his round-the-world trip, the most arresting of the photos reveal the pain and poverty that met his eyes in Nepal and India—haunting images of lepers, starving children, ragged men and women driven mad by hunger and despair.

"I saw a body being cremated and I met a holy man," he said. "I saw these starving kids walking around and I wanted to give them something, so I bought a whole carton of chewing gum and caused a riot. I started handing out gum to kids and they heard about it in a school. It was a literal riot. Kids heard about a crazy American giving away gum and ran out of their schoolroom into the streets. It was pandemonium over a tiny piece of gum."

Chapman also toured the Taj Mahal, but the story he remembers of the magnificent temple is a tale of pain and death.

"Around the Taj Mahal were these tremendous green grounds and trees and ponds. It was one of the most beautiful sights I've ever seen. But I learned that this beautiful temple had been built for a khan's wife and after it was built, they had the hands cut off of every artisan who had worked on it so they could never build another building like it.

"Later the son of the khan betrayed him and locked him in the Red Fort a few miles from the Taj Mahal. He confined his father in a cell with a tiny peephole where the only thing he could see was the beautiful temple."

Returning to Delhi from the Taj Mahal, Chapman was overwhelmed by the dichotomies of a world that he found "filthy, putrid. Children sleeping in streets with flies all over them, a man trying to grab my camera away from me and looking at me with these voodoo eyes.

"India was just a whole other world of desperate, desperate people," he recalled. "You can't imagine how horrible."

From India, Chapman briefly visited Iran and Israel, where he sought out the history of the "holy lands" in which his Christian beliefs were rooted.

When he arrived in Switzerland nearly a month after embarking on his adventure, he tried to explain to his friend and former boss, David Moore, the struggle he had undergone. He confessed that he felt himself a failure because he'd been forced to drop out of college. Moore assured Chapman that his life still had value and counseled him not to lose faith in himself. He said that lack of a college degree or an important job did not diminish his importance in the eyes of friends who continued to respect him for his past sacrifices.

"The only thing that's important," Moore told Chapman, "is that you are happy."

After attending a United Nations session with Moore in Geneva, Chapman left for England where he spent several days visiting ornate parks and photographing famous statues and buildings. In London, he recalls that he approached an elderly man on a bench. He asked the man to tell him the meaning of life. The man had no answer for him.

He left England a few days later, never thinking, he said, about John Lennon or about the English city of Liverpool where the Beatles had been born.

Before he returned to Hawaii, Chapman made a brief visit to Georgia where he saw his childhood friends and his parents. Back in Decatur, he made it a point to look up his old friend Dana Reeves. Although he and Reeves had argued during his last trip back home—Chapman felt that Reeves had not been appropriately shocked when told of his plan to commit suicide in Hawaii—he wanted Reeves to know that he would always be his friend.

On August 20, 1978, Chapman stepped from a plane back into the familiar and fragrant air of Honolulu. The first person he saw waving to him from the terminal gate was his travel agent. Gloria Abe ran excitedly into his arms.

Starting the next day, Mark and Gloria became virtually inseparable. Even on days when they didn't have a date, Gloria recalls that Mark would often ring her doorbell late at night. Sometimes he'd had too much to drink and sometimes he explained that he just felt depressed and needed to talk. Unlike his other friends and unlike his lovers of the past, Gloria never turned him away. She never protested that she was tired. She never said she had to get up early for work the next day. She would always let him in and he usually slept on her couch. Although he didn't tell her right away of the depression and the planned suicide that had brought him to Hawaii, Gloria quickly intuited his despair. It was part of the painful mystique that lay at the root of the sensitivity she believed she saw in him. His pain was a crucial element of the charm that attracted Gloria Abe, for better or worse, to Mark David Chapman.

"I believe it was some time during the first or second week back from his trip that he told me some serious things about himself," she said. "What helped him open up, I believe, was the statement I made on our first night together that he had been hurt a lot by others.

"I sensed this very strongly that night."

Gloria listened sympathetically as the peculiar and earnest young man held her hand and told her a tale of lost love. He talked about a girl back home in Georgia. The girl's name was Lynn, he said, a high school sweetheart he had loved and who had broken his heart.

He told her that he had fallen madly in love with Lynn after their first date, when she had invited him to an expensive French restaurant in Atlanta, an elegant restaurant where he had eaten gourmet food and tasted chocolate mousse for the first time. He also told her that Lynn had walked with a slight limp as the result of a childhood illness. Gloria, whose left leg had been atrophied by polio when she was a child, also walked with a slight limp. She seized upon the parallel between herself and Chapman's first love.

Although he told her it had happened long ago, he said he had never been able to overcome painful memories of first romance. It had been a pure, innocent, unconsummated love, he explained. It had happened back in the days when, he said, he had been "a strong Christian."

He also told her of another love, Jessica, a girl he had known since second grade. Although he had been engaged to Jessica, he said he could never forget about Lynn and that he and Jessica had called off a planned marriage two years before. Unlike him, he said, Jessica had remained "a strong Christian."

As he talked about his lapsed Christianity, describing his unique and compelling beliefs in the spiritual nature of human life, Gloria Abe was spellbound.

When he finally finished speaking, Gloria told him that she believed herself a spiritually attuned person, although she didn't know much about Christianity. Her father and mother had both emigrated from Japan to Hawaii, where her father had opened a restaurant and bakery business in suburban Honolulu before she was born. She told Mark that her mother was Buddhist and her father practiced the traditional Japanese religion of Shinto, paying homage to the departed spirits of family ancestors. Gloria hadn't received much religious training during her childhood, she said, although she had always felt a spiritual yearning. She devoted much of her spare time to the study of reincarnation, astrology, numerology, and parapsychology. Chapman warned that such things were "of the devil" and cautioned her to be careful.

As their relationship progressed, Gloria Abe became increasingly intrigued with Mark Chapman. She had never met anyone either as sensitive or as spiritual as she believed him to be.

"He explained to me in a powerful sermon the death and resurrection of Christ," Gloria said. "He spoke as if he was filled with the Holy Spirit, and I believe he was.

"I wasn't a Christian, but he was very patient and gentle with me even as I talked about reincarnation and astrology. He wasn't at all pushy. He just urged me to read the Bible.

"No one before has ever affected me the way he did that day. No one had explained Christ to me like he did.

"I told him that he should put his gift to good use, but he said he was not close anymore to Christ. When he was young he used to pass out tracts on the street. He used to preach in the streets. He couldn't do that now as he'd feel hypocritical."

Early in 1979, Mark Chapman and Gloria Abe announced wedding plans. Concerned about his ability to support a wife, Chapman at first wanted to postpone marriage until he and his fiancée had amassed a modest sum in a savings account. The Reverend Peter Anderson advised the couple not to postpone their wedding in the interest of financial security.

"We were going to wait a year and save our money, but Reverend Anderson said, 'There's no reason to wait. There's no real reason to wait. What's fifteen hundred dollars more or two thousand dollars more? What's that going to change?' So we agreed and it did make sense. It did make good sense. We were the first couple that he married, on June 2 of 1979."

Mark and Gloria Chapman's courtship and marriage were complicated almost from the beginning by Mark's parents' unexpected announcement that, after nearly twenty-five years as husband and wife, they were getting a divorce. It was further complicated when his mother, Diane, announced that she was moving to Hawaii. In the months before and after their wedding, Gloria recalls that her husband was often torn between spending time and money with her or with his mother. Mother Chapman would often accompany the newlyweds on dinner dates, cruises, and excursions that the new bride believed she should have been allowed to enjoy with her husband alone. Sometimes Gloria would protest the threesome, but her husband insisted that his first duty was to his mom.

After Chapman was arrested in New York City, Gloria recalled the conflict in a lengthy statement she prepared at the request of his defense attorney:

"Mark did all he could for his mom to set her up in a nice place and all, and I made things hard for him after a while. I got jealous and put pressure on Mark (not any real, physical pressure but an emotional-type pressure) to more-or-less choose between me and his mom. He decided not to have any contact with his mother for a while during the first part of 1979, just for my sake he told me later. I hated my jealousy, kept fighting it and finally overcame it a few months before Mark went to New York with a gun. But meanwhile, Mark had a lot of unnecessary pressure on him because of me and his mother."

Chapman became enraged at his father when he found out that his mother had been left without meaningful financial resources after the divorce. When he was being interviewed by psychologists and psychiatrists after the Lennon killing, he spoke of wanting to kill his father for what he had done to his mother during and after their marriage. He also told psychiatrists he became confused after the divorce. He described a parentlike responsibility that he assumed for his mother after she moved to Hawaii.

"I really didn't want her there," he told the psychiatrists, "because that was my island, it wasn't hers. She interfered. . . .

"She used to be a really good mother—take care of her kids, good cook—and then she came out to Hawaii, I guess to start a life of her own, and she became very conceited and would talk about nothing but herself . . . She could not talk about anything but herself and her boyfriends, and I tried to tell her, 'You're not talking about anything about me or Jessica or Gloria or nothing.' I said, 'Can't you see?' And she'd get mad as hell. I said, 'But can't you see, there you go again. You keep talking about yourself. You never structure your conversations about other people and about other people's lives. That's all you care about is your own life, you know.' She'd get mad as hell. She'd deny it, and I'd tell her she was menopausal and she'd deny it."

Chapman told the psychiatrists he was especially disturbed by his mother's liaisons with "beach bums," boyfriends who were about his own age.

"I would get mad with her, and say, you know, 'What are you going around with this bum for?' 'Cause she has big breasts, you know, and that's all they want."

Diane Chapman confided in her son that she didn't want his seventeen-year-old sister to come to Hawaii. Just as she had turned to him when he was a child to protect her from her husband, Chapman told the psychiatrists that his mother again thrust him into a role reversal as her confidant and adviser.

"She'd say, 'Well, I'm worried about Susan, and Susan wants to come out, but I can't have her out because I'm starting my own life.'

"I said, 'Don't worry about any of that stuff,' you know. I was the one who got her a lawyer for her divorce. She didn't know what to do. I had to take care of her. I found her a job at Sears.

"You know, I had to take care of her."

After her son was imprisoned for the murder of John Lennon, Diane Chapman told a reporter of her first concern:

"I loved my life and I wanted my life back," Diane Chapman said in a *People* magazine interview. "My first thought when this thing happened was 'My God, I'll never be happy again.' "

Nearly twelve years after John Lennon was killed, the killer's mother had visited her son twice at Attica prison.

In spite of the stress of coping with his forty-eight-year-old mother's midlife crisis and divorce, Mark and Gloria recall that they were reasonably happy for the first six months of their marriage. Gloria made peace with her mother-in-law, and the trio would often drive around the island in a Lincoln Continental that Chapman would rent for such evenings. They would stop for dinner or drinks at the Moana and other elegant hotels and beachfront night spots. The newlyweds' credit card bills began to pile ominously high, but Gloria soon learned better than to question her husband about his lavish spending sprees.

Spending money was a way of bolstering his sagging self-esteem, he explained. Toward the end of 1979, Chapman's self-esteem was again reaching dangerously low levels. Although still working at the hospital, he had left the housekeeping and maintenance job believing that, because he was married, he had to have a more important position in life. He applied and was accepted for a new job at Castle Memorial Hospital as a printer and public-relations representative.

"That was one of the biggest mistakes I ever made," Chapman recalled. "I felt like I had to do better, that I couldn't be a housekeeper when I was married. It was ridiculous—wanting to get ahead, feeling I had to have a more important job and be more responsible if I was getting married."

As Castle's printer and public-relations assistant, he conducted hospital tours, took photos of dignitaries at hospital awards ceremonies, and helped design and produce informational literature.

"It paid more and it was more prestigious. I got to go to the governor's office and take pictures of him greeting hospital volunteers," he said.

Although prestigious, the job also was demanding. In a short time, his still-fragile emotions began to overload. As hospital officials worried about his handling of the public relations portion of the job, he was assigned increasingly to the print shop, a place of solitude where his problems seemed to dilate the more he thought about them and where he tried to regain a sense of control.

"When I was a housekeeper, I was happy," he explained. "It was a busy day and it would go quickly. Then I was stuck, all alone, in this printing room, smelling chemicals, going crazy with the noise, the boredom. I was taken away from my element of being happy and being sociable because of my own strict 'should do's'—should do this and should be that—because I was married.

"I already was starting to cave in at that point. The pressures from marriage, which I should have been responsible for, and which I was in a lot of ways—I tried to be—but I started caving in. I started feeling desperation deep in me and the job wasn't helping any. The sickening smell of chemicals. And while the press was running, I would go to the kitchen and get a dozen huge chocolate chip cookies and three or four pints of milk and sit and eat all this sugar and fat. Just getting fatter, not exercising, constant noise, smells, no exercise. Never feeling that I had a good day.

"And the pressures kept building. We moved into an apartment down the street from the hospital and one night there was an incident where these two fellows were coming up the stairs and talking too loud. I started yelling at them, telling them to be quiet. I felt bad and later approached them in the driveway and apologized. Maybe I shouldn't have apologized. I remember one of them didn't even look at me, didn't even acknowledge my apology. Then a few days later, he started whistling at my wife as he would go by our apartment. I just wanted to jump out and grab him. But I didn't. I just got all frightened inside. I don't know why, but I started disintegrating and getting real paranoid about people then. I broke our lease and moved us out of there across the mountains to Kukui Plaza, where we lived anonymously on the twenty-first floor of this luxurious condominium.

"Inside the apartment complex was a shopping center, a park with a waterfall, and a pond. A pavilion for picnics. It was just beautiful. So things got a little better when we moved. I didn't feel as paranoid. I felt a little better.

"But then I started having run-ins with people, with Gloria's boss, with the people I worked with, with people I met on the streets.

"One day I got angry because Gloria didn't come right out of her office when I went to pick her up at the travel agency. So I laid on the horn and started yelling. I went into the office and started yelling at her boss. Then it happened again and her boss slammed the door in my face, so I made Gloria quit and get another job."

Supervisors and coworkers at the hospital also noticed the increasing hostility in Chapman, which eventually cost him his job.

Leilani Siegfried, a former supervisor, told police investigators that virtually everyone at the hospital liked Chapman, but that she and others worried about "perfectionist" attitudes that often caused him to become enraged when others failed to do a job the way he believed it should be done or to otherwise meet his expectations. Not content just to do his work, Chapman was constantly devising new programs and systems for himself and others.

He was fired, but almost immediately rehired and allowed to resign, after a confrontation with a nurse, Helen Tanaka, who had criticized him over his failure to complete a printing job on time. On the day after Christmas 1979, he started a new job as a security guard at a high-rise apartment complex at 444 Nahua Street near Waikiki Beach. He severed virtually all contacts with friends from the hospital who had helped him stabilize his life after the 1976 suicide attempt.

"It was bad, the wrong thing to do, removing myself from all my roots. I stopped going to church. Just becoming more and more isolationist. Isolated from church, from friends, and then the disaster at Castle where I quit, or was fired—asked, rather, to resign. That was the biggie.

"It's funny, my supervisor's wife, Mrs. Tharp, had a premonition. She said,

'I just don't want you to quit. You'll get sick again.' She worked in personnel.

"But after that incident with the nurse, when I resigned, I immediately started looking for another job but I couldn't find one on my own. I tried to get a job in housekeeping at the Hyatt Regency. I got a glowing recommendation for the job from Castle. But I remember the interview. I wasn't myself. I wasn't feeling good. I was all gooked up in my own self and I wouldn't have hired me at that point. That may have been a chance to turn around, if I'd got a good job at a nice hotel."

His former friend Judy Harvey encountered Mark unexpectedly during his job search at the Red Cross offices in Honolulu. He told her he had come in to sell blood and to apply for a job at the agency.

"He was just wearing a dirty T-shirt and a pair of ragged shorts and his appearance really alarmed me," Harvey said. "I remember thinking that I wouldn't have hired anybody who looked the way he did at that point."

"So I wound up back in security work. Working nights," Chapman recalled. "I bought a Sony Walkman and a collection of Todd Rundgren tapes and started going into debt for artwork. I had credit at a Korean grocery near the building where I worked and when my shift ended in the morning, I would buy these big, twenty-five-ounce cans of Foster's Lager, put them in a brown bag, and walk around and drink it on the way to the bus stop. I would drink down a huge can of beer in probably a half-block walk to the bus and ride home kind of pleasantly drunk.

"I began drinking heavy, becoming very unhappy and dissatisfied with my life. And at some point, I started talking to the Little People, the little government that I had in my head, again. I would address them on a little screen that used to drop down into a boardroom. I would tell them that we were going to be all right financially. It was like I was running a little country. It was the only thing that was keeping me functioning, was those Little People.

"The biggest pressure I felt at that time was paying off all our debts. We got hoodwinked into an art deal at an art gallery. We bought Salvador Dali's gold plaque for $5,000. We borrowed money from my wife's dad. The gallery promised us these plaques weren't even made anymore and they were going to raise in price and we would make a profit. Then we found out the gallery was raising their own prices on these things. They'd show you in the book where the price went up, but they were the ones making the price go up: the old game, the con game that I should have known about from the time I ran away to Miami and joined the carnival.

"At another gallery, I met a lady who knew all the tricks. I had come in to look at a signed copy of a print by Norman Rockwell, the 'Triple Self-

Portrait.' Something about it really appealed to me at the time. So I told this lady I already was in hock for the Dali piece. She said that was never going to go anywhere, so why not get the Rockwell piece, which was guaranteed to appreciate in value."

After taking legal action, Chapman got his money back for the Dali plaque. He then talked his mother into investing $2,500 that she had saved since coming to Hawaii and he purchased the Rockwell print for $7,500.

"He became obsessed with the whole art world," his wife recalled. "He himself began drawing with watercolors and pen and ink. He thought about being an art gallery salesperson. He visited the better art galleries in Honolulu and would talk at great length to different salespersons about art."

Gloria was astonished at the quality of some of the watercolors her husband produced, "pictures that you could have hung on the wall and been proud of," she said. "But it seemed like he could never leave them alone. He just kept going back and going back over and over them until these beautiful watercolors became a mass of blackness.

"It was like nothing he did was ever good enough until he destroyed it."

On March 13, 1980, Chapman abandoned his obsession with art for an obsession with personal finances that he code-named "Operation Freedom from Debt."

"And so began a terrible part of his life," his wife recalled, when he would get up early in the morning and at all hours of the night to sit at the kitchen table with a pencil and calculator. Sometimes he would stare into space and talk, as though to someone else. One day Gloria asked him who he was talking to, and he tried to explain to her about the Little People.

He told his wife that when he was a child the Little People were very tiny and that millions of them lived in a kingdom over which he had ruled in the walls of his family's home. Although he hadn't thought about the Little People for many years, he said they had unexpectedly returned a few months earlier to help him reorganize his life. They were bigger, he said, and there were fewer of them. Instead of a monarchy, the world inside his head had also matured into a more democratic, parliamentary form of government of which he was president.

Before making any decisions, especially regarding finances, he subjected his proposals to the review of cabinet officers, various committees, and then to a congressional body for approval, rejection, or further deliberation.

"This was a time when I was just always feeling bad," Chapman said. "I never had a good day. Just feeling bad and worn down. The only relief I had was in talking to my Little People, organizing things. My big thing was the operation for getting out of debt. We were so far in debt. We owed money on everything but our teeth. But I worked at it and worked at it with my Little People and got it all paid off, several months ahead of deadline.

"Eventually I couldn't and I didn't work anymore. I thought I could just stay at home and cook and clean and have dinner ready for Gloria when she got home. You know, be like Lennon was, kind of like a househusband.

"I felt so much pressure, getting in all these struggles and arguments with people everywhere. So finally I quit my job. I signed off for the last time—it was after I was at the library and saw the Lennon book—I signed out as John Lennon and quit my job there.

"When I quit, I already knew that I was going to go and kill John Lennon.

"Nothing was wrong. Nothing was physically wrong with me. But my own little world around me was, like, choking me in and I couldn't release my fury. I was just angry.

"My minister and all my former friends—I shut them all out. I just found reasons from each one of them to reject them. I was so sensitive to everything around me that everyone, every friend, hurt me in some way so that I could no longer let our friendship exist.

"I don't even think George Kaliope, the therapist at Castle who became my closest friend, I don't even think he could have reached me. Maybe if some stranger could have sensed something was wrong, maybe the right stranger could have reached me through some act of kindness or understanding. I just don't know. I just ran so much, I didn't want to even know if anything was wrong at all. I was driving toward self-destruction and nothing could stand in my way. I just had no self-worth.

"I made a big mistake by running from my problems and trying to isolate myself. My problems became mythical in proportion and then they became very, very real and very, very damaging. When you separate yourself from the world, you have to invent your own world. And that's what I did. I invented my own world. I became so withdrawn into myself and I just didn't even have a reason for living anymore. I became more and more sheltered, drawn in, paranoid—more and more sensitive and hurting. I started to hate people, despise people—people that I knew before, not strangers.

"I was in a lot of pain. I knew something was wrong, but I didn't realize it was that serious. I was headed down a deep, dark alley and I was running out of doors real quick.

"Other than talking to my Little People, my only respite was in the library. I would look at all the books in the library and sometimes that would give me a few moments of peace. I had a fantasy where I wanted to go to a spot in the back of the library where there was this tree. I just wanted to live under this tree with a book and when I finished a book, I would go back into the library and get another book. Everybody would come to me and say, 'Here's the guy that lives under the tree reading the books. He can tell you all about literature and books.'

"That was a fantasy I had. I was a very lonely man. I was walking around, lonely and hurting, in a fantasy world. And I finally just got to the point of absurdity—and where I am today."

CHAPTER NINETEEN

WITH LOOKING GLASS EYES

But it's spilt milk, or rather blood, and I
try not to have regrets and don't
intend to waste energy and time in an effort
to become anonymous. That's as dumb as
becoming famous in the first place.

—JOHN LENNON, *SKYWRITING BY WORD OF MOUTH*

"Have you ever woken up from a deep sleep with the sensation that something evil is in the room?

"You're not really awake, but you're not really dreaming, either. Your eyes won't open more than about halfway. You just feel paralyzed with a fear that's so powerful you don't know who you are. You're so frightened you've virtually lost your identity.

"Fear can do that, you know. It can strip you of your identity. There's nothing more frightening than that. I know.

"You try to scream but nothing comes out, just all this fear holding you down in your bed so you can't move. You can't even scream.

"My whole life was like that at that time, a half-waking nightmare. But I couldn't wake up and I couldn't sleep it away. I was scared to death, but I couldn't scream. I would try to scream and it would remain echoing in my chest without ever being vocalized. And that was what came out that night in December when John Lennon stepped out of his limousine. What came out of the barrel of that gun was that giant scream after all those years.

"My personality at that point, it was totally disheveled and cracked and bleeding. There wasn't much of me there, certainly not the me that is speaking now.

"You see, I had no real personality then. I was in a flux of the waves and the wind. Wherever the people or the world blew my thoughts to, that's where I would go. But this all began long before any thoughts of killing John Lennon entered into the picture.

"Perhaps someone who is insecure like I was, and who has no grasp on his life, needs books, needs explanations. They need their life in a Dewey decimal system mode, which is fantasy, but it can be very comforting.

"At that time in my life when things were going very haywire and the meaning of my life was escaping me—when I was so confused and discontent and angry and hurting—I turned back to something that I remembered from childhood that was orderly and neat and precise: an escape. And I began spending my days in the Honolulu Public Library.

"The library for me was a refuge from pain and confusion and the feeling of not knowing what was going on, not understanding the pain and confusion of the world around me, which it seems has always been the case.

"I flash back to when I was in elementary school and Mrs. Blakeslee was the librarian. Once a month she brought us in and taught us how to use the library. I remember she asked for volunteers to be library assistants. I volunteered and worked in the library for several years where Mrs. Blakeslee taught me the value of books.

"I remember going up and down the aisles selecting books. I was reading some pretty unusual books: Thurber and Ogden Nash and writers like that.

"Whatever the reason, when my life fell apart and I couldn't wake up from the nightmare years later, I felt a sense of peace and relief when I went into the library in Honolulu and climbed those four or five broad, stone stairs and passed through into that world of books and precision. It was a world that was neatly catalogued and mapped for me.

"I had kind of a fantastic goal at that point: of reading, or at least looking through, all the books in the library. I actually started doing this, going up and down the aisles, like when I was a child. I would literally start with one row and work to the end. I didn't start with anything in particular, with fictions or biographies or anything like that. I remember I mapped it out in my mind. I studied the map on the wall at the library. It was laid out in an upside-down U. Then I just started down at the base and worked around, then up and down, just pulling out the titles as I went along. I read an entire section of mysteries. Then I went to the travel section.

"I started going to the library before I quit the maintenance job that I had taken to relieve the pressure of being a security guard at a high-rise apartment building in downtown Waikiki. I started going to the library for refuge, to seek peace from the tornadoes that were beginning to unravel the corners of my mind.

"I also frequented the museum and art gallery. But I didn't like the cold, the unknowing and unknowledgeable—to me—nature of those places. I enjoyed artworks. But there was a complexity and a distance about art, especially modern art. So I spent most of my time in the library and I took comfort in being surrounded by all that knowledge, so carefully ordered in one place. Just the smell of books, of old books, especially. It's the essence of something orderly.

"At some point I quit working and began to hang around other public buildings of Honolulu as well as the library. I visited the King's Palace and the state legislature buildings, the House and the Senate. I also went into a courtroom and observed part of a trial, a rape trial, involving a man who went into a pizza shop and raped a woman at closing time. I remember the picking of the jury and one woman who didn't really want to be there. The judge ended up picking her for that very reason—that she didn't want to be there. It was cruel, really. The woman was frightened and the judge knew it, but he forced her to be there because, I guess, he smelled her fear, sort of like an animal. That disgusted me, and I was also a little confused by it. But mostly, I found it intriguing.

"Between the library and trips to the public buildings, I also would wander around the parks. I was drinking at the time. I would have some beer at probably about 9 or 10 o'clock in the morning, sometimes going so far as to put it in a brown paper bag and walking around with it. I'd go to this little twenty-four-hour store and open the refrigerator and buy a couple bottles of Budweiser. I was clearly trying to mask my pain by drinking that early in the morning. Nobody who is normal and who has himself together drinks beer in the morning.

"There's no history of alcoholism, or even heavy drinking, on either side of my family. But I was probably psychologically very much addicted to alcohol; probably an alcoholic, although I'm not sure about that. A lot of people drink.

"I also was doing watercolors, some rainbows and some birds. There are amazing rainbows and birds in Hawaii. I gave one of my watercolors, of a solitary rainbow in an empty sky, to an employment agency secretary who was real nice to me and who was trying to help me.

"I was a maniac around the house at that time, which is a whole other subject. But just to give you where my mind was, at that time, I was very lonely. I was extremely isolated. I wasn't talking with anyone because a little slight would send me into a frenzy. I just didn't know how to handle any rebuff or rejection because I was so insular with my life and personality, my feelings and experiences at that point.

"I probably wasn't even real at all, even with my wife, who was the person closest to me at that time, the only person close to me. She wanted to invite guests over, to have a normal social life, to enjoy the barbecue and picnic area of our apartment complex with other young married couples. I didn't want to have anything to do with that. I was very frightened and depressed and anxiety ridden and afraid of people. I hated people. Like John Lennon says in one of his songs, 'you love humanity and you hate people' or something like that. It was crazy. But if you look around you, you'll see that a lot of people are like that.

"Everything was happening and the shaky foundations of my personality were crumbling and it felt like the sky was falling down on me. And then, somehow, there was a spiritual dimension creeping into this.

"There was just a tremendous amount of—there was no esteem. Nothing had meaning or value. There was either manic happiness and joy about something new, or there was tremendous depression and drinking and fighting and anger and isolation and fear about other people.

"I needed to scream, but I had no mouth.

"John Lennon, when he was going through a tremendous time of confusion and depression in the sixties, from what I've read, in his own words, about the song 'Help!' that he wrote: The song was a genuine cry for help. It was his way of getting it out. Fortunately for him, he had the ability to put it out on a record and keep such feelings from poisoning his mind and taking total control of his life.

"That was a kind of preprimal scream therapy for him. But with me, I couldn't mouth the word *help.* I couldn't even scream.

"Listen to some of Lennon's records. Listen to the background of some of the Beatles songs. That screaming in the background, that's John Lennon. Listen to him scream when he's singing about not having his mother, about being abandoned by his mother and his father. The poor guy, his father left the family, then his mother left him to be raised by his aunt and uncle. Then his mother got killed after she came back to him years later.

"Just to think after a person had been through all that he had been through as a child, then to get murdered by somebody like me. . . ."

"I was out of work, but I had paid off the money that I owed, all the debts, the credit card debts that my wife and I had accumulated, the artwork debts that I had put on the Visa card. We had paid them all off, my wife and I working together. And I worked out very intricately that she could work and we could both live in this very nice apartment that we were living in with no problem—except that we would only have $100 extra a month or so. But it was enough once we stopped eating out in any fancy restaurants, renting Lincoln Continentals, and spending getaway weekends on Waikiki Beach at the elegant Moana Hotel—that sort of thing, the episodic spending and pleasure sprees that for some reason I needed to do from time to time. I can see now that those things were telltale signs. . . . I ran up debts renting fancy cars and staying in fancy hotels where people would think that I was somebody—because inside I knew that I was a nobody. 'Captain Nemo'—Captain Nobody, who had nothing, not even a job at that point.

"What had happened to me was that I couldn't work. I couldn't mentally work because of the pressures that were building inside my mind, the fear of being around other people. Not necessarily paranoia, though I did have fits of intense suspicion. I thought other people were talking about me or making fun of me, and maybe they were. I guess what bothered me most was just people. The only public place where I felt comfortable around people was the library.

"Perhaps people in the library were of a different nature. They were intellectual, more so than others. They were quiet people. I remember sitting in the open-air courtyard of the library, in the middle in these wooden chairs, deep-set chairs that you can just kind of sink into that have a little desk attached, a little wooden palette you can lay a book on or where you rest your arms. I remember getting the paper and reading the news and maybe *Time* magazine. It was just a very calm, soothing place for me. It was a place of searching and of hope.

"Even in the midst of depression and mental deterioration, I knew that I had to be doing something. So, in addition to spending long hours at the library, I also was checking out and reading a lot of books and trying to find out, you know, 'What is there for me in this world?'

"At one point, I checked out a series of books on editorial cartooning. I drew a cartoon of a French girl standing on a street corner with a placard draped over her shoulders, front and back—an advertising placard that was just plain and the girl had a little beret on. I sent it to *The New Yorker* magazine because I had seen the little line drawings and they appealed to something in me. They sent it back and they said they needed it in a larger size. But they didn't reject it.

"So, even though I was spending my days at the library and hanging around public places, I also was always trying to do things to get my life on track and make it have meaning. I had been painting and I had been doing watercolors. I remember this one watercolor that was supposed to be an ocean scene that I was painting. I kept messing it up because I kept trying too hard and it turned into a skull. It turned into this skull, this black and red and white mess. I remember it blew out the window. I had put it near the window on the air conditioner to let it dry in the sun and the wind came and blew it out the window and I never saw it again. But I was drawing this skull, from the ocean scene to a skull, which is probably pretty revealing about what was going on in my mind. Things were going on in my mind that I didn't even know about.

"I remember getting a T-shirt, a blue T-shirt, at this stand where you could buy such things and get anything that you wanted printed on them in about an hour. I had something printed on the back that said: I'M UNIQUE. I THINK FOR MYSELF.

"I didn't have that done because I believed that I was unique. I did that because I was angry at people and I was angry at their, what I perceived to be, their phoniness. Angry because I saw that everybody was afraid of being who they were, saying what they thought, and giving out their feelings.

"You see, that's how I was. I was that way, too. But I couldn't accept that. So the counteraction of that, the other spectrum of that—I was living at both ends of the spectrum at once in this mental state. I was never in the middle anywhere, so the counteraction of that, since I was so isolated, was to wear a shirt that said I THINK FOR MYSELF, if that makes any sense at all.

"I remember wearing the shirt and going to Sears to buy a yellow bicycle for my wife. I carried the bicycle out, on my head, out of the store and I remember there were these two women mocking and ridiculing me for this shirt that I had on.

"But I felt good that I had angered those people—that, you know, maybe it would get them to ask themselves, 'Gee, am I thinking for myself? Or am I letting the world tell me how to think?'

"Imagine, just for a second, how I was thinking that my solution resided in the library, my solution to my career. I should have been able to go out under a tree without a book and figure that out on my own. But I was just swept up by everything that was around me, and everything caused within me some extreme reaction. I don't know much about Freud and the ego and the id and all that. But my extreme reaction to the insincerity and the rejection that I found in other people was to wear a T-shirt that said I'M UNIQUE. I THINK FOR MYSELF.

"But it illustrates, in some way, the tremendous pressures and tugs and pulls—the 'Should-bes' and the 'Why-am-I-nots' and the 'Helps' that I never said.

"That was what I was feeling at that time, when I came across the book that ironically, paradoxically, said, 'One Day at a Time.' *John Lennon: One Day at a Time.* And shortly thereafter I began to think about killing John Lennon.

"I was in the library. It was 1980, but I don't recall the month. I wasn't looking for anything specifically about the Beatles or John Lennon. Some time in the course of that library visit—I wasn't centered on any one type of book. I'd bring home anything—novels, biographies, travel—but I had remembered reading *The Catcher in the Rye.* It just came to my mind to see if it was there. So I went to check it out and it wasn't there. And it wasn't there the next week or the next week or the next. So I went into a bookstore and actually bought a copy. And I read it again, for the first time since I was a teenager.

"I started reading *The Catcher in the Rye,* and I couldn't put it down until I got to the end. And I read it again. Then I held it between my hands. I put it against my face, and I inhaled deeply, drinking in the aroma, that sort of faintly antiseptic smell of a new book, through my nostrils and my skin. And I felt: 'Here is a way that I can identify with.' A way to live an honest life, an unphony way of life.

"But remember, my mind is disheveled. It's ripped and torn. There is a tornado in my mind, circling around my brain, bits and pieces crashing into the walls. A debris. Broken things. Cloudy things. Things I can't see, bits and pieces of memories like pieces of torn photographs just blowing across my mind. But at all times, at the forefront, the big, black cloud of the tornado. The hurt—the hurt, the frustration, the lack of esteem. And always, constantly, a loud, spiritual noise, echoing through my being, just ripping apart anything that I would try to build to get myself out of the maelstrom.

"You can't build anything against a tornado. You have to wait until it stops. You have to understand a tornado. You cannot build anything against it. And I think that's a very crucial primal truth of psychology and of people's problems. We want to build something against our tornadoes instead of trying to understand what causes them. That's what I was doing. I was trying to build a shelter against these spiritual winds. But when a tornado strikes any type of shelter, be it brick or wood, it rips it to shreds.

"As the famous parable in the New Testament goes, 'The storm came and the ruin of that house was very great.'

"That's what happened to me. My house was ruined. The storm ripped it up out of its very, very, very thin foundation.

"I have a pretty weak foundation. Perhaps some of that was pre–thought out by God and my life and my experiences. Perhaps that is the way I am designed, for His benefit, to make sure that I don't accomplish much without Him and have to stay close to Him in order to do any good for the world.

"But there I was in this tornado and I believe I found, if not a reason for it, an understanding why it was happening. I believe I found, in the reading of *The Catcher in the Rye,* a small anchor that, even if I was still pulled around, I wasn't pulled around as fast. I was more close to the ground with this anchor.

"*The Catcher in the Rye* gave me a pseudo-identity. I first read the book at about the same age that Holden Caulfield was, about sixteen. I don't believe I identified with it a great deal then, except perhaps the isolation part of it. But when I read it the second time, it was devastating. It represented a much more meaningful experience, a much more heartfelt anchor that, far from bringing me down to reality as I imagined it—it pulled me down and held me to a depth I would never know until later.

"As the extent of my *Catcher* obsession grew, I became actually projected onto the pages as Holden Caulfield. I actually became Holden Caulfield in my own mind, as a way of coping. So that book became for me an imaginary anchor in the midst of a real cyclone.

"The book became a comfort to me and I identified and became more enmeshed in it as the days and weeks passed. I became deeply involved in the book and identified with it so much that I went back to the bookstore and bought two more copies and gave a copy to my wife. I had inscribed in it—kind of as a harbinger of the inscription in the copy that I had with me at the time I killed John Lennon—I had inscribed 'To Gloria from Holden Caulfield.'

"Then, in the second book, the extra one that I had bought for myself in case something happened to the other one, I had written 'From Holden Caulfield to Holden Caulfield.' Of course, I knew that I was Mark David Chapman when I wrote that. But I was acting out in a minor way. I was saying, 'What if this were so?' But it was more than that. I had not totally felt that I was Holden Caulfield when I wrote that.

"But it was like a badge, it was like a pledge, like a statement of 'What if?' A statement of 'Here is my identity, here is what my pain is if it can be reduced to ink and paper. Here is what my pain is! Please help me.' That's what that was. 'Please help me.' I am deeply in trouble if I'm identifying with a sixteen-year-old boy in New York City and here I am a twenty-five-year-old man in Hawaii who is married. And inside this man, the tornado is ripping up everything around him right out of the ground, flinging bits and pieces of himself into his face. Silent cries and screams getting sucked up and going unspoken, unheard.

"So, it was with these things in mind, and these things of the mind, that I was going down an aisle at the Honolulu Public Library, not looking for any book in particular. Perhaps I was in the biography section. And I came across the book *John Lennon: One Day at a Time* by Anthony Fawcett.

"There was John Lennon on the cover. I believe he was flashing a peace sign. He was on Liberty Island, where the Statue of Liberty is. He was right at the base of the Statue of Liberty with his glasses and cap, with a scarf around his neck, having his photograph taken.

"I looked through the book at the pictures of John Lennon on the gabled roof of the Dakota building in New York. Of course I didn't know anything about the Dakota building. I didn't know anything about New York. I didn't even know where John Lennon was. But he was in that book.

"Just as Holden Caulfied had bled through the ink of the *Catcher* and entered my mind, John Lennon entered my mind through that book.

"Those photographs of him on the roof, they entered my mind and they took on a life of their own. And at some point, at the looking of those pictures, I became enraged at him.

"Of course there was jealousy. There was envy. But there was more than that. I didn't murder a man simply because I was envious and jealous of him. I didn't even think 'jealousy' and 'envy' at that time, of course, when I was looking at the book. But I remember standing there in the aisle of the Honolulu Library and burning that book into my brain.

"I remember thinking that there was a successful man who had the world on a chain. And there I was not even a link of that chain. Just a person who had no personality. A walking void who had given a great deal of my time and thoughts and energy into what John Lennon had said and had sung about and had done—and had told all of us to do—in the sixties and early seventies, when I was growing up, when I was first trying to make sense out of a world that was so painful and hurtful and sad. I thought I loved reality and I didn't want the world to be the way it was.

"I was thinking all these things, reliving my childhood, as I devoured page after page of that John Lennon book. And at that moment, something inside me just broke.

"That was when the winds that were swirling across my mind reached a fever pitch and swallowed up the few remaining fragments of decency and free will that I had left. That was when I turned so vile that my own mind vomited me into the pits of hell.

"I remember at that time, not having any thoughts of murder, but being very angered—angered enough to have destroyed the world, if I'd had control over nuclear weapons.

"I checked out the book and brought it home to my wife and pointed out the pictures to her, pictures of him smiling on the roof of the sumptuous Dakota building: the decadent bastard, the phony bastard, who had lied to children, who had used his music to mislead a generation of people who desperately needed to believe in love and a world at war that desperately needed to believe in peace.

"He told us to imagine no possessions, and there he was, with millions of dollars and yachts and farms and country estates, laughing at people like me who had believed the lies and bought the records and built a big part of our lives around his music.

"I remember seeing that he was in New York and I was kind of surprised that he was living in this country. I would think that he would have been living in England like Paul McCartney and George Harrison in their estates.

"But, still, no thoughts of murder.

"I remember being just totally enraged, wiped out by the fact that he had all these things, living off the fat of the land and that I was in such turmoil.

"Even if I had been normal, if I had been totally sane, if I had been doing okay at that time in my life—I probably still would have been a little hurt and felt a little betrayed. But not to the point that I was. I was actually cursing him to my wife, saying what a phony he was. I used the word *phony* because I was at the beginning infancy of *being* The Catcher in the Rye.

"I was . . . I, in context, in my mind, I was still fresh from the book. If you know the *Catcher,* you know the mind-set, or you feel the mind-set of the author, J. D. Salinger—his antiphoniness campaign. I was in that mode when I came across the pictures of Lennon. . . .

"*The Catcher in the Rye* was the stove and the Lennon book was the fire.

"*The Catcher in the Rye* was the mold and this portrait of my childhood hero, the Beatle who had molded many of my own ideals, poured very painfully into it.

"It reeked of phoniness.

"Another thing happened then, a few days later when I was back in the library. I was looking through *The New York Times* or *Honolulu Advertiser* and there was a picture of Lennon in the recording studio. He had long hair. He had a black hat, a straight brim and kind of round. He had his feet propped up on the studio mixing boards and he was looking into the camera and the paper was talking about Lennon coming out again, after he'd been a recluse all these years. Of course the Anthony Fawcett book was probably of the last years of his public life, right up till he became a recluse.

"So we had five years there of no John Lennon, no photographs. And this article was about the taping of his new album, which of course became *Double Fantasy,* and it talked about Lennon's past life, the things he'd been through and done and said. And in Lennon's own quotes, according to this article, he said, himself, that the thing about the bed-ins for peace, the concerts for peace, and the whole promotional packages that he and Yoko had done—he said in his own quote that those things were essentially put-ons, that they were phony, they were fake, and that they were a way of getting publicity. And I remember those were his quotes. He was quoted as saying that. It was not the reporter's own language. And I remember that that was a confirmation for me that Lennon was a phony. That was a tremendous confirmation.

"But still, no thoughts of murder had yet come into my mind.

"The next thing that occurred—that would destroy both our lives—the next thing that occurred was to push me to the point of no return. After it happened, there was no power on earth that would have saved John Lennon's life.

"I checked out some albums of his later music at the library and took them into the audio room with some cheap headphones. I listened to the album *Imagine,* and the song 'God,' which is one of his best songs as far as guttural honesty. Also, of course, the song 'Imagine' and a few other songs that I listened to. Again, this was before the idea of shooting him came to mind.

"But that, the music, was the third thing—after the *Catcher* and the

Lennon book. I would listen to this music and I would get angry at him, for saying that he didn't believe in God, that he just believed in him and Yoko, and that he didn't believe in the Beatles. This was just another thing that angered me, even though this record had been done at least ten years previously.

"I just wanted to scream out loud, 'Who does he think he is, saying these things about God and heaven and the Beatles?' Saying that he doesn't believe in Jesus and things like that. At that point, my mind was going through a total blackness of anger and rage.

"So I brought the Lennon book home, into this *Catcher in the Rye* milieu where my mind-set is Holden Caulfield and antiphoniness. While contemplating this new Lennon, I really delved into the ink of Holden Caulfield. I was swimming in the ink of *The Catcher in the Rye.* And I was blinded by it. The ink had gotten into my eyes and I was just dripping in the blackness of that ink. It would go on to blind my judgment for years to come.

"So, enter Lennon onto this stage of blackness and despair and my striking out at the world for its hypocrisy and its phoniness. Enter Lennon, who to me had been antiestablishment and counterculture and a hero. To find him in the coats of the rich on the roof of a million-dollar, a multimillion-dollar apartment complex was just too much, at that point in my life, for a disintegrating personality to bear.

"So there I was in the persona of Holden Caulfield, and I remember the exact moment that I thought about killing Mr. Lennon."

"I was sitting cross-legged on the carpet of the apartment, a nice apartment that my wife and I had at Kukui Plaza. We lived near downtown Honolulu. I was sitting there staring out the window. There was a coffee table, a cherry wood coffee table to my right, and a sofa.

"*The Catcher in the Rye* was prominent in my mind.

"Gloria had a series of Beatles albums in the apartment. As I've always done, I began leafing through album covers, reading the liner notes, looking at the pictures. Possibly in my childhood, as many people do in their teens, I had identified with the heroes and the legends and myths that surround pop culture and popular music.

"I remember opening up the *Sgt. Pepper* album and seeing that bright yellow photograph of all four of the Beatles in their fluorescent Day-Glo army uniforms. There's Lennon with his glasses and his little moustache.

"As soon as I saw his picture on that album, I remember thinking—I thought . . . I knew—that I was going to kill him.

"The Lennon book that I had checked out, which I kept way overdue, was on the coffee table. And what came together then was the juxtaposition of the Lennon that was and the Lennon that I perceived to be still living in the Dakota.

"I remember saying in my mind: 'What if I killed him?' I thought of the repercussions that would occur around the world. I felt, not in an ego way, or a prideful way at all, but I felt that perhaps my identity would be found in the killing of John Lennon. And there was a certain peace about that.

"It just was a 'What if?' thought. Like, 'Wouldn't it be something if I killed John Lennon?' It wasn't a decision that definitely I was going to do it and tomorrow going to go get the gun and all this. It was like a—a question I'd posed myself.

"But it was as though a black hand had reached out of the winds of that tornado in my mind and handed me a black book. And I took the book and I said, 'What if I open it?'

"And I began to think about what would happen if I did open it. And I thought about jail, about spending the rest of my life in prison. And it was an actual comfort to me, as odd as that sounds.

"I didn't know at that time that New York did not have the death penalty. For all I knew they could have had the electric chair. I didn't even question that. But I had posed the 'What if?' And I saw, sharp as a razor's edge, the contrast of what I perceived to be the phoniness of Lennon in the Fawcett book versus the Lennon that I felt I had known intimately, the Lennon of my childhood, the Lennon that I had practically worshipped as a Beatle.

"Lennon as a Beatle. Lennon as a phony. Just seeing these terrible inconsistencies, mirroring my own inconsistencies and my own pain and my own guilt at not having accomplished anything.

"The juxtaposition of the old and the new. This trinity—the Catcher, the new Lennon, the old Lennon—it was just kind of pointing out at me, like an arrow, like the sharpened tip of a triangle, pointing at me. And it was almost like I was handed something—that here was a solution: *Kill John Lennon.*

"And then these images came to my mind, like there was a door. A big, black, thick iron door with a ring on it set into the earth. And I lifted it up, this is in the middle of the tornado, and I descended a dark stone stairway and closed that door on top of myself. And I did indeed find shelter—the shelter that was made of the bottom of the ground. A pit is the only shelter you can have from a tornado. You cannot build your own. It has to be a pit. And I climbed down into that pit, or pictured myself climbing down into that pit. I pictured myself in the shelter of that pit and there was my solution.

"It's what Holden had envisioned and fantasized about, killing the big fat guy in the hotel: the pimp, the phony. I took it a step further than Holden. I got a gun.

"That was my shelter, my handle on things. That was how I would cope.

And every day that went by, my thought about killing Lennon became stronger and stronger until at some point that I don't remember I decided to actually do it. I actually did open that pit door on the bottom of the ground—open it, go down into it, and shut out the tornado. I entered a whole new realm then of living. It was just as desperate, but the winds stopped howling. It didn't hurt anymore. There was a goal, a substance to be grabbed onto then.

"I was to find that there was actually no way out of that iron pit door ever again. I had to go deeper, I had to go through chamber after chamber that finally ended up here at Attica.

"But the moment that I made that decision and climbed down into that pit and closed the door over me—the tornado stopped.

"I had found my identity. But I had lost my life."

CHAPTER TWENTY

THE LAST BOARD MEETING

For it might end, you know, in my going out altogether,
like a candle. I wonder what I should be like then?

—LEWIS CARROLL, *ALICE'S ADVENTURES IN WONDERLAND*

After his tornado had found a target for its final act of violence, Mark David Chapman found that his noisy and vexatious mind suddenly had become a place of haunting and unfamiliar quiet. Turning to *The Catcher in the Rye* for instruction and inspiration, he would sit for hours listening to the albums of John Lennon and the Beatles on the new stereo he had bought his wife. He had destroyed her old record player in a fit of rage several weeks earlier. Gloria Chapman had watched in horror as her wildly laughing husband, in frustration over his inability to repair a minor problem in the mechanism, brought a hammer crashing down again and again onto the turntable. It had been one of the few possessions she had brought into their marriage, just sixteen months before, that he hadn't sold, destroyed, or thrown away. It had been her last avenue of temporary escape from her husband's tyranny.

On this night, the 23rd of October, 1980, Chapman was celebrating a quiet victory over his tornado and the new life he was secretly planning for himself. Earlier that afternoon, he had stripped off the humiliating blue uniform with the embroidered white and red name tag, MARK. He had signed out for the last time from his maintenance job at the luxurious apartment complex at 444 Nahua Street in downtown Honolulu. When he signed out, however, it wasn't as Mark Chapman or even as Holden Caulfield. It was as John Lennon. He had also pasted Lennon's name over the tag on his uniform.

"A new identity," he thought to himself. "Not as John Lennon, but as . . . somebody."

Chapman wouldn't learn until several years later that on the same date, October 23, 1980, Lennon had also proclaimed a new identity of sorts. A few hours earlier in New York City, Lennon had officially released a new song, "(Just Like) Starting Over," that would be included on his new record album, *Double Fantasy,* scheduled for release the following month. After a reclusive five years holed up on the top floor of the Dakota building, the album was to symbolize Lennon's return to life.

As he sat listening to the voice of Lennon on the stereo, Chapman contemplated the vaporous creatures that seemed to be moving about inside him. He realized with an unaccustomed detachment that his mind continued to spin, but it wasn't the same unpleasant spin and tumble of the tornadoes to which he had become accustomed. He found this new motion an altogether pleasant sensation, like the gentle rocking of a ship on a calm sea, or the rhythmic spin and lift of a merry-go-round. For the first time in years, he found that all the thoughts in his mind were synchronized, spinning in one direction. Like jackals drawn to the smell of a bleeding animal, all of Mark David Chapman's thoughts moved toward an image of a bespectacled and leering John Lennon that seemed to flicker randomly into view on an electronic screen inside his head.

Believing himself to be once again in control of his thoughts and feelings, Chapman began moving with a rare sense of self-confidence among the tangle of misdirected rage and confusion that cluttered his head. He gathered together at last the bitter taproots of fury into the center of his soul. He pondered his rage like a hard-won treasure that he had decided to offer to the only force in the universe he believed powerful enough to see him through the evil act he had begun to plot. Slowly, ritualistically, he began removing his clothes. At last he sat before the record player, naked except for a pair of headphones clamped across his skull.

"Hear me, Satan," he prayed softly, bowing his head. "Accept these pearls of my evil and my rage. Accept these things from deep within me. In return, I ask only that you . . ."

He paused, lifting the headphones momentarily from his head to assure himself that his wife was still asleep behind the closed door in the next room. A chill passed through his body.

"I ask only that you give me the power," he continued, rocking gently in time to the Lennon song, "Lucy in the Sky with Diamonds," that had just begun to trickle into the headphones.

". . . The power to kill John Lennon. Give me the power of darkness. Give me the power of death. Let me be a somebody for once in my life. Give me the life of John Lennon."

Caught up in the music, Chapman's thoughts strayed from the diabolical trance. He began to realize that his mission would require a great deal more than the hardness of heart that he was seeking to purchase from Satan. It would require an elaborate and detailed plan. It would require a high degree of discipline, organization, and attention to detail—qualities that he had been unable to sustain against the tornadoes that had danced across his disintegrating mind.

He would need his Little People. The knowledge and strategic counsel of the Little People would help him to analyze the logistical problems that would be involved in carrying out an act as complex as premeditated murder.

The evening air settled upon his naked skin and Chapman wrapped his arms around himself. His large body began to tremble slightly. Ignoring the sudden chill, he forced his mind to a peak of clarity and began drawing up a mental checklist of the items he would need for his death kit.

He realized he had to get a gun and ammunition. He had to establish a plausible reason for traveling to New York City, to convince his wife and his mother that the mysterious and expensive trip was a venture he needed to undertake. He had to get money to finance the trip and he would need to be able to find his way around the labyrinth of the metropolis.

Recalling that he had visited the city many years ago, he thought warmly of his mother. When his grades had dropped, Diane Chapman had intervened at the last minute to persuade his seventh-grade teacher to allow him to go on the class trip to New York. The only thing he remembered from the brief sight-seeing tour was a long train ride to and from Georgia and the way everyone had laughed when another student had vomited in fear at the prospect of riding an elevator to the top of the Empire State Building. Aside from that distant memory, his only knowledge of the city where John Lennon lived had come from *The Catcher in the Rye.* The novel had been written before he was born, but Chapman believed that he had come to know the essence of New York from the book. He was certain that he would be able to find his way around the area of Central Park where Lennon lived; the part of New York where the ducks lived and where a melodious carousel carried laughing children; the place that his fictional hero, Holden Caulfield, had so vividly and painfully described for him. Summoning the spirit of Holden, he grew excited at the thought of the passions that the name Mark David Chapman would inspire around the world after his encounter with John Lennon. He thought of his father and all the phony friends who had let him down. He smiled.

Concentrating as hard as he could, Chapman tensed his body. Grinding his teeth, he moved himself back in time, into the relative purity of a childhood rage. He breathed deeply and rapidly, bathing himself in the flames of an imaginary fire, and beads of sweat began to appear across his forehead. Finally, he was there.

The quizzical face of Mark David Chapman loomed into view on an electronic screen in a large room. Peering from the screen into the boardroom, he saw that his Little People were gathered in anticipation of his arrival. Robert, the chief of staff, dressed immaculately in a dove-gray three-piece suit and shoes of soft black Italian leather, gazed somberly from a large plate-glass window. Outside the window, a large bird flew in small circles below the bruised clouds of a leaden sky.

The other members of the board were seated around a large mahogany table: the minister of finance, the defense minister, the interior minister, minister of personal relations, cultural attaché, health minister, attorney general, and a retinue of high-level aides. They sat in a circle before charts, maps, and reams of paperwork. Chapman realized in a moment of anxiety that they had been expecting him.

"They know," he thought, trying to look into the eyes of each of his ministers. As the Little People met his gaze and acknowledged his presence, however, he decided that they didn't know, that his initial suspicion was just another dimension of his paranoia.

President Chapman tingled with excitement as he pondered the magnitude of the secret he was about to unveil.

At last turning from the window and observing his president's curiously smiling face on the screen, the chief of staff broke off his contemplation of the bird and clouds. He stepped purposefully across the boardroom and took a seat at the head of the table. Clearing his throat, he called the meeting to order.

At Chapman's request, the board dispensed with a reading of minutes of the previous meeting, a routine discussion involving personal finances and a complex matter involving the purchase and resale by Chapman of signed copies of artworks by Dali and Rockwell. Chapman was glad that he had made the decision to keep the money he had borrowed from his father-in-law for the purchase of the art pieces. He would need it for the trip to New York. His wife would understand, he was sure. Sooner or later, Gloria Chapman always understood that it was necessary for her husband to have his way. It was in the Bible and he had pointed it out to her: woman had been created from man. It was her duty to submit in all matters to the will of her husband.

Hesitantly, Chapman began addressing the board. He began by saying that he was becoming concerned about his personal security. Because of such concerns, he said he had decided to buy a gun. The defense minister glanced briefly up at him and made a note on a yellow pad.

Addressing his finance minister, Chapman said his calculations revealed that his current savings would allow him to pay between $100 and $200 for the weapon, probably a .38 caliber handgun. After a brief pause, he added obliquely that he also would need about $500 for air fare for a proposed trip to New York City. The finance minister began punching numbers into a calculator. Chapman said he also would need an estimated $1,500 to $2,000 for hotels, entertainment, and "just in case."

He explained that he would need the money to effect a major new long-term plan within the next week. The finance and defense ministers exchanged wary looks across the table. The board chairman cleared his throat.

"If the president please," the chairman said deferentially, "the board would be grateful to learn more details of a plan that requires diversion of such large amounts of capital on such fleeting notice."

Chapman nodded his head and reflected for a moment before answering. He decided to be blunt.

"It's just because I've decided to be somebody," he replied. "I've decided that I can't go on being a nobody. Because I am rotting away on the inside. Because I'm dying."

After a brief pause, the Little People looked at him with alarm and expectation. He continued.

"According to my most recent plan, I've decided that I must leave these beautiful islands and go to New York. My identity lies in New York City and that is where I must go."

The Little People looked at each other quizzically.

"Someone from my childhood has caused me great pain," he tried to explain. "Someone you all will recall from our earliest times together, from our childhood—our innocent days when I used to play you the Beatles songs."

He explained to the Little People that he had become very upset after finding a book that pictured John Lennon and Yoko Ono living in a sumptuous New York apartment overlooking Central Park. After studying the book, he said he had been astonished to learn that the ex-Beatle had been living in New York City for nearly ten years.

"I thought he lived in England, in a castle or something like that, like the other Beatles," Chapman said. "But instead he lives in an apartment, a very expensive and elegant apartment, in New York City. All that stuff about peace and love that he sang about, it was all phony. He's just a rich bastard like the rest of the phony rich bastards that run the world."

Chapman spoke of the rage he had felt while leafing through the book. He said he had been betrayed by a childhood hero who had misled him, inspiring him with false idealism, in his youth.

"I've carried those ideals around all my life, and they've just crippled me," he said. "I believed the Beatles. I believed John Lennon. But they were just saying all that stuff. It didn't mean anything. It was all a big hoax, but I believed it."

He began crying.

"It's ruined my life," he said. "It's made me a nobody. John Lennon has ruined my life."

The boardroom was silent and Chapman's tear-streaked face had almost faded from the screen. Slowly, he began to speak again.

"I've decided that John Lennon has to be stopped," he said. "It's clear from this book that he is a phony who was never what he pretended to be. John Lennon is not what he told us he was long ago. Make no mistake. John Lennon has had a lot to do with what I have become, and probably what a lot of people like me have become as well.

"I have decided that I must kill John Lennon."

None of his ministers spoke. None moved.

"I've arrived at this decision after much thought," Chapman continued. "It will be a difficult task and I need your help."

After several moments, a murmur of voices began to rise from the table. Several of the little men exchanged rueful glances. Chapman was silent as the board members talked quietly, barely above a whisper, among themselves. After several minutes of debate, his chief of staff stood. Trying to conceal his fear, the little man looked up. He tried to see what was going on in other parts of the complex and fragmented mind that stretched behind the hard blue eyes on the electronic screen.

"We have unanimously agreed that this is a very foolish, a very nonproductive decision that you have made," the little man said, shaking his head. "We have agreed that we cannot be part of an act that will only cause you further difficulties. If you carry out this plan, you will cause great pain and grief. Not only for yourself but for very, very many people. Please, think of your wife. Please, Mr. President. Think of your mother. Think of yourself."

"I've thought of my wife," he responded. "I've thought of my mother.

"I also have thought of my pathetic father and all of my phony friends.

"And, without all of you without all of you who exist here only in my mind—I have no self."

The Little People trembled, recalling when, in childhood, they had been scapegoats for the anger and fear caused by his parents. They were surprised when he began to speak to them softly, with understanding.

"I respect your decision," he said. "I just want to thank you for the help that you have given me in the past. I owe you a great deal. Perhaps I owe you my life."

One by one, beginning with his defense minister, the Little People rose from their seats and walked from the secret chamber inside the mysterious mind of Mark David Chapman. Alone in his dangerous world at last, abandoned even by the endlessly forgiving Little People whom he had created within himself, the face of Mark David Chapman faded from the screen.

CHAPTER TWENTY-ONE

ANYONE COULD SHOOT ANYONE

If his inmost heart could have been laid open,
there would have been discovered that dream
of undying fame; which, dream as it is,
is more powerful than a thousand realities.

NATHANIEL HAWTHORNE, *FANSHAWE*

Gloria Chapman awoke from a razor's edge of sleep to muffled snaps of very loud music chattering against very small speakers. Her body convulsed as she heard again the rasp of the voice that had jarred her awake. Sounding as though it should somehow be familiar, the voice was nevertheless alien and guttural.

Erupting in phlegmy strands from a throat swollen and bleeding into itself, the voice seemed to arrange itself into a zombielike, disembodied life of its own as it intoned above the high-pitched scrape and wail of an old Beatles tune rattling against cheap headphones.

"I want you," the voice bellowed.

Gloria tried to leave her bed, but she was afraid. She feared she might find that the voice wasn't coming from her husband—or that it was. Pressing her hands against her ears, the frightened woman curled her sweat-chilled body into a ball in the center of the bed where she had slept mostly alone for the past twelve of sixteen months she had been married to Mark David Chapman. Scarcely able to control arms and legs that seemed to dance akimbo with a fear all their own, Gloria reached for a thin blanket that offered little comfort against gooseflesh that spread in frigid waves across her body.

"Mark!" she cried, unable to force her voice above a whisper. "Oh, Mark, please. Oh, please. You don't know. Oh, Mark. I . . ."

"Must die!" the voice bellowed from the next room. "The phony bastard must die."

The voice seemed to be coming from two people at once—one of them trying to scream and the other trying to call back the awful words. It shifted abruptly into a dull, staccato chant:

"The phony must die, says the Catcher in the Rye.

"The phony must die, says the Catcher in the Rye.

"The Catcher in the Rye is coming for you.

"Don't believe in John Lennon.

"Imagine John Lennon is dead, oh yeah, yeah, yeah.

"Imagine that it's over."

The music stopped and the voice was silent for several minutes, before it began muttering quietly to itself.

"The fool," Mark Chapman said. "The goddamn phony fool. He doesn't even realize that soon he's going to be dead.

"Just imagine that."

In his cell at Attica prison, Chapman has relived again and again the nightmare into which he plunged his wife during the months before he abandoned her in his frenzy to strike down Lennon.

"It was hideous," he confessed. "I would sit up all night and play Beatles records, speeding them up, slowing them down, interjecting my own words. I would strip naked, gritting my teeth and summoning the devil and wild things into my mind.

"I was sending out telegrams to Satan: 'Give me the opportunity to kill John Lennon.' "

Even without the help of his Little People, Chapman was sufficiently obsessed to put his elaborate plan into effect.

"People may ask, how could somebody going through a tornado of mental illness make all the elaborate plans that I made?

"It's because crazy people aren't all Jack Nicholsons. The person next to you, the person you live with, can be out of their mind. And if they're like I was, you'll never know it unless they want you to or unless you're very, very close to them and you've known them for many, many years. My mother *sensed* something was wrong with me when she knew I was going to go to New York. But she had no idea how far gone I was at that time."

As his plan unfolded, Chapman had doubts along the way. Each doubt, it seemed, was allayed by a series of random events that he interpreted as "synchronicities."

His resolve got an unexpected boost late one evening when he happened to tune in *Paul's Case,* a public television rendition of a classic American short story by Willa Cather.

Mark identified at once with Paul, a dreamy, sensitive, and rebellious youth on the brink of a great tragedy. Like him, Paul was a misunderstood young man of artistic sensibilities—a man with "a morbid desire for cool things and soft lights and fresh flowers."

Like Mark, Paul also was a sociopath who was planning to abscond with several thousand dollars that didn't belong to him for a final, first-class fling that would end in death in New York City. Paul had taken a suite at the exclusive Waldorf-Astoria Hotel in New York.

"Living it up means identity," Chapman explained. "Identity means security, warmth, and all those human things.

"Paul wasn't a thief, but he had to have a taste of that side of life. I wasn't a murderer, but I had to have an identity."

Reinforced by the synchronicity of uncanny parallels between himself and Paul, Chapman phoned the Waldorf in New York City to inquire about reservations. Told that no suites were available, he continued calling the famous luxury hotel for several days. Finally, he secured a small room for two nights at the end of October.

"When I had reserved my room at the Waldorf, I continued planning, like I had planned my trip to Hawaii. I knew where all the streets were, even though I had no maps of New York City until I got there. From reading *The Catcher in the Rye* and the Anthony Fawcett book about John Lennon, I knew in my mind where everything was that I needed to find."

Chapman fancied himself, like Paul, a connoisseur of the theater. Gloria recalled that her husband "often said that he could have been an actor, except for his looks. . . . He says that ever since he was a kid he knew he was meant for greatness, that he was destined to be someone big."

After making his travel and hotel arrangements in New York, he decided to get tickets to one or more of the acclaimed plays, including *The Elephant Man* being performed on Broadway at the time by John Lennon's friend David Bowie.

Virtually overnight, Chapman's wife observed, his mood improved. Although he had refused for months to visit her parents, he suggested that she invite them for dinner so he could thank his father-in-law for loaning him the $5,000. He had put the money into his own bank account after selling the Rockwell print. He noted the irony that the "Triple Self-Portrait" money would ultimately be spent to buy him a new identity.

On October 9, 1980—John Lennon's fortieth birthday—Chapman had stayed home from work. He had called in sick and taken his wife out for a Pearl Harbor cruise and dinner to celebrate the resale of "Triple Self-Portrait" to a California businessman.

During the October 9 dinner, Gloria recalls that her husband told her for the first time he was "seriously thinking about maybe going to London." He said nothing about John Lennon. It wasn't until two months later that she would check her diary and find that it had been Lennon's birthday when her husband first mentioned to her that he was planning to go away.

During a dinner with Gloria's parents on October 11, Chapman informed his wife and her parents, to the family's consternation, that he was thinking about taking Gloria away to live in England as early as the next year.

After Gloria spent several days worrying that she was going to have to move to a foreign country against her will, Chapman told her that he had changed his mind. He also told her on October 17 that "sometimes he gets so frustrated and bottled up that he just wants to blow somebody's head off."

The next day, he returned from the library with several books about England—and a book titled *John Lennon: One Day at a Time.*

"He would read a little of it and get angry," Gloria recalled, "saying Lennon was a 'bastard' . . . for preaching peace and love and having millions."

He informed his wife in unmistakable terms that the book was proof that John Lennon was "a phony." Gloria had paid little attention at the time. Her husband was often upset and she had endured far more violent outbursts from him in the past. The word *phony* was the way he commonly referred to people he didn't like.

After perusing the books on England, he had told his wife that he had decided they would definitely not move there. It would be too hard to get a visa that would enable them to find jobs, he explained.

Instead, he said, he would be going to New York City. Alone.

Several days earlier, Gloria recalls that her husband had purchased two copies of *The Catcher in the Rye.* He kept one copy for himself and gave the other one—which he signed "Holden Caulfield"—to her. He was pleased when Gloria immediately began reading the book. He was elated when she told him that the character Holden Caulfield reminded her of him "in the way his mind worked." Chapman had told his wife often in the past that she should read the book to help her better understand him.

Soon after Gloria started reading *The Catcher in the Rye,* Mark told her he was thinking about changing his name to Holden Caulfield. He seemed perplexed when she asked if she would then become "Mrs. Holden Caulfield."

On October 27, when his wife went to work, Chapman went shopping. He needed to pick up some supplies for his upcoming trip to New York City. His first stop was at J & S Enterprises, a weapons emporium near the Honolulu Police Department.

After explaining to a salesman named Robin Ono that he was a security guard and that he was looking for a gun for personal protection, he inspected several weapons that the salesman suggested would meet his needs.

"I walked along a long glass case looking at all the guns and I asked the salesman—Mr. Ono, ironically—which would be a good handgun for protection in my home.

"He said, 'Well, if you get a .22 and a burglar comes in, he's just going to laugh at you. But if you have a .38, nobody's going to laugh at you. Just one shot with a .38 and you're going to bring him down.'

"So, I looked at a Smith & Wesson snub-nosed revolver. It was lightweight, the kind of weapon I had carried on the job with Protective Services when I left Covenant College and worked with Dana Reeves as a security guard at De Kalb General Hospital. I knew a little bit about guns, but I was not a gun buff. The first gun I owned was a Ruger Blackhawk long barrel .38 that I bought for protection in a rough neighborhood where I lived for a while in Decatur. The next one was also a .38—that was for my security guard job.

"Then this fellow named Ono ended up selling me my third gun, the one I bought for killing purposes, for one hundred sixty-nine dollars."

While the gun was being fitted with specialized grips, Chapman walked a block to the police station where he filled out an application for a gun permit.

"I had to fill out a form where they ask if you were ever hospitalized for mental illness," Chapman recalled. "I answered no. If they had a computer check, they could have seen that I was lying on the permit application and perhaps delayed a weapon getting into my hands. But it would only have been a delay.

"My desire to kill John Lennon at that point was so strong, there was no law that could have kept me from getting my hands on a gun. I would have found one sooner or later.

"But anyway, I bought the gun without anyone asking any questions and hid it in a bedstand drawer my wife never opened. I never showed it to her."

On October 28, the day after he had secured his gun and permit, Chapman asked his mother to meet him for lunch.

Mark and Diane Chapman had a pleasant lunch, laughing and talking about their unusual family and about how much better they believed their lives had become since moving to Hawaii. Mark gave his mother a picture he had painted of an apple tree. She promised to frame it and put it on her wall.

Before the lunch ended, he explained to her that he was going to New York City. He said he needed to try to clear his mind and get a fresh start in life.

"She looked at me and she said, 'You aren't going to do anything funny there in New York, are you?'

"I said, 'No, Mom. Nothing at all.' "

The next day, October 29, at 3:30 P.M., Chapman boarded a plane with a suitcase containing a few personal items and most of the $5,000 he had borrowed from his father-in-law for his abortive investments in the art world. He told his wife he felt guilty about taking the money, but explained that he needed it "as insurance, in case something unexpected happens."

His wife thought it odd that, although he had returned the books about England to the library the day before, he was taking the John Lennon book with him to New York. There was so much that was odd about her husband, however, that she had virtually stopped questioning anything he said or did. She also thought it strange that, despite the pain her husband had put her through, she had never thought of leaving him. Vaguely, she recalled something that he had said to her the night before, when he had believed her to be asleep. She had half awakened when he had tiptoed into the room and rummaged for several seconds through a drawer in the bedstand.

After closing the drawer, he had started to leave the room. Turning slowly back around, he returned and stood beside the bed, gazing down at Gloria in the soft light that filtered through the slightly opened bedroom door. Although she had been half awake, Gloria hadn't opened her eyes. He believed her to be sound asleep.

"He said that he loved me very much, more than anyone else and there is no one else, and even though sometimes he may do things which don't make it seem like he does, he always loves me," Gloria recalled.

Unsure whether she was dreaming, Gloria didn't want to open her eyes. If her husband was speaking to her so gently in a dream, she didn't want to wake up. As she escaped back into the darkness of sleep, Chapman lightly stroked his wife's hair with his fingertips and said something else to her before leaving the bedside: "How can I do this to you?"

With the brand-new, unfired .38 caliber Charter Arms Special stored safely in the belly of the plane, Chapman's spirits picked up briefly with the exhilarating sensation of flight. He hadn't purchased ammunition for the gun, reasoning that punishment would be less severe if he were arrested for possession of a weapon without ammunition. He had phoned the airlines to inquire about laws and interstate travel regulations governing the transport of firearms. He had learned that, even though he had a legal permit, it was illegal to bring a handgun into New York City. To avoid unnecessary risks, he had decided to forego the purchase of ammunition until he got to New York.

Chapman had bought a new suit and topcoat for the trip. His wife had told him before he left that she couldn't believe the difference the clothing made in his appearance. After the plane landed in New York City, Chapman was approached by a similarly well-dressed man and woman who asked if he would like to share the expense of a limousine to the Waldorf. He refused, fearing that the man would ask personal questions he didn't want to answer about himself and his reasons for being in New York.

As he rode in a taxi through the teeming streets, he began to feel insecure, intimidated by masses of people and canyons of skyscrapers that leaped from acres of unbroken concrete.

"There's a smell in New York," he thought. "It's a scary smell and cold smell and I'm frightened. I'm frightened of someone attacking me. I'm frightened of someone finding out my secret."

At the Waldorf, Chapman registered for the two nights for which he had made reservations. Dismissing a bellhop, he carried his own bags to a small room. Observing that the room wasn't quite ready to be occupied, he left the hotel and headed instinctively in the direction of nearby Central Park. Fearful of entering the park, he approached a police officer and asked if it was safe to walk there. The officer told him he would be safe in the park during the day, but advised against walking there at night.

The officer stared blankly at Chapman when he asked about the ducks in Central Park.

"Do you know where the ducks go in winter?" he asked.

The officer walked away before Mark could explain about *The Catcher in the Rye.*

Chapman didn't seek out the Dakota, on the opposite side of Central Park from his hotel, during his first day in the city. He walked several miles around the park and through uptown Manhattan, so that his appetite was whetted for a good meal when he returned to the Waldorf. He dined that evening on filet mignon, Heineken beer, and chocolate mousse. He recalls that he slept very well his first night in the city.

Gloria noted on her calendar that her husband called her four times from New York City between October 30 and November 4. Battling a winter virus and loneliness, she told him each time that she was feeling very bad. He became angry each time she asked when he was coming home. During the phone calls, Chapman boasted that he had sat in front-row seats and seen three plays, including *The Elephant Man* and plays starring George C. Scott and other famous celebrity actors he had seen in the movies and on TV. He didn't tell her what he was thinking as he watched the demigods of his imagination walk before him as flesh-and-blood human beings on the live stage: How easy it would be to shoot them.

Neither did he tell his wife that he had gone on two occasions to the theater with women he had met while visiting the Statue of Liberty and

Central Park. He had been disappointed when, after taking the women to dinner, to the theater, on horse-drawn carriage rides through Central Park, and to the top of the Empire State Building, they had left without giving him their addresses or phone numbers. He had almost told one of the women, an English girl who said she worked as a nanny for rich people on Long Island, more than he wanted to reveal about himself.

"Something is going to be happening soon," he had told the girl over dinner. "You're going to hear about me."

"Oh?" the girl inquired. "Are you famous or something?"

Chapman brushed aside the inquiry the way he believed a celebrity might modestly respond to such a question.

"Oh no," he said. "No, I'm not famous."

Then, his sense of drama unable to leave the moment alone, he continued: "I just want you to be aware that something's going to be happening."

Initially, Chapman had been stung by the women's rejections after he had spent so much money on them. He found comfort in recalling the humiliations that his alter ego Holden Caulfield had gone through and the money Holden had spent trying to find a girl in New York. The cruel pain of rejection, he decided, was another synchronicity linking him to Holden.

He had thought a lot about Holden and *Catcher* synchronicities since his arrival in New York. As he wandered during the day through Central Park, sometimes sitting on benches outside the famous carousel and reading a hardcover book he had found about the history of the Dakota building, it appeared increasingly certain that his destiny was to become The Catcher in the Rye of his generation.

When he spoke on the phone to his wife from New York, Chapman was careful to avoid any mention of the Dakota building. He had visited the building on his second day in the city—and every day since. At first the building had frightened him. As he had sat on a park bench and studied the brown and gray tones of the austere, soot-stained building from the edge of Central Park, he thought of his childhood heroine Dorothy and her friends approaching the castles of Oz. Feeling more excitement than fear, he approached the building entrance and introduced himself as a Hawaiian tourist to the doorman, a Cuban refugee named Jose. Before the end of Chapman's first week in New York City, he had become friendly with Jose and with another doorman, a young Dakota employee who had talked with Chapman about rock 'n' roll and confided to him that his cousin was a rock celebrity, Eddie Money.

Chapman was forced to hide his frustrations when none of the doormen would give a straight answer to his questions about John Lennon. No one would tell him for sure whether the ex-Beatle was in residence at the Dakota.

"Mr. Lennon may be traveling" is all the doormen would tell him.

Gloria Chapman was surprised when her husband called her at work on November 4 to tell her that he had decided to fly to Georgia. He said he wanted to go there to see his old friend, Dana Reeves, and to look up other childhood acquaintances. Since his first call to her in Hawaii, Chapman had informed his wife that he had moved from the Waldorf-Astoria to the Vanderbilt YMCA and then to the Sheraton Centre near Broadway. On November 4, he said he was calling from a hotel called The Olcott. He didn't tell his wife that The Olcott, at 27 West 72nd Street, was less than half a city block from the Dakota. Nor did he tell Gloria the real reason he had decided to go to Georgia: to get .38 caliber bullets for his gun.

Earlier in the day, after checking into The Olcott, Chapman had decided that it was time to enter the second phase of his deadly plan. He had carefully positioned himself in proximity to his target and, despite what the doormen were telling him, he sensed that John Lennon was inside the Dakota. He recalled reading a news report that the musician was working on a new album and he reasoned that, unless the album was finished, Lennon would be in New York, close to the Hit Factory and the Record Plant recording studios where he worked. Chapman believed it was just a matter of time before his path and Lennon's would cross. When that happened, he wanted to be ready.

Consulting the Yellow Pages of the Manhattan phone book in his hotel room, he dialed the number of a gun dealer. He told the dealer he had a license to carry a gun and inquired about the price of ammunition for a .38 caliber pistol.

The voice on the phone laughed gruffly back at him. "You're not from around here, are you, buddy?"

"Well," Chapman stammered. "I . . ."

"You're not gonna find no .38 caliber bullets in New York City unless you're licensed and bonded. What are you, a cop from some place out of town?"

"Well, no but I . . ."

"Sorry buddy, but there ain't no point for us wastin' each other's time. You ain't gonna find no ammunition—unless you get it illegally—any place in New York City. You certainly ain't gonna get none from me."

Overcoming a momentary panic and rage after the abrupt conversation with the gun dealer, Chapman briefly pondered his alternatives. Moments later, he dialed Delta Airlines and made first-class reservations to and from Atlanta on the first available flight. Then he called his friend Dana Reeves, a sheriff's deputy in Henry County, Georgia.

Reeves was on duty in his patrol car when the dispatcher informed him over the radio that his friend Mark Chapman had called. Chapman wanted Reeves to call him back at a phone number in New York City. Reeves stopped at the first phone booth and returned the call. Chapman explained briefly that he was in New York "sort of for a vacation" and to take in a few Broadway plays. He said he wanted to come to Georgia for a few days and asked if his old friend would be able to pick him up the next day, November 5, at the Atlanta airport.

With the return to his native Georgia, Chapman felt for a few days as though he had recaptured some of the better moments from his later teenage years. He stayed at Reeves's apartment and the two old companions cruised the backroads of rural Henry County and the suburban Decatur area where they had grown up. Just as they had done nearly a decade before, Mark and Dana talked about religion and about the troubles of the violent and immoral world around them. Stopping at roadside diners and drive-ins, they ate hamburgers and drank sodas and reminisced about former friends.

Although he was married, Chapman said he still thought often about his first love, Lynn Watson, and carried a great pang of longing for her. He told Reeves that his wife was a wonderful woman, but that their marriage had been filled with "ups and downs." He said he had grown weary of Hawaii, where he believed people viewed him as an "outsider." He confided that he was thinking about moving back to Georgia if he could get out of his marriage.

Reeves agreed to take Chapman to see Madison Short, his high school chorus teacher at Columbia High School, and to meet with his former girlfriend, Lynn. Chapman was disappointed at the subdued welcome with which his former teacher acknowledged his return. It wasn't the way that Mr. Antolini had remembered and welcomed Holden to his home in *The Catcher in the Rye.*

Chapman's pride was further diminished after he called his old girlfriend to arrange a meeting. When Lynn agreed to meet him on the evening of November 6, Chapman prepared for the anticipated rendezvous by getting her an expensive brown teddy bear and roses. In Dana's pickup truck, the two men drove to the prearranged meeting site and waited for more than an hour. Reeves recalled that Chapman was embittered over the rejection. When the two men went driving later that night, Chapman angrily threw the teddy bear and roses in a ditch on the side of the road.

The following morning, Chapman asked his friend if he would bring his guns and go with him into the woods for some target practice. Reeves agreed and brought along his .22 caliber and .38 caliber pistols. Chapman wedged a quarter into a tree and stepped back several paces to fire at the coin. He missed.

After Reeves gave him a few pointers, Chapman placed another target in the tree. Before the session was over, the two men had fired more than 150 rounds of ammunition from both weapons. When they put the guns away, Chapman's aim was considerably improved. Returning to Reeves's apartment, Chapman confided that he had brought a gun with him from Honolulu to New York City. He brought the gun for personal protection, he said, because he was carrying a large amount of cash and he feared being attacked and robbed on the violent sidewalks of New York. He told Reeves he had brought no ammunition from Hawaii, and explained that he had been unable to get bullets in New York. He asked Dana if he could spare a few extra shells for the gun that was still in a suitcase under the bed at his hotel.

"It's for protection," he said, "just in case anything happens. Just in case I need to defend myself. New York City is a pretty frightening place."

Chapman refused to accept the standard, round-nosed, jacketed shells that Reeves initially offered him. He wanted something "with real stopping power," he said, "just in case." He selected five hollow-point Smith & Wesson Plus P cartridges designed to explode with the deadly effect of tiny hand grenades inside the soft tissue of anticipated human targets . . . just in case.

After the target session with the pistols on Friday, Chapman asked Reeves to take him shopping for a cassette player. He said he wanted to listen to the Todd Rundgren tapes he had brought with him from New York. Before his return to New York City on Sunday afternoon, Chapman visited the parents of his former fiancée, Jessica Blankenship, and found that Jessica was home recuperating from a tonsillectomy. He lingered at the Blankenship home with Jessica's father and mother, Harold and June, and told them about his new life in Hawaii. June Blankenship recalled that the conversation turned to the subjects of euthanasia and abortion and that Chapman expressed outrage over both the "mercy killing" of elderly and terminally ill persons and the termination of unwanted pregnancies.

"In either case," he said, "it's murder."

On Saturday, Mark and Dana decided to surprise Dana's mother, Nell, from whom he had rented a room for a while after finishing high school. Dana's sister, Jan, recalls that she was astonished by Chapman's physical appearance and the emotional cloud that seemed to hang over him.

"After he left, I was looking at pictures I took of Mark from years before and pictures I took on that visit, and it was like looking at Jekyll and Hyde," Jan Reeves said. "Except for all the weight he had put on, he seemed like the same old Mark. But when I looked at those pictures, I could see it was two different people."

After returning to Dana's apartment Saturday evening, Chapman called Delta Airlines to confirm his first-class seat on a return flight to New York on Sunday. As he packed, he asked Reeves again about the bullets.

"You're sure they're fresh?" he asked.

"They're not more than five years old," Reeves assured him. "I shoot them myself and they work just fine."

"I want them for protection," Chapman said again. "I wouldn't want to have an accident."

Reeves warned that the thick metal slugs would trigger the alarm of airport passenger security devices. Chapman said he intended to carry the bullets in his suitcase in the baggage compartment of the plane.

"What the . . . ?" Chapman muttered aloud as he settled into his seat and reached for the buckles of his safety belt. He was seated in the front row of the airplane beside a well-dressed woman and directly behind a rack displaying current issues of popular magazines. Without thinking, he threw aside the buckles of the safety belt and leaped in front of the startled woman who had begun to reach for a magazine on the rack. He was after the *Esquire* in front of her. On the cover of the magazine was a photograph of the man whose face he couldn't get out of his mind.

As the plane lifted from the ground and banked north toward New York City, Chapman was absorbed in the magazine's cover story, a critical and scathing commentary on the opulent life-style of sixties peacenik John Lennon. The article, by *Esquire* writer Laurence Shames, was yet another confirmation, another synchronicity, to buttress Chapman's deadly resolve. As he pondered the story about Lennon, Chapman thought of the five hollow-point bullets in his suitcase. He closed his eyes and smiled.

Shortly after returning to New York with everything he needed to carry out Lennon's murder, Chapman began to feel disoriented and confused. He began to have doubts. The Dakota doormen continued to tell him that Lennon was away. No one knew when he might be back, they told him. He could be in England. He could be in Japan. Maybe he had gone to Spain.

Chapman began to panic.

He still had several thousand dollars in his pocket, but he began to worry that his vigil might require a longer wait than he had anticipated a week before. He worried about the money he had spent on dates, on lavish theater and dinner reservations, and on the first-class flight to Georgia. He decided that he would have to move from the room at the Olcott to an inexpensive room at the West Side YMCA on West 63rd Street.

He found himself deeply depressed the following night, after a Monday spent lurking fruitlessly outside the Dakota. He had wandered about the boulders and lagoons of a wintry Central Park and returned to the spartan room at the Y, only to grow more depressed.

After returning from Georgia on Sunday night, Chapman had decided to go to a movie that had an interesting title: *Ordinary People* starring Mary Tyler Moore and Timothy Hutton. He had identified closely with the character played by Hutton in the story about a troubled and suicidal adolescent in a dysfunctional middle-class family.

Almost in tears when he left the movie, Chapman had phoned his wife afterward from a phone booth outside the theater to tell her that he would be coming home sooner than he had expected. Elated, Gloria pressed him to tell her when he would be back, but he remained vague. "Soon," he said. "Just sometime soon."

"I had an experience in that theater somehow," he recalled. "I came out and immediately called my wife. For that brief time, I had defeated, I had capped my volcano of rage toward John Lennon. I called my wife and I said, 'I'm coming home. I've won a great victory. Your love has saved me.'

"Then quickly, it was washed over with winds from the tornado."

For the next two days, however, Chapman continued to think about *Ordinary People,* about himself, and about his wife. He also continued to visit the Dakota and to listen to his Todd Rundgren tapes. He wandered through Central Park, watching laughing children kick soccer balls and tumble on the grassy knolls.

At 9:15 P.M. in Hawaii on Tuesday, November 11, Gloria Chapman's husband phoned again from the West Side YMCA. Although he told her he was very depressed, it was the call she had been praying for. He told her he was coming home. Then he began talking to her mysteriously about a gun and a planned killing.

"I was going to kill him, but your love has saved me," he said.

His puzzled wife said she didn't understand.

"You know what I'm talking about," he said, "don't you?"

"Mark, no. I don't know. Just come home."

At the other end of the phone line, his wife was simultaneously stunned at what he was telling her and ecstatic that he was coming home.

Chapman began whispering into the phone:

"Gloria, listen. I'm afraid to tell you this, but I've got to. I've got to say it now. John Lennon," he whispered. "I bought a gun in Honolulu and when I went to Georgia I got some bullets from Dana. I was going to kill him, but your love has saved me."

"Mark . . . What? Who?"

"Just listen," he said. "I was going to kill Lennon but our paths didn't cross. I was going to do it. You probably don't believe me, but I could have done it."

"Oh God, Mark, I believe you. Just please come home. Just please before something bad happens. Please. I love you, Mark. You don't know how much I love you."

"I got to know the doormen where Lennon lives," he continued. "I could have done it, but our paths didn't cross and now it's too late. Your love has saved me, Gloria. I just want to come back home to you, Gloria. No one else. There's no one else. I don't want anybody else, Gloria. You believe me, don't you? I don't need anybody else. I made such a big mistake in coming here.

"But I could have done it," he repeated. "You have to believe me. I really could have done it."

"Oh, Mark, I do. I do believe you. Just please, please come home. It's over now. Just please come home."

About two hours later, Gloria's phone rang again. Chapman told her he was calling from Newark Airport where he was waiting for a flight.

"I know it's late and I'm sorry," he said. "But the last time I called, I wasn't absolutely sure that I was coming home. It took me about another five minutes before I was sure, then I started packing my bags and I called the airport."

He said he would arrive back in Honolulu the next day at 3:15 P.M. He asked her not to meet his plane. He said he had dreamed of walking back into their apartment and sweeping her into his arms.

Late Thursday afternoon, November 12, Mark and Gloria Chapman embraced for a long moment when he walked through the door of their high-rise apartment and set down his bags.

"Oh, Mark," she said. "I've been so lonely. You just don't know. I've missed you so much."

"I know," he said. "I know."

Kissing the salty tears from his wife's eyes, Chapman pried himself slowly from her embrace. He turned away and snapped open his suitcase. When he turned back to face Gloria, his eyes were half open and a smile played about the corner of his lips. In his hand was a weighty and sinister chunk of steel. He also held a small container from which he shook five stubby, lead-tipped slugs.

Gloria withdrew in stunned silence at the sight of the lethal appearance of the weapon. Her husband, however, insisted that she feel with her own hands the reality of what he had told her over the phone.

"Here," he said. "Hold it in your hands. Don't worry. It isn't loaded. The bullets are here."

He ordered her to point the gun at the wall and pull the trigger several times. Then, he warned her to always be respectful of guns.

"It's not a toy," he said. "Never point it at anyone, whether or not it's loaded."

After the brief, incongruous lesson in gun safety, a familiar hood seemed to fall over Chapman's eyes. He stared in the vacant way that he used to stare when Gloria had observed him talking to his Little People.

"You probably don't believe me," he told his wife. "But it's true. You probably don't think I could have done it. But I could have.

"Anyone could shoot anyone."

CHAPTER TWENTY-TWO

PEOPLE AREN'T BORN LIKE THIS

"I can tell you this now because I'm a totally different person today. But I can remember what I was like, the sort of creature I had become in the months before I murdered John Lennon. God had been my anchor, but I cut the anchor line and God sunk to the bottom of my life.

"I made a decision to be crazy, or schizophrenic, a psychopath or a sociopath—whatever it is you have to be to do the things that I did. It's a choice anybody can make.

"When I try, I'm still able to put myself back into that 'thing' that I was. But it's very uncomfortable. It's frightening. I only let myself go far enough back into it to get a little of the feeling of it, a little of the atmosphere.

"I can remember when I abandoned all my feelings for other people, but the pain inside me still wouldn't go away. I was a person that could come across as so charming and so caring. But if you scratched the surface, you'd find just blackness, only a void. I believe people get this way because they at one time were sensitive, feeling people who got crushed somewhat out of alignment and have had to go into themselves and create these tremendously thick steel walls around themselves.

"I believe people become the way that I became because they're too sensitive. They just get to a point where they can't allow themselves to feel anything anymore for anybody except themselves. People aren't born like this.

"Just remember, as I'm telling you this, that I'm not the same person at all now that I was then. I still struggle with some defense mechanisms. I recognize that I still struggle with not wanting to deal with all of my feelings of rejection, anger, rage, jealousy, the whole assorted cornucopia of hurts. But I tell you of this incident only because I am a different person now, and to illustrate how far gone I was in the months before I became a killer.

"As I often did when I lived in Honolulu, many afternoons I would take the bus down to Waikiki. I would go there alone and hang around the Moana Hotel, at the Banyan Court. Right outside the Banyan Court is a little walkway with some park benches where you can sit and watch the people go by. One day, I came up to one of the benches and there was a woman, perhaps in her late thirties or early forties, but very attractive. I sat down on the bench with her and in a few moments I saw that she was very upset. She was crying.

"I had no feeling of sadness for her. I had no feeling in my heart at all for anybody.

"I was very attracted to this woman. I asked her what was wrong. She turned away.

"But I persisted, because she seemed vulnerable to me. . . . Not because she was crying, but because she was alone. She was an older woman and she was alone. Perhaps the crying made her seem more vulnerable. That gave me an idea that, if I just pretended to be very understanding and compassionate, it would give me an 'in.' So I kept asking her what was wrong. I came on to her in my most genteel manner. She wouldn't tell me, so I kept persisting, saying things like, 'Well, you can tell me. It's better to talk about the things that make you sad. It's better to get it off your chest.'

"This went on for about ten minutes or so, me trying to engage her in conversation.

"She wasn't crying greatly. She wasn't wailing or hysterical, nothing to cause alarm or attract a crowd or anything. Every now and then a tear would trickle down her face. Finally she told me that her son had been murdered. She had come to Hawaii to try to deal with the grief and pain.

"I kept talking to her, but I didn't feel anything when she told me that her son had been killed. I just continued to have this sexual desire for her. That was all. This was probably six months before any thoughts were in my mind of committing a murder.

"She didn't tell me at first that her son had been murdered. For some reason, though, I deduced that he had been murdered. She said he had been killed. I asked her if he had been murdered and she nodded her head and said yes.

"This woman had come to Hawaii to forget probably the greatest pain that any mother could ever feel. But at that time, inside myself, within the blackness of my cold and shut-off heart, I just wanted to take advantage of her grief and vulnerability to satisfy my desires.

"I tried to get her to go on a boat ride with me, a catamaran ride from the beach at the hotel. I said, 'Come on, let's ride the catamaran. They'll be leaving in a few minutes. You can forget about this for a while. We can go out on the ocean.'

"But she said no, she wouldn't do it. She said she just felt so bad, she didn't want to have any joy in her life. But I wasn't thinking of her. I didn't care if she had any joy in her life or not. There I was, just thinking totally of myself. And I began to feel angry at her for rejecting me.

"This whole episode came back to me about four years ago. I was out of my cell because I was working at the time and I was in an area of the prison where a television was tuned in to one of the talk shows.

"I looked up at the TV and I saw a woman on the show who seemed vaguely familiar. I would have sworn that I knew her from somewhere. The program was about the murdering of a child. Not a baby, but a teenage or young adult child. I remember this program was about parents who had been forced to come to grips with their children being murdered. The lady, the one who looked so familiar to me, said she had gone to Hawaii to recover and deal with her grief after her son had been killed. Then I knew.

"It sent a shiver through me. It shocked me, like some of the things that shock me about John Lennon when I hear them on the radio or see them on TV or in the newspapers and magazines. It was a memory I had tried to wipe out, a memory that I was ashamed of and there it was, on TV. I had forgotten about that woman until then. But when I saw her again on TV, it made me remember the kind of person I had allowed myself to become.

"Society meant nothing to me, except a tool to be used. People had become things, objects for my pleasure. When they caused me pain, I fled from them very quickly, and even rationalized that anything had ever happened. I forgot about the people as soon as I put the pain they had caused me inside my black box where I kept all my feelings and emotions. I had no conscience at that point. All my feelings went into a black box, where I wouldn't have to deal with the guilt or the pain.

"Less than three months before I became a murderer, something else happened. My mother and I had gone out to Pearl Harbor and taken the boat ride, the memorial tour that goes out so people can pay respect to all the soldiers and sailors who died there during World War II.

"As the tour boat neared the place where the *Arizona* was sunk with all the crew on board, people started throwing flowers into the water in honor of where the men had died.

"I started laughing. My mother looked at me and she was shocked. I couldn't explain why I laughed. I didn't think it was funny or anything. It's just that I was unable to feel the empathy or grief, the human emotion that I was supposed to feel. So I started laughing. . . .

"It was a time in my life when I had made a decision that I would live totally for myself. Even I wasn't aware of the depths that I had gone to.

"One day I went into a department store in Honolulu to get a bottle of perfume for my wife or my mother or somebody. The woman at the store acted like she didn't want to waste her time waiting on me. I stormed out of the store and hung around outside for hours, fantasizing that I would wait and follow this woman and hurt her.

"That anger built up and up, on top of all the angers that had stayed inside me all my life. It stayed in there because I couldn't deal with my feelings. I knew it was in there but I couldn't express it so it came out in all kinds of crazy, eccentric habits and behaviors and finally in violence.

"The only vent I had for my anger, my frustration, the rejection that I couldn't handle, was through my wife, who I could control at that point, and through purging the possessions we owned and her personal possessions from our apartment. That was something I had control over. I would purge a pot holder, or I would purge pens, anything that we didn't need: shoes, clothing, anything that we didn't essentially have to have at that moment in our apartment. I would just throw it away.

"That's something I had control over, my apartment—and my wife. I had control over her to where I would get my way and she wouldn't dare challenge me and risk my rage. If she questioned me or if I thought she was criticizing me even slightly, I would break something of hers or throw her against the wall or spit on her. Sometimes I would hit her.

"It was when I walked out of the apartment that I couldn't control anything. Out there on the streets, I was a time bomb walking in and out of a random series of events where anything could happen.

"There was the incident where I stood across the street from the Ili Kai Hotel, the hotel where you see Jack Lord on the balcony at the beginning of *Hawaii Five-O,* and I called in a bomb threat.

"I said, 'Listen, this is very serious. I'm not kidding around. I've planted a bomb in your hotel and I'm just letting you know. It'll go off in twenty minutes. This is very, very serious.' And they took it seriously and called the fire department and about twenty police cars. I stood there and watched from across the street as they evacuated the whole first floor of the hotel. I started getting paranoid when all the police cars came. I thought, 'They're going to catch me.' I started walking away saying to myself, 'They're going to know it's me! They're going to know it's me! They're going to find out it's me!'

"At this time, I had begun making a lot of threatening calls. One person I called regularly was our former landlord, from our first apartment. I used to call him up and harass him, send pizzas to his place, call in the middle of the night. I knew he could never change his phone number because he was a landlord.

"There was also a guy who ran a TV repair shop. Once I brought a TV in to be repaired and I felt that I had been treated rudely. So I called this guy up; I made life-threatening calls. I told him I was going to kill him and then I'd hang up.

"I would look out my apartment window, where there was a supermarket below with a pay phone in front. I would stand there at my window and call the pay phone. I had the number of that pay phone. And I would call and when some innocent bystander would answer, I would say, 'I'm watching you. I'm going to get you. I'm going to follow you home and kill you.'

"There was a doctor at Castle Hospital. He had never done one wrong thing to me. I just didn't like the way he looked. I kept calling his office and telling him he was going to die. I got one of those laughing boxes.

"I was out of my mind!

"Picture me in my apartment with a laughing box, calling this guy and holding up this little box that was laughing and laughing and telling this guy that I was going to get him and kill him—calling up just random people and saying, 'I'm going to get you, I'm going to kill you.' Horrible and paranoid incidents, one after another.

"There was an incident where I started harassing Hare Krishnas on one of the main tourist streets in Honolulu. I saw that they were ripping people off, and especially Japanese tourists. The Krishnas would hold a book up to the tourists and have a $20 bill inserted in the middle, pointing to it. They knew they weren't supposed to openly solicit.

"I learned the Japanese word for danger and I would go up to the Japanese people and I would go, '*Tsukete! Tsukete! Hayaku!*—Danger! Danger! Move on!'—and they would go.

"The Krishnas would look at me and walk away. They never confronted me. But I kept this up, day after day. In my spare time, I would intentionally go down to the street to harass the Hare Krishnas. I had to have some kind of purpose for my vengeance to come out, for my anger to come out. And the Krishnas were phonies to me. They were ripping people off. It was like I was doing something that was righteous, doing something that was against phoniness, something that—it was like all the phoniness and things that had hurt me all my life. I was coming full circle now, getting back at those things, picking my targets.

"So the harassment of the Krishnas went on for about three weeks and then this lady pulled me aside one day. She said, 'Look, I work in this dress shop around the corner. Let's have a cup of coffee and there's something I want to talk to you about.'

"We went to a little café and she said, 'Look there's something I've got to tell you about these Hare Krishnas. They're very dangerous. They don't play around. You are costing them money. There was a guy like you, a year ago here, that was harassing them and wouldn't leave them alone. A man came up to him after a few months of him doing this and squirted a hypodermic needle of acid into his face. He was disfigured for life. The only thing witnesses reported seeing was a man in blue jeans running away. They never found out who he was. The Krishnas hire these people. They bring them from California to do this kind of thing.'

"Now, I don't think that ever really happened, that they disfigured somebody with acid. I believe this lady just wanted me to stop harassing them, to frighten me away.

"I was basically a coward. Cowards make threatening calls to people and then hang up the phone. Even though I believed the Krishnas were phonies and I knew they were ripping people off, I quit harassing them when this woman made me think they could hurt me.

"It wasn't like I was consciously trying to spread evil or anything. I was picking targets. I thought I was doing good by standing up to these phony forces, the people around me that I believed to be phonies.

"But I had no feelings. I had to bypass them all. What happens to a person when he has to bypass all his feelings? What happens to a person, a person who still has a brain and a heart and still has to function? How can a person function if he cannot feel?"

PART V

HOLDEN IN HELL

CHAPTER TWENTY-THREE

YOU SAY YOU WANT A REVELATION

So I refuse to lead, and I'll always show
my genitals or something which prevents me
from being Martin Luther King or Gandhi,
and getting killed.

—JOHN LENNON

In the weeks after his arrest, Mark David Chapman was confined alternately to the New York City jail on Rikers Island and to the psychiatric wing for criminals at Bellevue Hospital. He had become depressed after spilling the blood of John Lennon, disappointed that his own blood had failed to turn into the Catcher's ink. Although he had taken his brand-new copy of *The Catcher in the Rye* from his coat pocket and begun meditating upon the words in the book—as the life flowed from Lennon's body a few feet away inside the Dakota building—Chapman remained unable to achieve the transubstantiation he had anticipated. His blood and flesh stubbornly refused to dematerialize. He was unable to disappear and escape into the book that was frozen, as the gun had been frozen moments before, in his hand.

In a symbolic sense, the killer had achieved his crude objective: He had gained an identity. The chronic "nobody" from a middle-class Georgia suburb had become one of the most notorious murderers in the world. The hour of his darkest personal glory, however, was another two months away.

After a night of bizarre cat-and-mouse tactics organized by police to shield Chapman from the press and from the vengeance of ever-growing lynch mobs of Lennon and Beatles fans threatening to kill him, the assassin was protectively wrapped in two bulletproof vests and arraigned at the Manhattan Court House on the afternoon of December 9. Under orders from his court-appointed lawyer, Herbert Adelberg, to say nothing during the legal proceedings, Chapman stood mutely before the judge and lawyers. He ignored a horde of media who had crowded into the small courtroom for a look at the man who, less than twelve hours earlier, had robbed the human spirit of one of its most poignant voices. As lawyers conferred, Chapman recalls that his eyes fell on a line of raised bronze letters that seemed to call to him from a dark mahogany panel above the judge's head. One of the words in particular caught his attention. The word was *God.* It leaped at him from the courthouse motto: *In God We Trust.*

"This is all about survival. The soul has to survive. If you're that sick it's got to survive and my brain couldn't handle any more of the subconscious guilt or whatever it was going through. My conscious mind couldn't handle any more of the deception. It wasn't even me anymore. I wasn't even there anymore. Whether that's called schizophrenic, I don't know.

"But I didn't make a decision about what happened to me later, when I became truly psychotic. That happened at the end of January in 1981, nearly two months after the killing.

"Several weeks earlier, my lawyer had given me another copy of *The Catcher in the Rye* while I was on the ward at Bellevue and I began reading it again there. I remember thinking that it was like I was reading a whole other book than the one I had read before—like I was reading a blueprint of what had happened to me. I found out that the book started on a Saturday and ended on a Monday, the whole time frame that Holden Caulfield had spent in New York and the same time frame that I spent in New York before the killing. And that was just one thing. In fact, I made a list of fifty total coincidences, things that were pretty frightening because there was no way that they could have been planned, no way that I could have set them up. It was like the whole killing was set up by destiny, just something that was meant to be.

"Yes, I did set up and follow a 'Holdenish' pattern by walking through Central Park and seeing the pond and asking the policeman where the ducks went in winter, the way Holden Caulfield did. But it was nothing like I could have ever planned, nothing like what I saw when I read it again after the killing. It was just eerie, like something more was going on than I had ever envisioned. Like it was out of my control.

"It was like all of those coincidences were not only confirmed, but they were magnified a thousand times and enlightened and new angles and nuances and the whole purpose was given to me to understand.

"During this time, I was being carried back and forth almost every day, wearing two bulletproof vests and in an armored van with lights and sirens between Bellevue and Rikers Island for all sorts of medical tests and psychiatric evaluations by the defense and the prosecution psychiatrists. But I didn't care at all what those doctors thought about me. I was above and beyond them. I was with a pure, holy purpose and there was nothing they could do that would touch it. They were down on some other level somewhere that didn't affect me at all.

"And it truly didn't, even to this day. What those psychiatrists did and said, some of the top psychiatrists in the country—Lee Salk and Bernard Diamond and all the others—it ended up having no effect on me in reality. I was so far above them, I could see far beyond them. I thought they were all phonies, all flunkies. There was nothing that could touch my noble purpose; it was so pure and real and I was so taken up in it. It was almost like an alternate heaven to me, another world that I had created. Not willfully, but my mind had created it, and, even though I realize now that it was a psychotic episode, at the time it was the most real and important thing in my life.

"After I had that revelation, my trial, my guilt or innocence, my life or death no longer meant anything. I honestly did not care about what would happen to me. Guilty? Not guilty? It did not matter one iota. All that mattered was that I do everything I possibly could to promote the reading of that book by people all over the world.

"Always until then I had freedom of choice. I chose to be 'quote crazy unquote' if that would end the pain. If I had to kill John Lennon to end my pain, and if I had to be crazy to kill John Lennon, then I would be crazy. I would rip off my clothes and summon demons and pray to the devil and if that was being crazy, then I was crazy. But through all of that, it was me. It wasn't the Little People. It wasn't the devil. It was me alone. I made the choice—right up to the moment that the bullets left the gun in my hand and ended John Lennon's life. I made a choice to pull the trigger. I made the choice—God forgive me—to destroy another man.

"But what happened to me two months later, in my cell on Rikers Island, that was a choice that was made by somebody or something else.

"It happened one night when I had been lying in my cell watching a movie about Adolf Hitler. That's when I had the psychotic epiphany in which it was revealed to me why John Lennon had been killed. The revelation had nothing to do with Hitler, nothing to do with what I had been watching on TV, except that maybe I identified with Hitler's isolation. Films do impress things on people in odd ways. Often, watching TV will put you in another state of mind and maybe that's what happened.

"The movie had just ended and the guards had switched off the TV sets in our cells. We had already locked in. All of a sudden, as I lay back on my bunk, it was like something burst forth from me. Like a million-watt light bulb switched on in the center of my brain. Like a nuclear fission and my brain expanded outward and there was no stopping the tremendous energy of this. I felt it physically. I cried. I shook. I laughed with absolute, pure joy. I was having a satori, a dark satori, a wicked satori of realization that I had been called by a far higher power to do this, that this was something much bigger than me. I did not equate it with demons. I didn't equate it with anything of God. It was something that I just felt. It was like I had opened a door and seen the cross-weaves of destiny. I could see several of the patterns of the universe and I became amazed and transported to a whole other plane of consciousness.

"That's when I realized, in that instant, that John Lennon had been killed to promote the reading of *The Catcher in the Rye.* And it was like an electric current had passed through my body and lit up all the cells in my brain.

"In a moment, I was on my feet and I came up off my bunk in the grip of a total, psychotic euphoria. I was as high as a kite, higher in my mind than I had ever been on marijuana or LSD or alcohol or anything. Just total euphoria, but without the side effects of drugs, without feeling woozy or clouded or aching in my head.

"There was just crystal clarity there for a few minutes. It was like the beginning of the TV show *The Outer Limits,* when a cloudy, foggy night comes into focus and then sharpens down to a crystal-clear image of the moon. That's what happened to me. The realization of why John Lennon was killed became just so clear, it was frightening.

"Suddenly I understood with every fiber of my being the reason that John Lennon had to die. I immediately wanted to make a statement to the press to promote this fact. My lawyer knew somebody at *The New York Times,* where I wanted it on the front page that Sunday. It was printed, but it was relegated to another section.

"I had no control over what I was doing then. I was completely, utterly compulsed and absorbed in my mission. I was on a mission, a genuine mission: Mission with a capital *M,* in neon with blinking lights over Broadway. The mission was that I was to promote *The Catcher in the Rye.* And I was going to use my trial—my lawyer, Jonathan Marks, told me it was going to be the trial of the decade, or maybe the trial of the century—to promote the reading of that book. I didn't care about being at the trial. I wanted the book to be at the trial. I wanted to carry the book into the courtroom. It was all about the book now. It was all the book.

"I didn't see then that I was crazy. At that time, it was important that I appear rational so that people would take me seriously and read the book. But more important than that, I knew then why John Lennon had to be killed and that's why I became euphoric—knowing that there was a reason beyond myself for what I had done.

"So, with my psyche being bathed in this new *realization* of why John Lennon had to be killed and my mission now clear to me, I spent the next few months excitedly pacing up and down the gallery outside my cell and talking to anyone who would listen to me about *The Catcher in the Rye,* saying they had to go out and read it, had to go out and buy it. Just get it and read it. It would be a grass-roots attempt, starting very slowly, starting with any correction officer or police officer or lawyer or nurse or doctor who was with me. There wasn't an officer who passed through the door that I did not tell them to read *The Catcher in the Rye.* There wasn't a doctor, a nurse, a psychiatrist, or psychologist who interviewed me that I didn't say, at the beginning and end and often insert in the middle of every taped conversation, that I was doing this to promote the reading of *The Catcher in the Rye.*

"To the corrections officers who guarded me and who took me back and forth from my cell to the hospital and the courtroom, all I talked about was *The Catcher in the Rye.* I had them bring in copies of the novel by the boxful. Doctors, too, the psychologists—I had them bring stacks of the book in so I could sign them. I signed them to make them keep them, so that they would never throw the books away. I didn't sign the books because I thought I was a celebrity or a big shot.

"I signed them because I knew it would give them a lasting value, that then no one would throw them away. They would give copies to their friends, and I knew it would increase the value of the books. My name became an extension of that book, and the officers kept bringing them in. I would sign my name and write 'The Catcher in the Rye' at the bottom of it. I know it's hard to believe there were no thoughts of celebrity when I was autographing those copies of the book, but there wasn't. I simply wanted to make the book as special as possible. That's why I would do that.

"When I was first arrested, a police officer had asked me for my autograph and I was disgusted. But when I became psychotic two months later, everything I could do was geared toward the book—every possible little thing.

"There wasn't a thought I had that didn't center around *The Catcher in the Rye.* I made a phone call to Bantam Books. I found out the phone number through the Yellow Pages and I called and asked to speak to their distribution representative.

"I asked him if he knew who I was, and he said he did. Then I explained that I wanted him to know that my trial was going to be highly publicized and that everything I was doing centered around *The Catcher in the Rye.* I assured him that I was really doing my best to promote it and told him to be sure to have enough copies printed up because they were going to be selling a lot.

"I had planned to read from the book the whole time during my trial and I was going to jump up at random moments and shout, 'Read *The Catcher in the Rye*! *I* am The Catcher in the Rye!'

"Wherever I went, from my cell to Bellevue to the courtroom, I took the book with me. In court, I made sure that I was always holding it in my hand so everyone would see it as I walked in and out. It would have been disastrous to me if the judge had said I couldn't bring the book into the courtroom. I held it crosswise so court reporters could see it, holding it very still so the newspaper and TV artists could sketch it.

"I remember that I would be delighted to no end when I would go back to my cell and see the sketches of the book on TV and realize how many hundreds of thousands of people, how many millions of people, had seen *The Catcher in the Rye* and how many of them would go out, just out of mere curiosity, and get the book.

"There was nothing that I couldn't do for *The Catcher in the Rye.* I was sacrificing my whole case for the reading of this book and it was well worth it to me. I knew what I was doing. I knew that the case didn't matter at all. It didn't matter where I was going or anything. It was all about *The Catcher in the Rye.* Nothing was going to stop me from promoting it. This trial was going to be a big one and it was all going to be about getting people to read the book. That's the only reason I cared about going on the witness stand. I really honestly did not care about whether I was found guilty or not. That wasn't part of the criteria. It didn't emotionally matter to me one way or the other.

"It was so real inside me that today, eleven years later when I'm totally sane and close to God, I still get caught up in it just talking about it. That's how powerful it was. If more than a decade later it can still affect me, I can still pick up the atmosphere of it, you can maybe understand some of the power there.

"I became a savior.

"That's how my brain handled that tremendous pressure and all that guilt of murdering John Lennon. By becoming the savior—The Catcher in the Rye—of my generation.

"The world thought I was a devil, so my brain had to re-create me as a savior, as someone who was sowing good.

"Yes, I understood that it had been necessary for a man to die. A phony man had to die. But what a beautiful foundation was laid by his death.

"There was no more hatred for Lennon. Just total understanding for what had happened. It was like a Zen moment: a realization, a total rapture.

"You take any person who did what I did, it's an awful thing to have to deal with and live with. So how did I deal with that? I dealt with it by becoming something other than a person. It was on the book now, all on the book. It didn't matter whether I was alive or dead. It didn't matter that John Lennon had to die. It was the book that was the focus, that would live long after us all and be read by the millions of people who would have never heard of the book if I hadn't murdered John Lennon. Everything was about *The Catcher in the Rye.* Everything, everything, everything! I lived and breathed that book. I became that book.

"It made me a new person, because my mind could not accept the thing that I had become after I shot John Lennon.

"I remember that I was shocked when I had heard my name on CBS news that night of December ninth at Bellevue Hospital, less than twenty-four hours after I had done the killing. When I heard Walter Cronkite speak my name, I tried to shut it out, despite what the prosecutor and other people said about me killing John Lennon just so I could become famous.

"I was frightened at what I had become. I had become notorious. I never thought of myself as a celebrity and I became instantly paranoid. I was paranoid of people wanting something—of lawyers who took my case, of former friends and ministers who tried to reach me and help me. I would scream at them, 'Why are you doing this? Why are you being nice to me? Why did you call on me, Reverend, just so you could be on TV? Why do you want to take my case, counselor, so you can become a famous phony celebrity lawyer like F. Lee Bailey?'

"I became a horror to my own self. I'm sure there was a part in me that enjoyed the attention, but there was a greater part of me that revolted against being an 'It.'

"I had become the thing that I thought I had killed: I became an 'It.'

"I had treated people like they were Its and then suddenly I became an It to everybody in the world.

"How did I deal with feelings like that, the feelings that came upon me after I had opened up Pandora's box and then the demons were really able to take control? I dealt with it as I had always dealt with the truly difficult problems in my life. I escaped. I ran into a box within a box: a black box. I had to do that, to save myself.

"The mind is an incredible thing. It really takes care of itself. Sometimes if it flips you out, it knows it's going to come back around the track again for another shot, but for that time period I was just in a totally other place. My mind couldn't handle anything else, so I became The Catcher in the Rye of my generation. I became almost a prophet."

"So why, after all this, did I plead guilty and destroy my chance for a trial, maybe for an acquittal on grounds of insanity? But most of all, why did I give up the chance of a lifetime to promote the book?

"You see, I still wasn't capable of feeling remorse and guilt. That wasn't the reason I had pleaded guilty. I didn't sit down in my cell and come out of the fog and come out of this fit and decide to plead guilty because I felt bad about killing John Lennon. I was beyond feeling any guilt or remorse about anything that I did to anybody.

"The reason I pleaded guilty—I believe to this day, I still believe this, as a clear, sane person now, as a rational person—I believe that I pleaded guilty because the Lord spoke to my heart. Not just to me—I was far beyond hearing God's voice at that point—but to my heart.

"It happened one day as I was sitting in my cell listening to rock music on the radio.

"God changed something in my heart and He spoke to my heart so that I could hear Him through all the sickness that was in my mind at that time. He told me twice to plead guilty, and for some reason I didn't question that. I was out of my mind and I wanted to go to that trial worse than anything in the world. That was my mission, to promote *The Catcher in the Rye.* So why would I plead guilty and just walk away from the best chance I would ever have to promote the book that had become my life—the book that held all the answers about why John Lennon had to die?

"Did I feel guilt, did I feel remorse? Did I come out of the psychotic cloud? No! No! No!

"I pled guilty because I recognized God's voice through all that—through all the insanity and through a mind that was totally obsessed and centered on the promotion of this book.

"I was out of control and this moment of sanity, of moral courage, it did not come to me on my own. But God came to me and it was God that took away that desire to go to trial and fulfill my mission.

"My lawyer didn't want me to plead guilty. The psychiatrists didn't want me to plead guilty, and they tried to stop me from doing it. One of the prosecution psychiatrists thought I was putting him on when I told him I was going to confess my guilt. He just said, 'Well, I'll see you at trial.' And I said, 'No, doctor. No, you won't.' And he didn't. There was no trial, because God had changed something in my heart. There's no other explanation, because if I didn't listen to Him the first time—when He told me not to kill somebody—then there's nothing that could have kept me from going to this trial that I wanted more than anything. There was nothing, not even the voice of God, that could have stopped me. God's voice alone? No. I wouldn't have been that strong. But God changed something in my heart before He spoke to me. It was a spiritual healing, and I did plead guilty.

"At the sentencing, I was no longer with the Lord. I wasn't listening anymore. I carried *The Catcher in the Rye* in there and I felt terrible that I had blown the trial. So I read from *The Catcher in the Rye* instead of the Bible. I knew down deep God had told me to plead guilty and that He would heal my mind. But when I came back for sentencing two months later, on

August 24, 1981, I wasn't the same person who had pled guilty. I believe I was sane when I pled guilty. I believe I knew exactly what I was doing when I went into the courtroom and admitted my guilt as a murderer. But then, I relapsed back into *being* The Catcher in the Rye and felt terribly that I had refused to go to trial. I felt like I had lost my mission. I felt like I had abandoned everything. That was why I read from *The Catcher* at my sentencing. I again wanted to get the message out. Even after I came here to Attica, I maintained a very strong belief in *The Catcher in the Rye* and I went through a long period of doing all I could to promote the book.

"That's why there seemed to be a dichotomy there, between when I pled guilty and when I was sentenced. I told the court when I pled guilty that God had promised me He would take care of me wherever I went, and He has kept that promise.

"But why didn't I say that at my sentencing? I read from *The Catcher in the Rye* at my sentencing and no one seemed to catch that. They would consider that all craziness. It wasn't all craziness. I was sane and healed enough to know what I was doing when I pled guilty. And then I realized on my own choosing and went back into the cloud with *The Catcher in the Rye.* It was very soothing, very, very comforting. And it remained very, very comforting even up to a period of about five years ago, when things would get rough here, and I was not quite this close to the Lord. It was an option I always had, to once again become The Catcher in the Rye. Early on I chose it once or twice. Then, as I started getting better—I knew I had it there. It was a comfort, a pillow for me to lay my head on: knowing that I could go back into *The Catcher in the Rye* and begin promoting it again.

"It didn't finally change until I made a decision that I would not allow myself to slip back into that psychotic comfort of being a fictional character. It didn't finally change until I finally said that I would not allow myself to be Holden Caulfield. You don't know how hard it was for me to do that. Nobody will ever know how hard it was for me to do that.

"Even now, after all these years, I feel my blood stir just thinking about Holden Caulfield. I guess it's like a drug addict. To me, slipping into the mind of Holden Caulfield was as comforting as a needle full of heroin to an addict. You can't imagine what it was like."

CHAPTER TWENTY-FOUR

A WICKED SCENE

From the beginning, the Little People were forces of good.

Whenever Mark David Chapman had visited his childhood wrath upon the benevolent kingdom within his mind, the Little People had always understood. They had forgiven him and he had shown his remorse by broadcasting from his mind all the Beatles music they wanted to hear.

When Chapman was twenty-five years old and the Little People returned, all grown up and wearing three-piece suits, it was to help him arrange his finances and try to stabilize his marriage and personal life. When he advised them that he was planning to murder one of their childhood heroes and asked for their help, "they were appalled," Chapman recalled. "They were the inner government within me which was basically good and they wanted nothing to do with this evil plan. They tried to warn me. When I didn't listen, they abandoned me."

One of the Little People, an especially loyal minister whose name was Robert, reappeared to Chapman while he was in jail awaiting trial early in 1981. Robert briefly explained that he could reconvene the government to try to help Chapman cope with the aftermath of the tragedy that he had allowed the small, Evil One inside him to create. Chapman considered the offer, but decided against it. He was too ashamed, he said.

Although Chapman had invited demons to help commit murder, he never believed himself to be possessed of them. The voice in his head, the one that commanded "Do it, do it, do it" as he aimed and pulled the trigger of the .38 caliber pistol, was his own voice, he later told psychiatrists.

When other people told him they sensed the presence of demons inside him after he killed John Lennon, Chapman laughed. He refused to cooperate with exorcisms that were attempted by a Christian guard at Rikers Island, a former hometown minister who visited him in jail, and a chaplain who visited his prison cell.

"I was a Christian," he said. "I believed that it wasn't possible for a Christian to be really possessed. Even though I was the one that did the inviting, I didn't believe there could be really demons inside me. It made me angry when these people were commanding demons to come out of me.

"When an officer with a Bible commanded Satan to come out of me, I didn't believe it. I didn't believe these things were inside of me at the time. Not really. Not *really.* Not deep in my heart. I could summon them and use them, but they had to stay outside.

"When the officer said, 'I command you, in Jesus's name, come out, you demons! You demons, I know you, Satan!' He made me angry by saying these things."

After Chapman decided to plead guilty to murder, when his identity as The Catcher in the Rye of his generation began to crumble around him, he began to feel the demons stir inside. The slayer who had calmly and apologetically confessed to the killing of John Lennon and cooperated fully with police and psychiatrists became a raging monster almost overnight. Calling demons by name, he stripped naked and destroyed television sets, radios, toilet facilities, and other items on the gallery outside his Rikers Island cell. It took eight guards to bring him under control.

Although temporarily restrained and returned to his cell, Chapman continued to cry out to the demons that danced in his brain. He climbed and hung like a beast from the bars of his cage, taunting jailers with the curses of an alien tongue. He sent the demons forth against a fellow murderer, Craig Crimmins.

Crimmins, dubbed "The Phantom of the Opera" for killing a young violinist at the Metropolitan Opera, was the only other prisoner with Chapman on the protective-custody block at Rikers Island. Chapman's demons began speaking in a high-pitched, fearful voice in mimicry of the young woman that Crimmins had murdered. Cackling with glee, they repeated the same story day and night to the Phantom: that he belonged to their master and that his soul would roast for eternity in the flames of hell.

"I was speaking in the voices of two demons," Chapman recalls. "It was a wicked scene."

In response, the Phantom began lighting cigarettes and throwing them into the cell against Chapman's naked flesh. Arguing that Lennon's killer was driving his client insane, the Phantom's lawyer went to court to have Crimmins removed from the cell block and protected from further persecution by Chapman's demons.

Dragged from his cell and injected with Stelazine, a potent antipsychotic drug, Chapman suffered a violent reaction to the medication that resulted in paralysis of his head, throat, and vocal apparatus. Fearing further medication and paralysis, he promised to confine within himself the violence of demons sent by the Evil One.

The second possession and demonic outburst occurred after Chapman was taken from the city jail at Rikers Island. On June 22, 1981, he pleaded guilty to second-degree murder and was sentenced on August 24, 1981, to serve a minimum of twenty years and a maximum of life in prison. Shortly after sentencing, he was taken from Rikers Island and committed to the state prison system at Downstate Correctional Facility. When he found that he was being sent to Attica—where forty-three men had died during September 1971 in the bloodiest prison revolt in U.S. history—the killer panicked. Chapman also feared Attica for another reason: John Lennon's first public performance after immigrating to the United States in 1971 had been a benefit for the survivors and families of prisoners killed by state police at Attica. The song he wrote and sang for the benefit at the Apollo Theater and later recorded on the Plastic Ono Band album *Sometime in New York City,* was titled "Attica State."

When Chapman learned he had been sentenced to twenty years at Attica, he curled into a fetal position, refusing to come out from beneath a blanket in his cell. In a peaceful effort by prison authorities to allay his fears, a Correction Department chaplain asked to visit him in his cell. Still curled in a ball, refusing to speak or remove the blanket from his head, Chapman listened as the chaplain attempted to reassure him that he would be protected from outraged Beatles-generation convicts who threatened to avenge Lennon's death. He would be confined with other notorious murderers in protective custody. The chaplain also told Chapman he sensed "a demonic presence" about him and prayed that the demons would come out. Several hours later, Chapman boarded an armored bus for the four-hundred-mile drive to Attica in the rolling farmlands of western New York. When he stepped in chains to stand before his new home, his heart sank. The high-walled fortress, with soaring towers and its dismal tones of brown and black, loomed as a nightmarish distortion of the Dakota building.

. . .

Gloria Chapman quit her job in Honolulu and moved to an upstate New York village near Attica shortly after her husband began serving his sentence. Almost every day, she would visit the prison where the couple sat beneath surveillance cameras in a caged room holding hands, reading from the Bible and from religious instruction manuals. After a while, Gloria found a job at a nearby department store and rented a room from members of her church group in a small community near Attica. Even though there was little hope that they would be allowed overnight conjugal visits, Gloria was prepared to wait twenty years, if necessary, outside the walls of the penitentiary that separated her from the man she still loved with all her heart. She believed that her husband loved her, too, even though he had written long, rambling letters from Rikers Island telling her that he would never see her or speak to her again.

He had begun the first letter with a quote from Ernesto Sabato:

> "Cunning, the will to live, desperation have caused me to imagine a thousand ways of escaping my fate. But how can one escape one's own destiny?"

> Dear Gloria,
>
> It is with great sadness that I write to you this farewell letter. I'm sorry that I cannot see you again—it would be impossible. I don't really know how to begin except to apologize for what has happened. Many times I can't believe it myself—but I have an understanding of it that no one else seems to really understand. It is very simple yet ironically quite complicated. Please re-read *The Catcher in the Rye.* You above all people would be able to understand my deep sensitivity and thoughts. It is such a beautiful thing and had such a tragic ending—but didn't we know it would end up this way? It was inevitable—it was destined. I have fallen off the cliff, I fell a horrible kind of fall—I cannot bring you with me. There is no hope, even for me. My own sensitivity and perceptions have destroyed me. I tried to be close to Christ but I couldn't stay—It's not meant for me. As a Christian you must still feel hope—you always will—but you must try to forget me. I shouldn't have married you. I knew better because of who I was. You never really knew me—you think you do but I'm far more complicated than you can imagine. There is so much that you don't know about me. I'm sorry to be doing this to you but I cannot drag you down with me. The end is near—I must complete my mission.
>
> Don't be valiant and hold out for me—I cannot return to society—you must face this fact. I have died to society—only a few select people will be able to understand what has really happened to me—only a few. You

must remember the good experiences we've had together—Remember me on the beach at Kailua—Remember me when you see *The Wizard of Oz.* Remember me when you hear Todd Rundgren's music esp. these songs "The Last Ride," "Zen Archer," "[I'm in the] Clique" and "Freedom Fighter." Also those Don McLean songs, "Bronco Bill's Lament," and "Vincent." Remember me through the movies *Heroes* and *You Can't Take It with You.*

Gloria, I cannot love you—My heart was broken by Lynn and I couldn't love anything after that—That was the beginning of my problems, I guess.

I was destined for madness, despair and gloom—It was just your fate to have been involved with me. I am an odd creature. You cannot have me. No one ever had me.

Remember me through "Paul's Case" and Jimi Hendrix's "All Along the Watchtower."

You must not write me—I will read no further mail from anyone—I will not see you or anyone again. After I read from *The Catcher in the Rye* in the courtroom I will never speak again. I have known this for a long time. Do not worry—it is destiny. I will suffer, I will be mistreated terribly, but it must happen. I am a sacrifice of kindness and sensitivity for all. I am The Catcher in the Rye. You are in my life no more—what has happened has happened. You must forget—do not try to understand it—I will be where I belong. The end is near. I am fearful for the first time in my life. My only message to anyone would be to read *The Catcher in the Rye.* There is nothing more to say than this.

And so I say farewell to you—thank you for treating me kind and giving to me all you had. You are a very rare person—I'm sorry for mistreating you—I'm sorry our paths crossed.

The end is here—Goodbye, My Fancy

Mark David Chapman

The Catcher in the Rye

P.S. "That's all I'd do all day. I'd just be the Catcher in the Rye."—Holden Caulfield (—J. D. Salinger)

"Madness is surely a quiet, hidden tomb designed to carefully protect one's sacred innocence and sensitivity from the evil devices of men."—Mark David Chapman

In spite of what he said in his letters, Gloria believed that he would never send her away from her vigil outside his prison. She did not count on his demons, who would command that he banish her back to Honolulu.

Gloria recalls warning her husband some time in 1982 that she believed the creatures from the dark side of his spirit were again taking possession of his mind. She could see it in his eyes, she said. She could hear them playing in the random, unguarded words that slipped from the corners of his conversation. Bible in hand, she closed her eyes and rebuked the demonic forces with all the power she could muster within her soul and mind.

Scoffing at his wife's attempts to pray the demons out of him, Chapman began burning red lamp bulbs in his cell and praying once again to Satan. Vowing to starve himself, he refused to eat for thirty days. He was transferred to Marcy, a prison psychiatric facility near Albany. State corrections authorities went to court to obtain a court order that allowed the starving prisoner to be force fed with intravenous tubes. His wife also visited him at the prison hospital, urging him to break his fast.

After being nourished back to health and treated for several weeks at the prison hospital at Marcy, Chapman recalls that he was "back to God," singing hymns in the armored van that returned him to Attica.

Gloria Chapman had purchased a car and their visits became more regular. Then, in the late summer of 1983, the demons returned.

Ignoring his wife's pleas, Chapman refused to meet with her. Except for an occasional shower, he refused to come out of the prison cell where he held himself as a hostage to the devil. For eighteen months, Chapman burned his red lamp, invoking the name of Satan all hours of the day and night. He composed hymns to his demons that he sang and played on the guitar he was allowed to keep in his cell. After his wife was threatened by an ex-Beatles fan, a prison parolee from the congregation of her church who was returned to prison after being found in possession of an illegal gun, she returned to Honolulu. She didn't hear from her husband for more than a year.

"I got scared and told her to go back home. I invited the devil into me again and went through an eighteen-month period where I couldn't communicate with her. I was lost; I was gone, a bag of chaos to myself. I sat in my cell up there and drank sodas and listened to rock music and talked to Satan and had to go to Marcy again. The first episode was early in 1982, and then, during the summer of the next year, I became very, very violent again.

"They put me in the hospital here. I was yelling at people, threatening them. So they put me in the van to go back to Marcy and when I got there, I began threatening everybody, saying, 'This is the New Mark, I'm rated X. Watch out. I'm very, very bad.'

"I refused to move. They came in and had to lift me up, on my stomach, to put a straitjacket on me so they could give me a shot. I was very violent and one of the psychiatric aides got on my back and tried to strangle me. After they got the jacket on me, they were pulling me down the hall by my hair. Dragging me by my hair, literally, and I'm yelling, 'Pull it all out! I love it! Yank it! I love this! Yank it out!'

"Then a doctor came in when these guys are still riding me like a horse, pulling my head back, to cut off my breath so I couldn't scream. I got up on my knees when the doctor came in. It's very hard to do in a straitjacket with two big guys on your back. But I was terrified when the doctor came in. I begged him not to give me any medication. I said, 'Please, please.' I didn't want a repeat of the Stelazine episode where I was paralyzed at Rikers.

"Then there was one scene when they dragged me into the sleeping area, put me over a bed, pulled my pants down, and the nurse took out a hypodermic needle.

"I said, 'Break that needle off in my ass! Break it off there! Just stick it up in there and break it off. I know that's what you want to do.'

"Finally, they overcame my chaotic mind with brute force and sometimes that's what you need."

But they didn't overcome the demons that came back shortly after he was returned to his cell at Attica. The demons didn't go away until some time in 1985, after a series of prison exorcisms that Chapman performed alone and with the help of a minister who agreed to pray outside the prison at prearranged times. The exorcisms were conducted late at night when the prison was quiet and guards weren't as apt to discover Chapman writhing on the floor of his cell.

As fluids poured from the corner of his mouth, the murderer vomited seven evil spirits before he recalls that his mind began to feel restored. Snarling and cursing, the creatures evaporated through the walls of the prison, he says.

"When they're coming out, there's a grinding inside you. When you really feel them is when they're coming out, with these squelched screams and cries and languages and cursings. You just feel this filthiness. It's like a shower when you're covered in filth, with filth in your nose, your hair, your ears. Filth caked to your skin.

"Imagine how you would feel if the dirt was inside you. That's what it's like. . . . You feel the demons' personalities as they're coming out. Some of them are nasty. Some of them are weak. Some are filthy mouthed. Some are very, very strong and don't want to let go. They hang on as they're being pulled out of you. Sometimes it takes an hour and a half to get one of them out. You're exhausted at the end of one of these sessions."

After cleansing himself of demons, Chapman began penetrating the various other identities, including the fictive Catcher in the Rye persona, that continued to grip him. The grip became especially powerful each October 9 when news reports that he read and heard inside the prison always carried stories detailing how John Lennon would have had a birthday, except for Mark David Chapman. On December 8, Chapman says the memorial tributes marking the date of the murder triggered violent episodes of remorse.

It wasn't until after the tenth anniversary of Lennon's murder in 1990 that he says he achieved a perspective that allowed him to understand connections between his Little People, his demons, Holden Caulfield, and assorted other fictional characters that have struggled for control of his mind. They pursued him even through the books, magazines, and therapeutic recordings that he would play on a tape recorder in his cell to try to find peace.

"Through my many years in prison, I have experimented with different types of self-help. One mode is tapes, hypnotic and subliminal tapes. I got this tape from a mail-order learning-system company, a hypnotic tape that's supposed to bring you to a peaceful place in your mind and bring you back to some place where you have control of your life. The tape had me walking along the beach, and finding this cave, and I went in this cave and there was this door and I opened this door and there was this really nice upholstered chair. It's really strange, but I sat in the chair and there were buttons—now, this is all on tape. I didn't create this. This was created by a psychologist and I bought his tape. It's all hypnotic imagery—and there were buttons on the arm of this chair.

"It was a parallel to the buttons I had on the arm of the sofa, where I used to push buttons and blow people out of the walls when I was a child. Whenever I'd get mad, I'd do that to the Little People.

"On tape, this psychologist would tell you to push this button and go back to a certain time in your life. This was all to help you regress mentally to this time period and help you understand why you did the things you did, what your background is, your identity. Well, lo and behold, after he had done that, the button thing, he went into this spiel—remember, this is while I'm in prison; this is long after my own created world—he went into this spiel how you could have people helping you, like committees, and you could assign experts in your mind to work on problems. I thought that was fascinating because that was exactly what I had done on my own. And I don't ever remember reading that anywhere. That wasn't planted in my mind beforehand to do that. But as soon as I heard that, that bothered me and I quit listening to the tape and I no longer listen to any of the tapes at all. I don't even have them anymore.

"But anyway, that's what it was: a board and people were formed into committees. It's exactly like I had when the Little People returned just before I killed John Lennon. One committee worked on my finances. And every night or once a week they would give me these reports on how we were doing. And these were all highly trained, efficient people. I even sensed their personalities. One of them even had a name. He was like the chief of staff. He was very aloof and efficient. I would often see him sitting by the window alone in the boardroom, just looking out the window and thinking. We had on the board an equivalent of like a military general, who was head of the defense department, a defense committee and the financial committee, the relationship committee. Just maybe five or six committees that worked there to help me and I would turn to them and they would tell me what to do. Of course they were answerable to me, but they would often give me advice. And this is what this tape was saying, that you could go to them for advice about anything. And I just didn't like that. It was almost demonic.

"It seemed to me like you were stepping too far out of yourself to get advice. But yet, these committees proved to be probably—not demonic—but probably, in my own mind, more helpful because they were appalled when they were informed that I wanted to murder John Lennon. And they did leave me at that point. So I think it was probably, to a very confused person, they were probably the last attempt at my own scrambled disheveled entity at survival. They were an attempt at survival, at order—to end the chaos, or to at least placate it each day. They gave me order. They gave me responsibility. They gave me rationality. The irony is that they were not real, and it's kind of interesting how the mind kind of takes care of itself when it's enveloped in chaos, whether the chaos is demonic or—that's another thing, the demonic world that I summoned, I think that was another side of me. I don't think I even shared it with the Little People. I never thought about it. This is the first time I've ever talked about this. However, I believed, and still believe, that the demonic world was the real world. The demons were real. And of course the Little People are not real, were not real.

"But we're talking about a very scrambled mind in a person and that's the way I was in the final months before I became a murderer. No person who is healthy summons demons wanting to kill somebody."

CHAPTER TWENTY-FIVE

FAN MAIL

We're all Christ and we're all Hitler.

—JOHN LENNON

When he murdered John Lennon, Mark David Chapman gained a notoriety that the world won't let him forget. He also got a famous address at Attica prison, where Beatles fans worldwide could send him a staggering amount of mail to remind him of the horrible thing he had done.

Lennon's killer has received thousands of letters. His mail spans the gamut of tortured human emotion, from suicidal and homicidal rage to hero worship and forgiveness.

The envelopes and packages, sometimes bearing colorful and collectible John Lennon stamps and postal commemoratives issued by Germany and several Caribbean Island nations, come from all over North and South America, Europe, the former Soviet republics, Japan, Australia, New Zealand, and the Scandinavian and Slavic countries.

Chapman reads all his mail, but he answers virtually none. After categorizing each letter—"nut case," "hate/threat," "autograph seeker," "hero worshiper," "sincere," "semisincere," or "fake"—he places it in the appropriate folder in a corner of his cell.

Many of Chapman's correspondents want to save his soul. A number of women have offered to visit him, professing romantic interests.

The hate mail is chilling in the depth of loathing that distraught Lennon fans struggle to express in their efforts to inflict pain upon Chapman and exact a measure of revenge for the death of their idol. More frightening than his hate mail are letters from those who write to say they admire him. Some confide that they have stalked other rock stars and celebrities.

After years of reading and sorting mail, Chapman has developed a keen awareness of the artifice employed by aspiring pen pals. Adults often send him photographs of their children or letters copied in childish scrawl in desperate efforts to elicit a response. Some say they're on their deathbeds, and that a letter or autograph from the man who murdered John Lennon would allow them to die happily.

"They'll do anything for an autograph," Chapman said, puzzling over a child's wide-ruled tablet paper bearing the scrawl of a woman who had bared her soul to him. The woman detailed a soap opera litany of intimately personal and family woes in an effort to gain a sympathetic reply.

"They use their own kids," Chapman exclaimed. "They write me and say they've had operations and they're dying, or they're people in old folks' homes. I can understand the hate mail. I can understand some of the letters from people who are sincere and just want to know why I murdered John Lennon. But the hero worship and autograph collectors, they're really pathetic."

It Was Only a Song

Some write regularly to Mark David Chapman to tell him they're going to kill him when he gets out of prison.

"Remember me?" asks one anonymous correspondent who periodically sends a brief, unsigned letter with a Royal Oak, Michigan, postmark. The letter always states the same grim message: "The day you get out of prison is the day you die, Bastard."

From Australia, with a December 1990 postmark, a distressed Lennon fan raged:

> Mark,
>
> I am writing to you in disgust. I hope you rot in hell. How on earth could you call yourself a fan of John Lennon and do what you did to him, you Mungle. You sicken me. I can tell every time they ask you why you did it, you say something different, because I don't think you really know. It's a waste of a life someone as talented as that. I did not agree with everything he did but it doesn't give anyone the right to take anyone's life like you did, you Mungle. I hope you get your just deserve one of these days, and I think you will. As for saying he was a fake, you are the fake, Mate.
>
> IT WAS ONLY A SONG!, you nut case. I hope you know how many

lives you have wrecked and how many people out here in the real world hate you. One day it will happen to you if they let you out of there. No worries.

In another letter from Royal Oak, Michigan, the writer sketched a tombstone with Chapman's name on it and the inscription:

DIED: MURDERER, WON'T BE MISSED.

BORN: WHO CARES, DIED: NOW!!!

Below the tombstone, the writer has penned:

Asshole!

You killed my hero! You're so fucking insane. Watch out when you get out of jail (your home forever), because I'm gonna blow your brains in!!!! You're the worst person ever!!! From, The World.

P.S. I hope you feel awful!

P.S.S. I can't believe I wasted a whole stamp on such a nothing!!!!

Other correspondents, like Katie, a distraught teenager from Nice, France, say they're driven to contact Chapman out of their love for Lennon's music and message.

"John Lennon for me is a genius," Katie struggled to explain during an interview. "His music is very good, super, and extraordinary. John is my god. I believe in John. He is my love and my life."

The girl said she "fell in love with John Lennon" through his music when she was nine years old. It wasn't until three years later, when she was twelve, that a friend told her she'd fallen in love with a dead man.

"I think he is alive, like the rest of the Beatles," she said. "I don't know he is died until a friend tell me that Mark Chapman have kill him in December 8, 1980. I am very hurt for all of my life."

In her letter to Chapman, written over a period of several hours with the help of an English-language dictionary, she tried to express her hatred of the man who gunned down her idol. Almost politely, she advises Chapman of her hopes he will be released from prison—so that he can be killed by a Lennon fan. Curiously, except for the letters he gets from other Americans, most of the international correspondents, including those who write even the most venomous letters, are virtually always courteous in their efforts to explain to him their compulsion to communicate. Many ask, some demand, that he reply.

In a letter postmarked August 2, 1991, Katie wrote:

Mr. Chapman,

My name is Katie, I'm French and I'm 17 years. I didn't know John Lennon, but I should do if you were not in front of the Dakota, the December 8th, 1980, at 10:45 P.M.

Today I have all his records, and the Beatles, too.

I would like know him!

I want tell you that you have ten years to stay in Jail now, and then your case will be examined. I wish you'll be executed, not by law, but by a John's fan who avenge him.

You have bungled your life, and John's, too, and lot of persons like his sons, his friends, his fans. I had to write this letter, and hope an answer.

Thank you,

More to the point, and more typical of the unsigned letters and packages he receives, is a scurrilous attack from the bowels of an anonymous Detroit housewife who wrote:

I think you are a crazy SOB. Why did you kill John Lennon? I hope you rot in the Attica State Prison. I hope they never let you out. If they do let you out someone will kill you and I would die laughing. It would serve you right. Maybe someone in prison will kill you. Your day is coming. If God comes before you die, you will get yours. You are a sick bastard. You are unable to live the nice life I do since you shot John Lennon. I get up everyday and cook my family breakfast and get my husband off to work and then my little boy gets up and plays and we have a good day. We are able to go anywhere we want, anytime we want and do anything we want. But you showed your ass and are in prison eating slop while us normal people are here eating hamburgers, pizza, stew beef and rice and good cornbread. You will never have the good life again but you did it to yourself. Well maybe someone will kill you and end your life just as you did to John Lennon, a slow gruesome death would be even better.

From—Well, it doesn't matter.

I have said my peace. I may write you again and remind you of the things you are missing out on by being in prison.

P.S. When was the last time you had sex (with a woman). Remember a hot woman's tits swinging in your face and your xxx cock in her hot pussy, well you probably never experienced that since you are of a crazy and sick mind.

An overwrought British fan from Lennon's native Liverpool sent the killer a short article and picture of Chapman clipped from *The Liverpool Echo,* a local newspaper. The writer had scratched Satanic symbols with a ballpoint pen across the photograph of the cherubic, smiling face of the murderer reprinted from his high school yearbook. The photograph had been photocopied and transmitted around the world after the Lennon killing.

"You belong to Satan, and you will meet The Beast, whose footsteps you follow," the Lennon fan wrote, advising Chapman that Lennon's "hymn, 'Imagine,' is played at all our funerals." (When he received the letter, Chapman underscored the above line and noted in the margin that he found it "interesting.")

The letter writer continued: "John Lennon will never be forgotten. He was The Beatles and yes The Beatles ARE more popular than Almighty Jesus. . . . Well, your past and your future is in the Holy Bible. Try reading the Ten Commandments. You might learn something. I pray that John Lennon's voice will haunt you, until you are in The Pit alongside of Satan."

From Lima, Ohio, December 1990:

> Dear Mr. Chapman,
>
> I've just finished reading the article about you in *USA Today.* You are pathetic.
>
> Many of us listened to John Lennon, many of us were inspired by Lennon. Most of us could understand that it was the dream, not the dreamer that was important.
>
> You have seen to it that "the dream is over" . . . You have prevented John and the rest of us from enjoying growing old together, for it was his occasional quip or quote that would let us know we were all right. You have done this Mr. Chapman, just like all the other failures in your life, you and only you are responsible for it.
>
> I do not forgive you, most of us will not forgive you and most of all I hope God will not forgive you. My only wish for you is that your pathetic soul burn in hell.
>
> A Lennon Fan

From South Carolina, a letter emblazoned with peace symbols:

> Chapman,
>
> I am writing to you for one purpose. To tell you that you are a fucking monster. I can hardly believe that some dickfaced asshole like you, with no direction, no intelligence and no talent at anything, shot a brilliant man like John Lennon. What the fuck were you thinking?! He inspired more people than you could have imagined in your puny little brain. He was a great man and then some scumbag like you comes along and shoots him down. Well, I'll tell you this right now you son of a bitch. You will never

get out on parole and do this again. And I am going to do everything I can to make sure that you fry in the electric chair. And you better hope to God that you never get parole because I guarantee that some good soul out there will terminate it. You are a filthy fucking scumbag and I hope you rot in hell.

John Lennon Forever

Most of the letters are handwritten and many are lengthy, like the following bitterly cathartic questionnaire from a London correspondent who identifies himself as "John Lennon Fan Number One."

The letter is dated February 4, 1988, after the correspondent viewed a BBC documentary based largely on interviews with one of Chapman's former girlfriends, Lynn Watson. Chapman says that Watson visited him at the prison later.

Mark Chapman,

My blood ran cold when I saw you on TV last night in a documentary about how you cowardly shot chunks out of the world's best singer/songwriter John Lennon, a genuine, sincere man of peace who had at last found true happiness and was really enjoying life. Where did you come from? Were you a disciple of the devil? Who are your real heroes? Hitler? Idi Amin? Charles Manson? I bet you wouldn't have had the guts to kill someone as notorious as them!

John Lennon was unarmed! If he'd been as phony as you said, he wouldn't have been as naive to think he could walk around signing autographs without a gun, no bodyguards, no bulletproof vest!

You're the phony, Chapman. You wish you'd been John Lennon, that's why you signed his name on a register. You're not fit to have been privileged to have even met the great man as I did when they filmed *Magical Mystery Tour* in 1967 in my hometown and then he was witty, friendly, kind, open, John Lennon.

You outraged and hurt so many people who'd never done you any harm, you were and are the most hated person by a vast majority, a cowardly, pathetic excuse for a human being. All the crap about being influenced by a book *Catcher in the Rye,* I wouldn't even read such rot if it had any connection with you. Fools without minds of their own get taken in by other people's words. If you'd been a somebody then you'd have written your own book. You called yourself a Christian but you were and are a vicious, cowardly killer and you call John a phony. Look at yourself, Chapman, what are you? Are you even as good a creation as a maggot—or a beetle? I doubt it. You didn't change The Beatles. They'd already split up, you didn't even kill him, just destroyed his body. John Lennon, the man, the legend, will live on forever. His music is ageless.

You're too pathetic to hate, a Nowhere Man who killed a great man out of jealousy for his greatness.

. . . In a way, by writing this to you, some of the hate is going away from me.

A lot of people have the view that someone will get you in the end like you got John, if you don't commit suicide first.

In one sentence, could you tell me? Did you want to be him? Are you still unrepentant about your cowardly, cruel act? Are you such an evil person to feel nothing for the grief, the heartache that you caused?

You'll go down in history as one of the world's most hated and cowardly killers of all time.

The Fan Club

In 1988, a fan wrote: "I just finished reading that brand new book, *The Many Lives of John Lennon* by Albert Goldman. Mr. Chapman, sir, why did you wait so long to kill that rotten piece of drug addict slime?? In my book, you're a hero. They should release you and give you a medal."

Others agree, like a man who wrote to ask permission to start a "Mark David Chapman Fan Club."

Dear Mr. Chapman,

The reason I am writing is to let you know that I am a great fan of yours. What you did ten years ago in killing John Lennon was remove from our planet a great menace whose fame, popularity, and power with the young people of this and many other countries posed a great threat to the stability of our nation. The good Lord only knows what havoc Lennon would have wreaked had you not eliminated him when you did.

I'm trying to get a Mark David Fan Club organized. But few people if any share our moralistic values.

In August 1988, an imprisoned British admirer wrote:

Dear Mark,

I hope you don't mind me writing to you. Today I read an article in the *Daily Mail* paper about your life in prison. It said you glory in your celebrity status. You're right to glory in it. You've done something that you will always be remembered for, killing John Lennon. To tell the truth, I'd like a status like that but I don't think I'd have the bottle to do it. I've slashed a person up and got 9 years. I got celebrity status down my end of the country. It's nice, isn't it? I came into the world just another baby, but I'll go out of it being remembered for what I did. . . . I'm just a woman that wants to be remembered wherever I go.

The writer closes the letter with a sketch of a smile face wearing John Lennon–style round-rimmed glasses.

Back in the USSR

From Alma-Ata in Kazakhstan, a former Soviet republic in the remote mountains of Central Asia, eighteen-year-old Maria wrote to Chapman explaining that she is the distraught president of a two-hundred-member John Lennon Fan Club. Maria, suicidal over the tragedy of Lennon's death, tells Chapman he can save her by revealing why her idol had to die. She writes:

> Dear Mark,
>
> Forgive me for this letter please, but I can't wait any more.
>
> So, my name is Maria and I'm 18 years old. I live in the USSR. I love John Lennon and 2 years ago I became a president of Soviet John Lennon Fan Club named "Come Together" and including about 200 young people all over the republic. And also I love yourself (strange thing, yeh?) I think we have much in common. Now I'm writing my own book about December 1980 events (so you can see I'm a journalist) But . . . I needed your help now. Not for a book, but for myself. I understand that my mental state is very difficult now. I want to commit suicide because of John's death. But I have one foolish belief that it can't be true if you are really good man. I hope you can find what I mean. I want to deceive my heart because I want to live.
>
> Would you be so kind to help me?
>
> Write me if you can and if you have some free time.
>
> Sincerely,
> Maria
> 25-04-91

In an interview and subsequent correspondence with the author, Maria explained that Lennon's life and death continue to have a powerful impact on youth raised under communism.

"My letter to Mark Chapman was my scream for help," Maria said. "I was in deep mental crisis then because of John's death."

Maria's home phone is a twenty-four-hour hotline for "John's fans who want to commit suicide because of his death," she said, sometimes taking calls from Beatles fans all over Europe. The Lennon Fan Club in the former USSR is spreading, she said, into a "world council" of Lennon devotees like herself.

Lennon's simple message of honesty and peace is especially appealing to the youth of a country "dissuaded in the false ideas of the older generation.

We don't want to believe our politicians and military men, and we are not accustomed to religion. That is why many of us, the most sincere and talented, go into the Beatles' music and the ideals of John Lennon," Maria said.

Despite the lack of books, recording equipment, videos, tapes, and compact discs, and despite the language barrier, Maria said Lennon's message has penetrated her distant corner of the world.

"We manage to get in some mysterious places the old, shabby records, paying incredible prices, and we translate the songs," she said. "The Soviet fans are very united. The most widespread age of the Soviet John fans is sixteen to twenty years, 80 percent of whom are girls. There are the fans of the first generation, the age of thirty to forty, and also the little children, ten to thirteen, who love John desperately."

Maria has difficulty explaining her own fascination with Lennon.

"It was not the music that affected me. It was the man and the personality," she said. "I don't know why I'm his fan, really. It's only love, and that is all."

Catcher 22

University of California psychologist Jay Martin has identified a "Catcher syndrome" in case studies culled from the psychiatric literature. Martin includes an analysis of Chapman's case and the John Lennon murder in his book, *Who Am I This Time? Uncovering the Fictive Personality.*

In their own struggles to find an identity, many borderline personalities like Chapman have sought shelter from their confusion between the covers of *The Catcher in the Rye,* Martin has found. Few have acted out their fantasies of violence against the world of "phonies" they blame for their confusion and personal woes. But many have become similarly intoxicated by the Catcher's ink and emerged Chapmanlike in the twisted guise of Holden Caulfield. Chapman prophetically signed a copy of the book he purchased before the Lennon murder: "To Holden Caulfield from Holden Caulfield." Others who have cloaked themselves in the image of his onetime alter ego write to him at Attica from the various fractured personalities they inhabit, male and female, around the world.

From Ottawa, Canada, the "Female Catcher in the Rye" wrote to Chapman:

> . . . I have no friends as I am extremely shy and withdrawn and I'm not very trusting of people. I've been in trouble with the law for harassment and sending death threats (which I never did—I don't think). I don't know if you want to talk about it or not, but like you I think sometimes I am Holden Caulfield's alter ego. *The Catcher in the Rye* has been my favorite

book for the last 15 years . . . I have also read all Salinger's other books—I like "A Perfect Day for Bananafish" and *Franny and Zooey.* None of them come close to *The Catcher in the Rye.* So forget about all those other phonies. I won't let you down.

The reputed son of a British Lord, declaring that he, too, had identified with Holden, wrote to Chapman to offer financial assistance:

Dear David,

I hope this letter finds you well and in good spirits. It would seem you have not received my earlier letters for one reason or another. I know that you neither seek charity or pity but I do feel you have had a "rough deal" because it was a "celebrity" you shot and I would like to befriend you and help if possible. My father, Lord———, has over the years sheltered me from the real world somewhat. I feel that as a result of his over protection, I have missed out and been robbed of a sense of realism. I have seen and read a lot about your life here in England on television and in the newspaper. I found it absolutely fascinating, David.

All you say you saw in life and things like the book *The Catcher in the Rye* I too saw. Holden Caulfield had a true sense of reality and saw through life's falsehoods without effort. It is this perception I lack. By becoming friends you and I could learn from one another. I would if it was possible be happy to pop on over to N.Y. to see you. Should you be in need of personal effects or financial assistance, please do not hesitate to ask. I know you do not seek charity David but this is from one friend to another—Okay? I look forward to your reply and perhaps our eventual meeting—Good Luck David and God Bless.

All the Best

Your Friend

P.S. "Don't ever tell anybody anything. If you do, you start missing everybody."—Holden Caulfield, 1951

P.P.S. I am told you prefer David to Mark, if this is untrue—please do not take offence and I shall rectify this in the future.

P.P.P.S. Would you like copies of articles on you which are written in the U.K.?

Forgiveness

Other letter writers, saying they identify with Chapman's Christianity, write, like this anonymous correspondent, to forgive him:

My Dear Brother in Christ,

A few days ago I read your sad story in our local newspaper. It broke my heart, and I felt very prompted to start praying for you . . . I guess you'd say I am a survivor of the 60's since I became a Christian after a very awful L.S.D. experience in 1969. It may also interest you to know that I've been a Beatle fan since I was 14, when they first appeared here in America. I've never stopped liking them and enjoying their music. I was as sad as anyone else when John Lennon was killed all those years ago and that brings me to the only present I could send to you in this letter: I forgive you and am praying for you. . . .

Please don't keep on condemning yourself when God does not. The world may hate and condemn you but God does not. And isn't that the most important thing, not what man thinks of us, but what God thinks. . . . He bore your sins (yes, even your sin of killing John Lennon) on the cross.

So as a Beatle fan and a Christian sister in Christ I can only offer you my forgiveness and prayers. God has so much more to offer you, please let Him do so. I only mean for your good and encouragement.

Your Friend in Christ

Chapman received the following unsigned card in an envelope with a Reno, Nevada, postmark after a lengthy newspaper article and interview was circulated by Gannett News Service in December, 1990, on the tenth anniversary of the Lennon murder:

David:

I have been touched by a lengthy article about you in my local newspaper, entitled "I Am Not An Evil Person." For the first time I am able to understand how it is possible for someone to commit such a crime. I believe you must be punished, but I also believe you are not an "evil person." I hope you can make peace with your Maker. I wish you strength to want to be restored mentally. I hope you will spend your time searching for a way to benefit mankind at a later time. The world will have to wait a little longer, now, to know what you could have been, but have inner peace that you know. The Muslims believe that God is offended by perfection. That is why an intentional flaw is woven into every Persian rug.

In God's eyes your mistake will be forgiven. Forgive yourself and go forward. I am 70 and will not be here to see the good you can do, but the rest of the world can. Bless you.

The following unsigned letter, which arrived at the prison Jan. 3, 1991, bore a British postmark:

Mark:

Listen what happened to me a few years ago. I went to work one morning and during the course of the morning the name JOHN LENNON kept thudding into my brain repeating over and over again. JOHN LENNON . . . JOHN LENNON . . . JOHN LENNON . . .

It nearly split my head open. A little later in the day I heard the following voice inside my head, not out loud you understand. The voice said "I am the son of God. He that believeth in me though he were dead yet shall he live and he that liveth and believeth in me shall never die. For I say unto you, John Lennon he shall die for he has offended my Father who is in heaven."

You were used as an instrument of divine will, nothing more, nothing less. Have you taken a lie detector test on the voice that told you to "do it now . . . do it now." That will prove you were telling the truth. I know for a fact that John Lennon died because he offended God. In fact the devil sent orders for John Lennon's soul. I don't suppose for one minute you will believe me, but everything I have written is true. I am an ordinary 9-5 worker who lives in England. I haven't put my name and address on, because I don't expect you or anyone else will believe me. I have written to newspapers over here, anonymously, because I don't expect to be believed, but what I have told you is the truth about what happened to me. The day after it happened, the very next day, John Lennon died.

You were just used as an instrument. I know. I am probably the only other person on earth apart from you who knows why John Lennon died.

Please Mr. Chapman

Chapman says that he is astonished, and sometimes disgusted, by the way that people attempt to flatter him into responding to their requests for autographs, letters or interviews.

A man claiming to represent his city council requests that Chapman sign his name and send "a brief message for world peace" that will be displayed along with the messages of local school children in a fund raising project.

A woman who has written several letters to Chapman tells the murderer that he is "the man who turned John Lennon into an eternal legend." She says that she wants to discuss with Chapman issues "superstars in the music world, politics, fame and so on."

He routinely receives letters from high school students whose teachers have assigned projects requiring them to write Chapman, often in connection with the reading of *The Catcher in the Rye.* Many organizations write to request autographs or photographs to be auctioned off to raise money for various charities.

Chapman says that he was particularly upset by a letter he received "from the Red Cross, of all organizations," asking him to donate autographed material for a celebrity auction.

"I'm a man who brutally murdered another human being," Chapman said, tossing the letter abruptly across a table in the interview room at Attica prison. "That human being bled to death. His blood was all over the place. And I get a letter from the Red Cross, of all organizations, saying they want a signed photograph of me to auction off so they can raise money.

"Anybody in jail for murder should not be treated this way, given celebrity status. They shouldn't be able to take a signed letter or photograph from somebody like me and auction it off to raise money.

"That tells you that something is truly sick in our society."

CHAPTER TWENTY-SIX

ALL THE LONELY PEOPLE

When I was twelve, I used to think
I must be a genius but nobody's noticed.

—JOHN LENNON

The thought that I might be able to leave a mark on the world
excited me tremendously.

—YOKO ONO

I was crazy. I thought I was destined for something special.

—MARK DAVID CHAPMAN

Robert John Bardo had carefully studied the newspaper and magazine articles about the murder of John Lennon. Armed with a copy of *The Catcher in the Rye* and a .38 caliber Charter Arms revolver, he struck out in search of his own identity. On an afternoon in June of 1989, as Rebecca Schaeffer lay dying at his feet just outside the door of her Los Angeles apartment, he found it. Bardo had tracked down the precocious twenty-one-year-old celebrity, rising star of the TV series *My Sister Sam* and the movie *Class Struggle,* and fired a bullet into her heart. The vibrant young actress was simply "an image on a screen" with which Bardo had become fatally obsessed.

"Even after I met John Lennon," Chapman recalls, "I didn't think he was a real person."

Before he wounded former president Ronald Reagan and crippled White House aide James Brady in a 1981 assassination attempt, John Hinckley wrote a letter to actress Jodie Foster. He told her he was distraught over Chapman's killing of Lennon. Somehow, Hinckley reasoned, the assassination of a president was supposed to avenge the rock star's death and win the affections of the actress with whose celebrity persona Hinckley had become obsessed. The list of ingredients on Hinckley's murder recipe, like Chapman's and Bardo's, included a .38 caliber Charter Arms Special and a copy of *The Catcher in the Rye.*

Before he wounded Reagan and paralyzed White House press aide James Brady, Hinckley wrote to Foster boasting that he would become a Chapman-like celebrity, idolized and "loved" by "millions of Americans."

Other celebrities—including David Letterman, Michael J. Fox, Theresa Saldana, Olivia Newton-John, Anne Murray, and Justine Bateman—have been the targets of threats by obsessed fans compelled to act out on a public stage the counterfeit identities that they believe link them to the fame they crave. Some, like Saldana, after surviving a near-fatal stabbing by a demented drifter who still vows to kill her, live surrounded by security guards and in terror of their lives.

Since John Lennon was just "an image on a screen" in the mind of Mark David Chapman, the former Beatles fan found it relatively easy to incorporate the superstar into an intricate narrative that controlled his life. To justify the act of murder, Chapman also found it necessary to transform himself into the fictional character Holden Caulfield. According to the *Catcher* script as Chapman interpreted it, Lennon's blood would give him an identity as The Catcher in the Rye of his generation. His new identity would, in turn, lend an aura of literary dignity to the desperate and cowardly act of shooting a man in the back.

After firing the fatal shots, Chapman was dumbfounded when John Lennon failed to sprawl dead, as the gunman had envisioned, at his feet. Although mortally wounded, Lennon sprinted up a half-dozen stone steps and crashed through a glass door into the foyer of the Dakota building before he collapsed. Chapman had expected to curl into a fetal ball beside Lennon's bleeding body and flow at last into the inky world of The Catcher. At the anticipated moment of his rebirth, when the gun stopped firing in his fist, his greatest fear was that nothing had changed.

It would be another two months before the killer finally got his wish, of becoming The Catcher in the Rye of his generation. While awaiting trial in his cell at Rikers Island, Chapman became suddenly entangled in the deceptive web he had spun from the Catcher's message. After numerous extended sessions with defense lawyers and psychiatrists in preparation for "the trial of the decade," Chapman collapsed finally into his own fictive persona as a bizarre mutation of Holden Caulfield. With an ironic touch of poetic justice, it was Holden himself who would destroy an elaborate insanity defense calculated to keep Mark David Chapman from being punished for the murder of John Lennon.

A verdict of insanity would have returned Chapman, a keenly intelligent and practiced sociopath, to the setting of a mental hospital where he already had proved himself able to manipulate psychiatrists and therapists. With his metamorphosis at last into Holden Caulfield, Chapman took the "terrible kind of fall" described by Salinger into the web of his own self-delusion and deceit.

University of California psychologist Jay Martin is one of the foremost authorities on Holden Caulfield. In his book *Who Am I This Time? Uncovering the Fictive Personality,* Martin writes of Chapman and details the cases of several Holden Caulfields—along with several Elvis Presleys, Marilyn Monroes, Batmen, Supermen, and others the therapist has helped extricate from borderline worlds of dangerous fantasy.

To a person like Chapman, a person devoid of a personality of his own, "a fictional character is unchangeable and safe. It gives a guarantee of a hold upon reality and has stories about it that can be imitated," said Martin. *The Catcher in the Rye,* he says, is an especially appealing identity for depressed young adults who, like Chapman, suffered psychological trauma in childhood or adolescence that impairs their ability to function in the adult world.

"People who read *The Catcher in the Rye* twenty or thirty years ago don't tend to remember how depressed and psychically injured Holden Caulfield is. But if you go back and read the book, it's very apparent how wounded and how depressed he is," Martin said.

Recalling the depression that drove Chapman to attempt suicide and that struck again on the eve of the Lennon killing, Martin suggests that it was easy for Chapman to imagine himself in the tortured adolescent disguise of Holden Caulfield. Fictive personalities, says Martin, "become a substitute for a self that is threatened with annihilation"—the sort of self Chapman has described.

Chapman put on and discarded the personalities of friends with whom he sought to identify. In some cases, he says he virtually became the people that he admired. Until he became Holden Caulfield, the killer denies that he ever had a personality apart from "the alter ego of whoever I was closest to at a given point in my life, usually a friend a few years older than myself. I was always somebody's sidekick. Anybody I was with, I became them. I had no personality of my own. Why didn't I have any substance to myself? What happened? Why was my personality always so fragmented?"

According to Martin, alter egos and fictive personalities are common features of a healthy personality—unless the fantasy overpowers the fantasizer.

"It is neither possible nor desirable to dispense with fictions," the psychologist said. "But to possess *only* fictions means to be possessed by them. However many roles we play for others, we must play as few as possible for ourselves."

. . .

The line between reality and fiction has become further blurred in the aftermath of the John Lennon killing, a murder that itself has been transformed into the grist of pop culture and novels. The Lennon-Chapman tragedy, which inspired an outpouring of songs by superstar musicians like Elton John and David Gilmour, has also inspired books, including at least two recent works by Stephen King, the contemporary master of the literary horror genre. King's novel *The Dark Half,* based on preliminary psychological profiles that described the killer as Lennon's twisted alter ego, anchors itself in reality with repeated references to Chapman's cold-blooded act. King, himself an object of public adulation by virtue of his fame and success, alludes frequently in the novel to the phenomenon of celebrityhood and the fatal obsessions it inspires in fans on whose fascinations a celebrity's fame and fortunes depend. As the "dark half" of John Lennon, Chapman is described by King as a "crocodile hunter." The writer explains the deadly sport of celebrity stalking as "see-the-living-crocodile-syndrome . . . about the fellow who shot John Lennon and the one who tried to kill Ronald Reagan to impress Jodie Foster. They *are* out there . . . Look at Oswald. Look at Chapman."

Similarly, the contemporary novel *Pinball,* by the late Jerzy Kosinski, grapples with the numbing effect of Lennon's murder on the celebrity world. Based on the life of a fictional rock 'n' roll legend whose fears force him into two separate lives, Kosinski wrote in *Pinball:*

> If, out of occasional loneliness, he had ever doubted the wisdom of his choice to remain anonymous, his doubt had vanished when John Lennon was murdered. Osten had been in New York City at the time, and he had gone to stand with the thousands of anguished mourners outside the Lennons' apartment building.
>
> He realized that Lennon, by stepping too easily and too often into the midst of his fans—whether to sing for them, shake their hands, or autograph their albums—had unwittingly undermined his separation from ordinary people, which was the essence of his charisma.
>
> Given an easy chance to be close to the famous man, the assassin . . . had seized the opportunity to kill him, as if by doing so he could usurp the very greatness Lennon had sacrificed by stepping down to the crowd, by attempting to prove himself ordinary. . . .

Misery, King's best-selling book and box-office hit, is a chilling tale of a celebrity novelist who falls prey to Annie Wilkes, an adoring "Number One Fan." Wilkes, like Lennon's killer, is an intelligent and perceptive psychopath unable to make the distinction between reality and a fictional world of "perfection" inside her mind.

In the movie version of *Misery,* Hollywood actress Kathy Bates portrayed the mercurial behavior of a celebrity-obsessed psychopath with haunting effect.

In his cell at Attica, Chapman says he's heard radio talk shows and received clippings of news interviews in which King has spoken of him and the Lennon murder as the basis for some of the author's most horrifying tales.

"Stephen King has a fascination with me," said Chapman. "Those stories he's writing now, about 'the celebrity's worst nightmare,' he got that from me."

During the summer of 1992, King himself was being stalked by a John Lennon fan who, noting the look-alike appearance of the murderer and the writer, accused King of being Lennon's killer. The obsessed fan, barred by a court order from approaching the writer's home or office, drove his van for several days through King's hometown of Bangor, Maine, with a poster saying: "Photos prove it's Stephen King, not Mark David Chapman, getting John Lennon's autograph. No joke, folks."

American pop culture, a phenomenon of celebrity worship and fame, has created a false sense of self-importance that can become fatally twisted in the minds of star stalkers like Chapman, Bardo, and Hinckley. Social critic Christopher Lasch, in his 1978 book, *The Culture of Narcissism,* details a collapsing social and family order that appears to be spawning a new and dangerous kind of insanity of which Chapman is perhaps the best known contemporary example. According to Lasch, the very nature of mental illness has changed in modern times—from the obvious "hysterical reactions" of earlier eras to a more dangerous and deceptive "borderline personality." Lasch describes a world in which a generation of children have grown up without knowledge of how or where to define the boundaries that demarcate their own illusions from the flesh-and-blood realities of other humans.

"And pop culture is the backdrop to this stuff," said Lasch. "The fascination with celebrity and the tendency to live vicariously through celebrities and the enormous ambivalent feelings about those people: envy, hatred, as well as admiration—you have to understand how deeply that pervades people's sensibilities who grow up on that stuff. I mean, those are the heroes, the demigods of our time.

"I think that people who are in this business, reflective people like Lennon, probably have some inkling that they're in a very dangerous racket."

The inability to distinguish "between the self and the object" is a hallmark of the narcissism that Lasch believes to be a defining psychosocial condition of modern American life. The need for attention and recognition pushes many rock stars and actors onto the stage. It pushes many untalented fame seekers and "nobodies," like Mark David Chapman, John Hinckley, and Robert John Bardo, over the edge.

"Any actor or rock star is somebody who is in the fantasy business, whose stock and trade is the creation of illusions and wish fulfillment and making people's fantasies come true. And it seems to encourage forms of identification that tend to eradicate the distinction between the self and the object," said Lasch.

Chapman recalls that, encouraged by his mother, he believed from an early age that he would someday "be famous."

Jan Reeves, a friend who knew Chapman as a teenager in Georgia, recalls him saying that, more than anything, he wanted the world to know his name.

"He told my brother [Dana Reeves, the former police officer who unwittingly supplied the bullets that Chapman used to kill Lennon] that the worst thing in the world would be to go through life and die without anybody remembering your name," Reeves said. "That was the first thing I thought about when I heard his name all over the radio and television the day after John Lennon was killed."

In a jail interview at Rikers Island three months after he killed Lennon, Chapman told psychologist Richard Bloom:

"I've always known I'd be different and I've always known I was destined for greatness, and I don't mean greatness in an ego sense of the word. Hitler was great, wasn't he? Not in an ego sense of the word, but Hitler had tremendous greatness and there's a tremendous thing about Hitler that a lot of people don't know. He was a genius, there's no question. I know he was crazy in some aspects, but he was brilliant. There's no question about it. John F. Kennedy was brilliant, a tremendous man. What makes me different is the fact that I was always destined for greatness, and I don't mean in an ego sense. I mean in a real, rational sense. I told my mother this ten years ago, and she told me I was. She agreed with me, and I said, 'I don't know if it's I'm going to be a great actor or a great musician or what. A political—I don't know what, but something. I'm going to be very great. I'm going to be very famous, and I don't necessarily mean in a good way.' And then even before I shot Lennon, when I was home, I told my mother, I said, 'Mama I just know I'm going to be something great,' and I said, 'I don't know whether it's going to be good or bad.' But I always knew in the future that this was going to happen. . . . I always knew the whole world would know who I was. I always felt different and felt special and felt odd and peculiar."

University of California sociologist Todd Gitlin, who has specialized in the study of the chaotic 1960s era, agrees with Lasch that pop culture is at the heart of the modern dementia that impelled Chapman.

"Lots of people, anybody in this culture who becomes renowned becomes a projective screen for a lot of insanity. And in the sixties, the Beatles were the biggest and most luminous screen around," said Gitlin. "Celebrity worship is a phenomenon from a media-saturated society, for which no purer example exists than the United States. It has to do with the elevation of celebrity as social fad. It's a new notion that comes with the star system that starts with the movies. As other authorities decline in their power, as people therefore look to celebrities to be their angels and devils, celebrities become the objects of all kinds of fixation; objects of delight and vast expectation, which usually turn into objects of loathing. And it can turn into homicide in the end. Devotion to Ronald Reagan is on the same order as devotion to Elvis or Madonna or John Lennon in the end. People look to [idols] to solve their problems. In a sense, people invest these guys with enormous power and meaning and understand them as larger-than-life embodiments of enormous virtues.

"In this sense, we see that John Lennon was right when he said, 'We're bigger than Jesus.' This is the sense in which it was true.

"Assassination is a worldwide phenomenon. What's new is that pop culture has become a field in which people have expressed deep aspects of their identity, their love and hate, aspirations and fears—they're mythic lives. In pop culture, people look to celebrities for a tribal identity. From that perspective, the killing of John Lennon was on the same order as the assassination of Lincoln or Gandhi . . ."

Lasch calls the illusion of fame "a mirror effect . . . that tends to refer not to any actual achievement but simply to this quality of celebrity, which turns out to refer to nothing but itself. It's as if you're dealing with two equally fantastic images of reality: the fantasies projected by the celebrity and fantasies projected onto the celebrity.

"And the importance of this is that it makes it so hard for any kind of solid, substantial reality to intrude into this process of identification."

When he wrote *The Culture of Narcissism,* which was published the year before the Lennon murder, Lasch wasn't thinking of celebrities who have become the targets of nonentities like Chapman and Bardo since 1980. He began researching the book out of concern over the disintegration of the traditional American family and the rise of a dubious "me first" code of personal fulfillment that appears to have displaced social consciousness and the ethics of individual responsibility.

The "second generation narcissist" that Lasch describes in his book could have been modeled on the "corporate" family in which Mark David Chapman describes growing up as a surrogate spouse to a self-absorbed mother who used him as her personal security guard against the outbursts of a father he recalls as "rigid" and "emotionless." In his book, Lasch also foretold a bureaucratic consciousness echoing the language and images that Chapman uses to describe the workings of a "corporate board" of Little People inside his mind and the technocratic walls that he attempted to erect between himself and other humans the killer says he regarded as "tools for my personal pleasure."

The narcissistic family Lasch describes is "characterized by parents who either are not there or, just the opposite, who are intrusively there, with all kinds of well-meaning but very bad attention, trying to produce the perfect child or trying to make the child a substitute for a husband or wife. Studies from childhood suggest the danger of a narcissistic parent displacing the wish for admiration on a child and using the child in effect as a substitute for the spouse."

Lasch said that in his research he discovered "many books on the changing structure of personality in a new kind of society and a lot of this resonated with what clinical psychoanalysts were saying about narcissism.

"I was struck by the fact that what they were saying supported what I had found by approaching the problem from the sociological direction. And what the mental health people were saying was that the kind of patients they were treating had changed over the years. They said they were seeing more patients with various kinds of character disorders rather than the classical hysterical neuroses. That seemed to me to make a lot of sense in view of what I'd learned about other things, and I began to wonder whether there weren't other influences at work in our culture that might bring out narcissistic traits, reinforce them, encourage them, even reward them. I was struck, for example, about what people were saying about the kind of people who do well in the modern corporation, in an atmosphere where manipulation of personal relations counts for more than doing a good job, essentially, or working with materials.

"The corporate master of interpersonal relations was also a pretty good description of a narcissistic personality. They had the same traits: the charm, the ability to inspire enormous loyalty and affection in people, but at the same time the incredible distance from themselves and others. The way these people tended to burn out at a certain point in midcareer when the youthful charm begins to fade and they find they can no longer manipulate people in this way. An inner emptiness floods to the surface and a lot of these people become suicidal. It sounds very much in some ways like Chapman's description of himself."

The deadly parallel is that many of the self-serving values adopted by narcissistic "nobodies" like Mark David Chapman darkly mirror the values of narcissistic "somebodies" like John Lennon.

Chapman recalls that he happened upon Lasch's book several years ago in a library at a prison hospital. He had been taken from Attica in a straitjacket and was being treated at the hospital after a self-described psychotic episode that he ascribes to demons he had invited into himself in preparation for the Lennon murder. Although he tried to read Lasch's book, he said, "I got scared because I saw too much of myself in it. Some of the doctors at Bellevue also said I had a narcissistic personality disorder, but I didn't really understand what it meant at the time.

"There was a point in my life, however, before I murdered John Lennon, when I became a very narcissistic person. I decided that, really, nobody could love me better than I could love myself."

The pathological self-absorption described by Lasch and psychiatrists also would perhaps explain Chapman's 1977 suicide attempt and Lennon's killing as a substitute suicide.

"One of the things that struck me in connection with suicide was the explanation that narcissists are curiously indifferent to threats to their bodily integrity and existence, so that they can't take suicide seriously. It's the most compelling explanation I've seen of the suicidal side of this syndrome."

Lasch says he's encouraged that U.S. Secret Service psychologists and psychiatrists have begun a study of celebrity stalkers and killers like Chapman, who in prison has cooperated with federal officials trying to save others from the fate of John Lennon. Secret Service agent Brian Vossekuil, who visited Chapman inside Attica with a team of psychiatric experts from Harvard University late in 1991, says federal officials expect that celebrities will face even greater threats from celebrity stalkers in the future.

"We're taking a closer look at people who have acted violently toward persons of public stature," said Vossekuil. "I think we're at the front of a real big problem and we don't know very much about it. We're trying to look at and isolate the behaviors of celebrity stalkers, in both the public and the political arenas."

During his meeting with the Secret Service team, Chapman explained that he felt himself a "nobody" at a time when he viewed Lennon as the most important "somebody" in the world. After finding the Anthony Fawcett book about Lennon's life-style and the Dakota—a book that caused him to realize the gulf between being "nobody" and "somebody"—Chapman says he passed the "point of no return," when he stopped thinking about killing Lennon and started making plans to do it.

"I was an acute nobody. I had to usurp someone else's importance, someone else's success. I was 'Mr. Nobody' until I killed the biggest Somebody on earth.

"It's important to understand how nobodies see celebrities," Chapman explained during his meeting with the Secret Service consultants. "These people aren't real. They don't flush the toilet. They don't have bad days. They're on TV. They're on albums."

After he found the book about Lennon—picturing his childhood hero on top of his sumptuous home in New York City—Chapman believed that he had been extended an invitation he couldn't resist.

"People aren't pictures. I know that now. I didn't know that then. People aren't still frames. They're beating hearts and there's pain and trouble inside those hearts that can never be captured on film. But I assumed so much from a photograph, and from an address, where he lived: the Dakota, the home of phony rich people. Actually, it was that building that kind of cinched the deal. The building is like something out of a fantasy, like something out of *The Wizard of Oz.*

"Those pictures of him at the Dakota made him, somehow, even more unreal to me. He wasn't three dimensional to me. He was two dimensional. John Lennon was not a person. In my naïveté, I couldn't see beyond that. I assumed from pictures in a book and the pictures were very misleading. I picked up the book and just flipped through it, reading bits and pieces about the Dakota, seeing what I wanted to see.

"After that, I couldn't sit still. In my mind at the time, I really wasn't taking a life here. But after I passed my point of no return, there was no turning back. If there was anything there that could have stopped me, I wouldn't let it in. I met his son that day. If that wouldn't change my mind, nothing would."

Forensic and psychiatric experts look to studies of celebrity assassins in hopes of helping mental health and law enforcement professionals identify stalkers and prevent future tragedies. Lasch suggests that any study of the assassins' psychological profiles would be incomplete without a companion analysis of modern society and the culture that spawns deadly fantasies of celebrity and of fame at any price.

"I guess the most typical kind of easy psychologizing about such cases is that they're in search of celebrity themselves and this is the easiest way to get attention, get into the limelight, which is true as far as it goes," said Lasch. "But I don't think that kind of explanation takes you very far.

"It's tempting to make easy psychiatric judgments, especially when you're dealing with such flagrant material that lends itself to such judgments.

"Is there any way to identify such people? It's always so much easier after the fact. Then everybody can look back and say, 'It was so obvious, how could anyone have missed it?' But Chapman, on the surface at least, was a person that everybody loved, a person who had these enormous personal successes everywhere. A person with people loving him and he's doing a great job. That's the last person you'd single out as somebody who was dangerous. That leads me to the rather pessimistic conclusion that there probably isn't any way to identify such people ahead of time.

"In some ways I think the explanation has to start, not even with psychology, but with some attempt to study the whole culture of mass communication, mass celebrity. At least that seems to me to be the most, if you had to choose only one, the most important background factor in all this. The thing that has changed most dramatically has been the saturation of public space by these images of high-flying celebrities.

"Celebrities have taken the place of heroes and they exist in a culture where it seems almost impossible for heroes to exist. They're pure figures of fantasy from the beginning. Almost all of them arise out of the entertainment industry, which traffics in fantasy. They hardly have any existence, actually, aside from their celebrity and the celebrity status is quite devoid of substance or content. That of course is an exaggeration but it does serve to distinguish heroes from celebrities and to distinguish the kind of feelings they evoke in people, which is a much more intense kind of identification. And that's where the distinction between the celebrity and the fan seems to get obliterated. It's hard to remember they're not you, because they're so fully invested with your fantasies and they are addressing them so directly, invoking them, asking for just that kind of identification.

"So many pop culture celebrities themselves are so flagrantly narcissistic that it makes identification with them easy. That's the kind of response they invite."

The fanatical obsessions inspired by rock stars like John Lennon is a phenomenon that transcends life. Even in the grave, celebrities like Elvis Presley and Jim Morrison have been unable to escape the depredations of obsessed and troubled fans. Recalling that the body of Elvis had to be exhumed after threats by grave robbers, Lennon's friends and family have kept secret the location of the ex-Beatle's remains.

Elliot Mintz, Yoko Ono's Hollywood publicist, said Lennon's widow wanted from the outset to avoid the spectacle of "Lennon's tomb." In death, Mintz said, John Lennon should be accorded some of the peace that eluded him in life.

"The John Lennon experience did not turn into the Elvis Presley exploitation experience," Mintz said. "This is not an attack on Priscilla Presley or any member of the Presley estate. It's just that Yoko did it differently. At the very first moment, she decided there would be no funeral. The absence of a funeral set the tone for this not to be like what occurred in Memphis with forty white Cadillacs going down Elvis Presley Boulevard and the attendant mourners.

"Instead of a eulogy or statements, Yoko asked for a few moments of silence for people to reflect, and John was cremated. There is no place where people can go to visit John's remains."

Lennon was cremated rather than buried "so it wouldn't become a situation like what we've seen in Paris, around Jim Morrison's grave or people going off to visit James Dean's grave," Mintz said.

The day after he was murdered, the ashes of John Lennon's body were brought back to Yoko Ono at the Dakota and placed at the foot of her bed.

"I was there when [Doug McDougall, a retired FBI agent] brought back the remains," Mintz said. "He was in charge of seeing that the cremation took place privately and that there would be no confusion ever as to the legitimacy of his remains. He brought them back to the Dakota building and Yoko's attorney, David Warmflash, and I brought them upstairs to Yoko. She was in the bedroom at the time. We gave them to her. She simply asked how he appeared prior to the cremation. MacDougall said he just appeared as though he was asleep. The clothing that John wore the night of his murder was later returned to us from the hospital in a brown paper bag. The clothing, the glasses, the personal effects that he had on him. Yoko asked me to give her the glasses, but she, to the best of my knowledge, never, ever wanted to open the bag."

After an attempt to steal Lennon's diaries, Mintz urged Ono to remove Lennon's ashes from the Dakota, where they had been kept since the day after the murder. She agreed. The ashes were removed to a location that, Mintz said, will remain forever secret from all but family members and the slain star's closest friends.

CHAPTER TWENTY-SEVEN

DECEMBER 8

John spoke with our voice. That's what made him a brother, and that's what made his death appear to be a death in the family.

—ELLIOT MINTZ

Every year they come.

On October 9, the date of his birth, and on December 8, the date of his death, they come by the thousands to a quiet, boulder-strewn knoll in Central Park called Strawberry Fields. On December 8, 1991, they came from India, Egypt, Japan, Poland, England, and all across the United States.

In lieu of a funeral, Lennon's death was commemorated by a candlelight vigil and a moment of silence. In lieu of a grave, Lennon's spirit was set free in a quiet corner of the park near the spot where he died.

Anchored in a large stone at the edge of the park a metal plaque stands as testimony to the impact on the world of Lennon's life and music. Bearing the names of virtually all the countries of the earth, the plaque notes that Strawberry Fields was dedicated as a place of peace in an unprecedented action by the General Assembly of the United Nations.

Less than one hundred yards from the Dakota archway where Lennon was felled by an act of violence, Strawberry Fields sits almost as an afterthought—a subtle oasis of tranquility in the center of one of the most violent cities on earth—evoking questions of human life and death and the choices that are made in between. The peaceful memorial was built by Yoko Ono in a calculated effort to blunt the tabloid hysteria and carnival spectacles that have marred the memories of Elvis Presley, Jim Morrison, and other celebrity icons.

Still, the fans come.

. . .

"I have come here before. I came from a very long way," said Sharif Attar, a thirty-nine-year-old international businessman from Cairo, Egypt. "I am a very great and old fan of John Lennon and the Beatles."

Sitting quietly on a park bench, Attar smiled softly as he watched crowds of young people laughing, crying, and singing in small groups around him. He said he plans his business trips to coincide with Beatles and Lennon memorials that are held each year in the United States and England. No matter where he is in the world, Attar said he always finds a John Lennon tribute occurring on December 8. In 1990, he found himself in Istanbul, Turkey.

"In Istanbul, of all places, they had a special John Lennon memorial day," he said. "There was a massive audience in the city to hear local bands play Beatles music. In Istanbul. It was utterly astonishing."

Attar said he seldom thinks of Mark David Chapman.

"I think the guy who killed him must have been mentally disturbed," Attar said. "I don't believe that people think of hate when they think of Mark David Chapman. The loss was so great, we can only think of how much we lost."

"I'll kill the son of a bitch. I'll kill the son of a bitch if I ever see him."

Katie has traveled from her home in Florida to pay tribute to John Lennon outside the Dakota and at Strawberry Fields every year since his death. On December 8, 1991, she sat with flowers in her hair before a shrine of incense, blossoms, and candles. She sat all day and long into the night before the impromptu shrine set up by Lennon fans on the large "Imagine" mosaic imbedded in a wide concrete walkway in the heart of Strawberry Fields.

"I was seven years old when I fell in love with John Lennon and I'm not a violent person," she said. "But I would kill that bastard if I could."

"I wanted to kill him at first," said Suzan, a twenty-one-year-old Bard College senior who has come to every Lennon tribute at Strawberry Fields since 1984. "But at this point, I think he's just another human being. The things that were going on in his head are impossible for me to understand. If you kill him, maybe that would be liberating him. Whatever guilt he feels, he should have to go through that.

"I've thought about the guy a lot. It's intriguing to me, the whole thing.

I think he's got to be a sick guy. He should never get out of prison. He hurt too many people."

"When I came to the United States this year, I told all my friends, one place I want to be is here on eighth day of December," said Dorothy Glebocka, a twenty-five-year-old student from northeastern Poland. "I was fourteen years old when I first heard John Lennon and the Beatles, and it gave me a hope for the world.

"When I was in class and a friend tells me that John Lennon has been killed, I cannot believe it. I cried for three days and I want to die myself. Crying, crying, crying.

"And now I am all day crying here. A stupid thing, I am crying all the time. I think Americans are not like this, with their eyes filled with tears. They come and take pictures and go away. But I am sitting here five hours crying. But I am glad. I am going back to Poland in two weeks, but I am glad. I am here and I will always remember being here. At least I am here.

"I didn't love John Lennon because he died. I wish him to still be alive. I loved him because he was like he was. He was not the person like Paul McCartney who I think is trying to sell only himself in all the ways that are possible. John Lennon didn't want to sell himself. I think he gave the world as much love as he could.

"Love. Just love. And what? He was killed!

"This man who killed him, it's like this. I even don't blame this man. I even don't blame Mark because he was crazy and you can't blame crazy people. He did the worst thing in the world. John Lennon could do so many things, so many more things, if he had not been killed. To me, it was the end of the world. I wish I died. . . .

"This man should never be out of prison. Never."

"Men of peace. Victims of violence. It happens all the time. The Gandhis keep getting assassinated over and over," said Prateek Patnaik, a thirty-four-year-old microbiologist from Bombay, India. As in England and the United States, each anniversary of John Lennon's birth and death is widely commemorated with music festivals and prayer services in India, Patnaik says, where the musician is held in special esteem.

"These gatherings are proof of his universal appeal. His music reached out to everybody, even to other generations in other cultures. He is someone who Indians recognize as a Western person who understood Hindu spiritualism. In a lot of films, we see John Lennon and the Beatles on the banks of the Ganges and dressed in the saffron robes of the spiritual seekers.

"He also used a lot of Indian instruments that added a new dimension to his music. His later music was very different from the Beatles. He almost sounds like one of those people on his way to being enlightened, or understanding that there is more to life than just going ahead and doing material things, making a career of just singing plain love songs. I think most of his later tapes have a very deep spiritual undertone to them.

"We have music festivals in India where groups come and perform and there is always a solid following for the Beatles, which keeps lasting. At every music festival, there is a solid Beatles contingent. There's something about it. You don't have to be a follower or a fan. The music just draws you to it. There is something very real about it.

"The spirituality in the later Lennon music was a very real dimension. Lennon himself, I think he realized something in his later years.

"It's funny. It's very eerie. Lennon talked about his own death. He looked up to people like Gandhi and Martin Luther King more than he looked up to politicians. Politicians are just people from show business. But someone like Gandhi and King were real people who really wanted to do something and didn't really care about the cost of doing those things. It's very odd that he said just before he was killed that he didn't want to be shot like Gandhi or King. He said he didn't want to be shot because he didn't want to become a martyr.

"I come here from far away because it's my little way of holding up a little light to a person who seems to have discovered his own spiritual self."

"I think most people gather here because death means different things to different people," Marie, a Lennon fan from New Jersey, said. "This is our cemetery because there is no other place where we can go. Where is John's body? He was cremated. But where are the ashes?"

"Without belittling any of the other Beatles, and at the risk of sounding in bad taste, had any of the other three run out of time that evening, there would of course have been a tremendous amount of grief and sadness," said John Lennon's friend Elliot Mintz. "But I don't think it would have cut as deeply as it did with John.

"There was an attempt on President Reagan's life shortly after John was killed. It was frightening. It was terrible. But there's something more three dimensional about this. This was an end of an era. One runs into the risk of cliché. No doubt everything that could be said has already been said. But what is significant is this: We are still doing this eleven years after the fact. That is one of the things that puts it into a sphere all its own."

NOTHING IS REAL

In a recurring dream, Mark David Chapman wakes in the middle of the night beside his sleeping wife. He is back in the bedroom of the high-rise Honolulu apartment building where he used to live.

Slipping quietly from bed, Chapman pauses for a moment beside the nightstand where he had once hidden a .38 caliber Charter Arms handgun. Briefly, he wonders if the gun is still there. He is afraid to slide open the drawer of the nightstand and look. Leaving the bedside, he tiptoes across the carpeted floor and closes the door gently behind him.

The living room is softly aglow from reflected city lights that filter through thin, white curtains covering a sliding glass door. The door leads to a balcony that hangs from the edge of the apartment, twenty-one floors above the earth. Chapman steps to the window and stares for a silent moment at vacant streets below. He has a momentary urge to slide open the door and step outside onto the balcony, but he's afraid.

Turning back to the living room, he sits for a moment on the sofa. In shadows and silence, he recalls something horrible that almost happened a long time ago. To reassure himself, he turns his head and looks at a picture on the living-room wall. Mounted in a rectangular frame with a large white border, the picture hangs prominently above a mantel. It seems to glow with an inner light.

Getting up from the sofa, Chapman walks across the room to stand before the eerie luminescence of the picture frame. Resting his hands on the edge of the mantel, he studies the large, square print beneath the glass. He reads the words *Double Fantasy.*

In the soft light, he can barely see the signature scrawled in ink at the corner of the album cover. He knows the name is there and he wills it into focus:

John Lennon, December, 1980.

Suddenly, Chapman is seized with the urge to go back to bed. He wants to lie close to the soft, warm body of his sleeping wife. Before he turns around, he closes his eyes to say a brief, silent prayer.

In his dream, Chapman looks again at the album. He touches the edge of the frame. He whispers to himself:

"Thank God you're still alive. Make us some more great music."

APPENDIX

I always remember to thank Jesus for the end of my touring days;
if I hadn't said that the Beatles were "bigger than Jesus," and
upset the very Christian Ku Klux Klan, well, Lord, I might
still be up there with all those other performing fleas!
God Bless America. Thank you Jesus.

—JOHN LENNON, *SKYWRITING BY WORD OF MOUTH*

In the literature of both religion and psychology, macabre spirits stand guard at the unfamiliar portals that separate sanity and madness. Whether crying out to God's angels or invoking Satan's demons, humans who have come and gone from that awful chamber in the mind tend to speak in hushed and reverent tones of things they have encountered there.

Whatever these spirits might be—superstition or separate reality—psychiatry and science seem unable to make them go away. Neither has religion or parapsychology been able to provide tangible evidence of their existence.

Do they exist? The argument is irrelevant to those who, like Mark David Chapman, become absorbed in their embrace. To those of great spiritual faith and to those who stand in utter helplessness before the creations of their own minds, angels and demons are forces to be denied only at great peril.

Rid at last, he says, of his demons, Chapman remains anchored in a spiritual world where he describes a near-constant dialogue with God. Largely isolated for his own protection from other inmates in a maximum security prison, he spends hours in his six-by-eight-foot prison cell writing poems, short stories, and religious tracts that he says are inspired by God. Seeking to escape from the darkness of a mind in which he became lost, his writings are fraught with images of light, like the following untitled poem he wrote on August 28, 1991:

Somewhere, somebody at night
waved a high torch
across the universe

A small flicker from distant skies

Later that evening as we lit the lantern
the fog rolled in off the lake
and talk turned to next day's fish and weather and trails.
At the mention of obscured stars
I thought of an old, steady candle
left burning up at the cabin

Why would the light of a single wick
be so important to me?
Why near midnight did I twist quietly toward the heavens,
my zippered bag sandy and damp,
not wanting to sleep without the sight of the stars?

After writing and discarding more than 3,000 pages in tenacity or obsession, John Lennon's killer on August 9, 1992, completed a short story that he had begun writing more than three years before.

"The Prisoner's Letter" will provide the critical and careful reader with cryptic insights into the workings of an imaginative mind desperate for contrition, forgiveness, and recognition—a mind that still is driven to save the world. Chapman seeks to tell the story of a fictional cellmate of Christ, struggling toward images of light through scenes of fear, darkness, and the desperation of a life lived without meaning or purpose. Chapman's Stephanas is an innocently accused man, who dies, like John Lennon, over a misunderstanding—and because he had the courage to speak out publicly in defense of beliefs deemed heresy by self-appointed truth-makers of the moment.

The Prisoner's Letter

Aulus Alexander
Counsel to Aristarchus
Thessalonica

Greetings:

May this letter find you at peace, my friend, and in good health. My affection and deepest love to you and your family at this time and always.

Alexander, I have but a short time in which to write this, my last letter to you, for tomorrow I am to be executed by the authorities. I urge you to read it carefully for it contains information of great importance. For some time I have wanted to explain these matters to you in detail, all the extraordinary events taking place here and what they have come to mean for me.

Do you recall that windy day of years ago, during the war, as we stood together outside the charred remains of what was once the beauty of Kashra? As we watched, the bravely fallen of our mercenary forces were hauled away in the wood carts. That very hour we pledged together our most solemn oath. We agreed, should a similar fate look to befall one of us, the one left standing might grant the other a final desire, a request to be fulfilled regardless of circumstance, whatever it may be. How well I remember that day as I sit here, recalling the vow we had sworn as death's own procession creaked by, wondering which of us would be first to feel its hand.

In view now of my imminent death, Alexander, I seek this day the honoring of our agreement, for you to kindly fulfill the promise we had placed upon our hearts those many years ago.

My request is a simple one: I ask that upon reading these words, you would not only accept them as a true and worthy account, but make every possible effort to pass them on to our countrymen. Though I realize you are but one man, my dream is the letter might be read by everyone in your considerable realm of influence.

Yet who can know, when one writes of such eternal things? Perhaps one day all of Greece might gaze upon it, the letter bearing an influence of its own, reaching far beyond the border of any one man's expectations.

My story begins in a place that even now I hesitate to recall.

I was lying in a cold, dark prison cell, half-frozen in the depths of what is called in this mountain city the Fortress of Antonia. A huge stone building, it is here the Roman governor, Pilate, resides and keeps his numerous troops. They are needed in this rebellious town, at least according to Caesar. Words cannot describe a more troubled country.

In the rabid blackness around me, the sound of dripping water echoed through the chamber like a death knell. An ancient, musty smell clung to everything, even my skin. High near the ceiling, a small barred window framed the sight of a glorious expanse of stars. It was difficult to believe that the dawning of a new day would find me in such misery. Only hours before I had stood beneath the heavens and wondered if there was anything so beautiful.

Dining at the home of a close friend, we had just walked out under the evening sky when a large man suddenly charged at us through the trees. Grabbing my neck, he began screaming that I was a thief, responsible for stealing a collection of rare vases from his home. I had barely begun my defense when a patrol of Roman soldiers stormed the grounds and arrested me. Dragged before the local magistrate, to my disbelief I was ordered imprisoned at the fortress, and led from the courtroom in chains. My freedom gone and my spirits broken, I remember each of my feelings as I approached the forbidding walls of the castle. My hopes seemed to desert me as the soldiers led me down a long, dark stairway and cast me into a cell, beating me unconscious.

Awakening in the bowels of a dungeon I could never have imagined in my nightmares, fearing for my life—they hang people on crosses, these Romans—I loudly cursed the fortune that had brought me to the hellish chamber. Declaring my innocence to every guard that passed by, I fell to the dungeon floor and howled like a beast when informed that my accuser sat upon the city council.

At the very height of my panic, wishing a swift end to it all, I was startled when a voice spoke to me from the darkness:

"Do not be frightened. You have nothing to fear in this place."

I lifted my head from the floor. The gloom of the cell betrayed no human presence as the voice spoke again:

"The charges against you will soon be dismissed. In four days, they will release you."

Four days? Release me? I was hearing voices! How quickly the madness of imprisonment had broken me; how else could I have explained it?

Lying back on the stone, angry that my fears had overcome me, I had just closed my eyes when the sound of a man's breathing could be heard from the other side of the chamber.

Twisting my head and squinting into the darkness, to my amazement I saw a man sitting there, leaning against the wall not ten feet from me, barely visible in the soft rays of starlight that shone from the window above us.

"Who are you?" I demanded. "What are you talking about?"

I could hardly make out the figure, the shoulders and head of a man who appeared to have been injured, his chest rising out of the shadows with each labored breath. I reasoned that they had thrown him into the cell while I lay unconscious.

"My name is Jesus. From Nazareth. Why are you so troubled?"

Why was I troubled? What was wrong with this man? Could he not know of our circumstance, what it meant to be waiting down here? From the edge of blackness, I heard his voice again:

"You have no reason to worry. I have told you the truth. If you care to accept it, we will meet again, not many days following your release."

Meet again? We were both going to be dead in a matter of hours, if not from the crosses, then surely from this cold.

As though reading my mind, he replied:

"Death can only conquer those with no life within, my friend."

At these words, Alexander, I began to feel that something extraordinary was happening. I could no longer deny the force I felt move within me each time he spoke. There seemed to be a reason that this man had been placed in the cell with me.

Once again, as though sensing my thoughts, he answered my unspoken questions:

"I am here to stand trial before the governor, before Pilate. I await him now. Perhaps you have heard why these things are taking place."

Suddenly it came to me.

As you know, dear friend, though I am absent from the country for months at a time, I had heard something about a "Jesus" in a merchant's home at Joppa. From what I had learned, he was the cause of a very dangerous upheaval in the religious communities here, proclaiming a powerful message of a new and controversial belief. Some of the acts he had performed had been labeled as miracles. The city's worshipers had gathered about the temple in protest of the man, denouncing the growing number of his followers as sheeplike and ignorant of the prophecies of old. The Romans had issued warnings against him.

According to some reports, the man's ideas had spread to distant regions as well. Journeying through the upper country last spring, I had overheard whisperings that he might be the coming "Messiah," the Chosen One of God awaited by the faithful for years. A special man sent from Heaven, he would arrive in unmistakable power and glory to establish a great kingdom, ending all foreign rule. Ushering his people into a new era, he would forever reign among them, faithfully guarding his kingdom against every evil.

Clearly, however, the broken figure who slumped against the stone across from me was not this Messiah. Whoever he was, if indeed he was the teacher known as Jesus, I soon began to pity him. It was evident that some kind of mob had set upon him on his way to the fortress. Even in the dim light, I could tell that he had been brutalized. I wondered if the captain of the guards had ordered him temporarily held like this for his own protection—at least while awaiting Pilate. Contrary to what I had first suspected, imprisonment had saved his life.

As I pondered his troubles, he again seemed to sense my thoughts and began to reveal the true meaning of his plight. Not realizing that his words would prove the most important statement on life I would ever hear, I thought, as I listened, that I had encountered—a lunatic.

"I am here because the Father has sent me to die. To offer up my life as the substitute penalty for every man's wrongs committed here on the earth. My blood will be shed as the sacrifice for the sins of all mankind."

The man said that anyone who believed that, and who asked for forgiveness from his father, would be given eternal life. But those who chose to reject this offer would suffer a penalty far greater than death: eternal separation from God.

His words had a peculiar ring of authority to them as they came from the void. Although the words of an insane man, they ran as clear as a brook.

"I am the Good Shepherd," he said, "and my sheep hear my voice. If anyone not of my flock hears my voice and comes to me, I will not turn him away, regardless of his wrongs, but will instead make him one of my sheep and bring him into my Father's kingdom forever."

He said he was the one the prophets had spoken of. He said that though he sat condemned to die in this rotting hole with me that he was the King many had been waiting for—a ruler not of this world, but of the next. And he said that he would come back—even after the grim death that surely awaited him—to gather his people from the farthest corners of the earth.

He paused then, and in that moment I wondered again whether I was not simply imagining all of this. Then from the darkness he asked me this: "Do you believe these things?"

I could not answer him, my friend. And as the moment lengthened and the sound of dripping water marked the time until our deaths, he asked me yet another question:

"May I ask you then, what you do believe in?"

From the words I was hearing, Alexander, it was clear the man was very troubled. I didn't even want to consider the possibilities of what might have happened to him. As he looked up at the window, his face illumined in the quiet starlight, I understood why they had brought him here: The Romans brooked no dissent, not even from a man who appeared as innocent as he. Had he incited the people to some kind of revolt? It was a crime punishable by death in any part of the empire. His very statement to me an act of treason, I felt from my heart genuine sorrow for him. Of all his grand predictions of kingdoms and peace, I sensed but one of them would become a reality—he was indeed going to die.

Growing very tired in the cell, what the man had said had been too much for me. Worries of my own death were pressing heavily against my mind, and I wanted only to rest. What had any of his words to do with me, anyway? They would soon be as rain on the wind for the both of us.

Sinking back to the floor, I buried my face deep in my arms. As I slowly drifted down to sleep, the man's shadowy image faded from my thoughts like a dying candle.

Suddenly I was no longer in my cell, but out among the bright fields of wheat in which I had played as a child, the man still with me talking as we sat together under the warmth of a great glowing sun. In my dream, his question began to haunt me as I watched his eyes, his hands slowly gesturing. "What do you believe in?" The words touched a part of my life I had abandoned in these fields years before.

As he pressed me for an answer, I was up and running as fast as my legs would carry me. Across the fields I ran, stumbling through the land of my youth, my knees torn and bloody from the many falls. Coming to the edge of the fields, I soon collapsed in a large meadow. My entire body bruised and broken, I sank to the sustaining earth. I knew that I could not escape the question that pursued me. I had to offer up an answer to it, one that I knew must come from somewhere deep within me. "What did I believe in?" The question penetrated my heart. It pried into my secret corners, sifting through each hardened layer of stubborn ideas—false and feeble excuses I had used to hide from myself. What *did* I believe in?

The horrible emptiness that had robbed my life was now made plain to me in a memory I had buried deep in my past.

Many years ago in my wanderings, I had dived for pearls near Pereta, a tiny coastal town near my father's home. I remember the day I chose to chart all my dreams from this secluded port, to find if on my own I could recover a share of the sunken gems.

I dove by moonlight, a map of the murky underwater caves etched upon my memory. Over the side of the boat and into the chilly waters, taking as much air into my lungs as they would hold, I fought my way many darkened feet down a rocky slope to the black mouth of a cave. As my lungs nearly tore themselves from my ribs I searched within the cave until I came upon an entire bed of exotic shells. With a knife, I quickly freed several and burst to the surface and the air above me.

Over and over I dove, my body nearly exhausted, my hands pale and frozen. And as dawn crept up, I knelt to pry open each barnacled treasure chest.

Imagine my heartache at finding nothing in any of them but a few sandy bits. I could have searched those waters forever and never found the treasures that I desired.

Is this what I feared from the man's question? If I dove beneath the surface of myself, would I find nothing but worthless sand? That would have been too painful to bear. Was it the fear of emptiness that had kept me from exploring my own heart?

Years later, on a voyage to Athens with my father, Curtisius, I had often walked about the ship in the evening hours, staring into the star-filled skies. Afraid of the most simple answers, what had drawn me to the more distant, elusive ones?

Compelled to search the heavens for these things, I spent many nights on the rolling deck of the *Gloria Wind* pondering the meaning of those stars. I had even fancied a particular set of them was calling out to me through the darkness. How I had longed for this, for a power greater than my own to bless me with true understanding, to reveal to me the reason I was alive.

The sound of distant chains woke me from the dream with a shudder; my escape had ended. The anguished cries of men could be heard from above. Who knew what fate awaited them? A cold wind blew across my face as I looked about the cell for the stranger. Had they taken him away as I slept? A misty dream was all that remained of my fitful sleep on the stone.

I called to him, but heard no answer. Peering into the darkness, I saw he still sat in the rays of starlight shining from the window. No, they had not come to get him, not yet. I could see from the shadows he had lowered his head and was fast asleep.

Despite the man's alleged acts of treason, I believed his crimes were unworthy of the punishment soon to be rendered him—the cross. I imagined the agony. The man was to be stripped of all clothing and stretched upon two fastened beams of wood. Iron spikes would be driven through his hands and feet. As those around him watched, the man would then be lifted high above the crowds, the cross carving a sharp dagger into the sky. A slow and painful death would follow.

As I pondered this image, an icy wind howled through the window above. How would they justify the death of a man such as this? What he had explained to me had all the markings of a man gone mad. Yet I knew in my heart there was something more powerful here than madness.

As if to settle these things within me, just as he had seemed earlier to know and answer all of the questions I had been harboring, the man called to me from across the chamber.

At first I thought he was calling for help. God knows his wounds were bad enough. But something was wrong. Something in his voice had changed. As I groped my way through the darkness, I couldn't believe what I saw as I approached him. My God, I thought, the man *had not moved an inch.* His head still lay upon his chest, his arms as gray as the walls.

I was gazing upon a corpse.

Drawing back from him, I stopped dead against the wall. Who had spoken? This couldn't be real, I thought.

Another fear gripped me as I realized that I would be the one blamed for his death. The commander had let a man as controversial as this Jesus die under his authority and I would make the perfect scapegoat. The bizarre nature of it all—that I would be blamed for the death of a man who said he was going to die for *me.*

Inexplicably, I began to laugh. The insanity, the futility, the hopelessness of it all. Grains of sand. All my life, grains of sand. And nothing I could do.

Sinking to the floor, sickened by the thought of how I would be judged by my fellow men—perhaps even you, Alexander—my mind grew black with anger and contempt toward the man.

The approaching footsteps of soldiers quickly ended these thoughts. Startled, I turned to look upon the man for the last time.

A key rattled noisily into the lock of our tomb. My rage seemed to melt away into the walls. All my bitterness ceased, and I resigned myself to the end that would soon befall me.

A squad of four armor-laden soldiers crashed into the dungeon. One of the soldiers bent and slapped the lifeless body of the man, as two others lifted him by the shoulders. I stared at the curious soul with whom I had shared my last hours.

As the soldiers turned the body toward the door, the man came to, his head twisting slowly, alive to meet my horrified eyes.

The truth of what had happened struck me as hard as any fist. *I had mistaken his exhaustion for death.* And as a strange strength began to calm me, I found myself standing to face him, mindless of the danger.

A soldier fixed me with a warning glare, and ordered me to sit down. Yet from what I had seen, I was unable to obey.

For in a moment that could only be described as the beginning of everything I had searched for, the radiance that I beheld deep in his eyes shone brightly out of the darkness to the very emptiness of my soul.

Alexander, the candle grows dim within the walls of my new cell at the fortress and I must end this letter quickly. From the hall, I hear the moving of many chains; I will soon be led to my execution. I have but a few things left to say, matters which, I pray, I will have time to inscribe upon these pages.

Just as the man had predicted, I was released from the dungeon cell four days following my arrest for the theft at the councilman's home. As you can imagine, I was astonished. But the experiences that were to follow, Alexander, would make this sweet moment crumble to dust by comparison.

As I wandered in the intoxicating air of freedom from the iron gates of the citadel, I chanced upon a youth who beckoned me to follow him. After a journey of several miles from the city, I was brought inside a modest village home filled to the walls with courteous and smiling people. Standing in the midst of them, speaking words that were as familiar to me as when I had first heard them, was the man I had last seen being taken from the prison cell.

The breath seemed to go out of my body as I realized and accepted what was truly happening—that this was the man I had watched being led to his death.

As I looked upon the man and accepted this truth, Alexander, I saw my own destiny and purpose clearly—to follow him, even to my own death if required. Little did I know how soon I would be called to make this, my final decision.

Within a fortnight, I was arrested and charged with treason when I began telling others of the things I had witnessed. My trial was brief. I refused to deny before the Roman judges the fact of his resurrection, that the man Jesus had actually risen from the dead and walked among us. They sentenced me to die.

Without shame, I endured the ridicule and indignities of a leper as I was cursed, spat upon, and led roughly from the courtroom.

Yet I must share with you one final scene before closing this account, Alexander.

Not many days following our gathering at the village home, he began to assemble a small group of his closest friends. To my joy, he invited me to accompany them to a nearby hilltop where he had often turned for solitude. As we made our way in the silence of early morning, he spoke to us carefully, instructing us to tell the world of the miracles we had seen, the truths we had heard. He told us that he loved us, and promised that his spirit would always be with us.

Bidding us then to leave him with just his disciples, we descended the hilltop as a strong wind began to blow from the east. Lagging behind the rest of the scattering group, I turned for a final look. A huge cloud had gathered itself about the mount and I fixed my eyes within it to see if I could spot him but once more. Suddenly I caught sight of a billowing robe deep inside the rising cloud cover. Was it my imagination, or had I seen a miracle too great to comprehend? An instant later, my friend, the cloud dispersed. He was gone.

Remember our oath, Alexander. I await you in the place he himself has reserved for all those who have believed in him and called out to him.

Stephanas

BIBLIOGRAPHY

Bresler, Fenton. *Who Killed John Lennon?* New York: St. Martin's Press, 1989.

Bugliosi, Vincent, and Curt Gentry. *Helter Skelter.* New York: Bantam Books, 1975.

Cather, Willa. *Willa Cather, Collected Short Fiction, 1892–1912.* Lincoln: University of Nebraska Press, 1965.

Clarke, James W. *American Assassins.* Princeton: Princeton University Press, 1982.

Clarke, James W. *On Being Mad or Merely Angry: John W. Hinckley Jr. and Other Dangerous People.* Princeton: Princeton University Press, 1990.

Coleman, Ray. *John Lennon.* New York: McGraw-Hill Book Co., 1985.

Daws, Gavan. *A Shoal of Time* Honolulu: University of Hawaii Press, 1968.

Dowlding, William J. *Beatlesongs.* New York: Simon and Schuster, 1989.

Exley, Frederick. *A Fan's Notes.* New York: Vintage Books, 1985.

Fawcett, Anthony. *John Lennon: One Day at a Time.* New York: Grove Press, Inc., 1976.

French, Warren. *J. D. Salinger.* New York: Twayne Publishers, 1963.

Gaines, James R. "The Man Who Shot John Lennon." *People,* February 23, 1987.

Gaines, James R. "A Killer Takes His Fall." *People,* March 2, 1987.

Gitlin, Todd. *The Sixties: Years of Hope, Days of Rage.* New York: Bantam Books, 1987.

Goldman, Albert. *The Lives of John Lennon.* New York: William Morrow and Co., Inc., 1988.

Green, John. *Dakota Days.* New York: St. Martin's Press, 1983.

Greenberg, Joanne. *I Never Promised You a Rose Garden.* New York: Signet Books, 1964.

Guest, Judith. *Ordinary People.* New York: Viking Press, 1976.

Hamilton, Ian. *In Search of J. D. Salinger.* London: William Heinemann Ltd., 1988.

Kaye, Marvin, ed. *Devils and Demons: Fiendish Tales.* New York: Dorset Press, 1987.

King, Stephen. *The Dark Half.* New York: Viking Penguin Books, 1989.

Kosinski, Jerzy. *Pinball.* New York: Bantam Books, 1982.

Lasch, Christopher. *The Culture of Narcissism.* New York: W. W. Norton & Co., Inc., 1979.

Lennon, John. *Skywriting by Word of Mouth.* New York: Harper and Row, Inc., 1986.

Lennon, John and Yoko Ono interview, December 8, 1980, RKO Radio Network, Inc.,

Lewisohn, Mark. *The Beatles Day by Day.* New York: Crown Publishers, Inc., 1987.

Martin, Jay. *Who Am I This Time? Uncovering the Fictive Personality.* New York: W. W. Norton & Co., Inc., 1988.

Michener, James. *Hawaii.* New York: Random House, 1959.

Norman, Philip. *Shout! The True Story of the Beatles.* New York: Simon & Schuster, 1981.

Robertson, John. *The Art and Music of John Lennon.* New York: Birch Lane Press, 1990.

Ryan, David Stuart. *John Lennon's Secret.* London: Kozmik Press, 1990.

Salinger, J. D. *The Catcher in the Rye.* New York: Bantam Books, 1964.

Seaman, Frederic. *The Last Days of John Lennon.* New York: Birch Lane Press, 1991.

Sheff, David. *The Playboy Interviews with John Lennon and Yoko Ono.* New York: Playboy Books, 1982.

Sheff, David and Victoria. "The Betrayal of John Lennon." *Playboy,* March 1984.

Solt, Andrew, and Sam Egan. *Imagine.* New York: MacMillan Publishing Company, 1988.

Somach, Denny, Kathleen Somach and Kevin Gunn. *Ticket to Ride.* New York: William Morrow and Co., Inc., 1989.

Strauss, William, and Neil Howe. *Generations.* New York: William Morrow and Company, Inc., 1991.

Thomson, Elizabeth, and David Gutman. *The Lennon Companion.* New York: Schirmer Books, 1987.

Under, Merrill F. *Demons in the World Today.* Wheaton, IL: Tyndale House, 1983.

Ward, Ed, Geoffrey Stokes and Ken Tucker. *Rock of Ages: The Rolling Stone History of Rock & Roll.* New York: Summit Books, 1986.

Watson, Charles "Tex" as told to Chaplain Ray Hoekstra. *Will You Die for Me?* Dallas: Cross Roads Publications, Inc., 1978.

Wiener, Jon. *Come Together.* New York: Random House, 1984.

INDEX

ABOUT THE AUTHOR

JACK JONES, recipient of numerous journalism awards, conducted the first prison interviews with David Berkowitz, the Son of Sam. He has been visiting and speaking with Mark David Chapman since 1986. Jones resides in Canandaigua, New York.